One Way Ticket to Anywhere

A Memoir

Rich Ochoa

Vera,
My good friend. Thanks for helping to spread the word about my book. I always look forward to seeing you at our social gatherings.

Rich Ochoa

A Createspace Book

Published in the United States of America by Createspace, an Amazon.com company. www.amazon.com

Copyright © 2011 by Rich Ochoa

All Rights reserved

ISBN 9781461142997

Second Edition

To My Great Grandmother, "Big Grandma", Helen.

You ended every visit standing on your front porch as we drove away; waving with one hand, wiping tears from your face with the other. I wondered, "What's wrong with Big Grandma? We're gonna see her again soon." And we always did, until the last time she stood on the porch waving and crying. Now I understand: There was nothing wrong with Big Grandma.

Table of Contents

Acknowledgements

Note to My Readers

Introduction

I'm Gonna Die

Abducted

Chocolate Milk

Bouncing Baby Sister

A Scarred Childhood

The Pee Desk

My Favorite Song

Man of the House

Will You Be My Friend?

California Is the Place You Wanna Be

Pet Cows and Dogfights

The End of the World as We Know It

The Olympics

Pole Vaulting

I Bet Bruce Jenner Didn't Have This Problem

Selling Roses

Could Someone Give Me a Ride?

There Ain't No Free Lunch

Yeah...About that Ride...Not Right Now

Cocktails

Are You My Dad?

Grandpa and Grandma

Letters to Me and My Mother

Who Shot J.R.?

We're Going Home Kids

Brother Sal Ahmey

March 30, 1981

The Last Supper

Kill or Be Killed

The Stolen Lawn Chair

One Way Ticket to Anywhere

The Lady on the Bus

The Clothes on My Back and a Broken Sack

A Friend with a Bed

My Own Place

"I Thought You Was Roadkill"

My Wheels are Coming Off

One of Us Needs a Car

Squeal Like a Pig

Tuna and Potato Chips

The Blackberry Relays

Worms in My Turds

Sumpin to Eat

Flagrant Foul

What's an Editorial?

Icees and Nukes

Money for Nothing

To Study or Not To Study? That Is the Question

Acknowledgements

I thought I knew how to write until I finished the first draft of this, my first book, and then solicited feedback. I realized how much there was to learn, even about something as subjective as this craft. Without the critique of my friends and fellow writers at Trinity Writer's Workshop in Bedford, TX, this manuscript would never have been publishable. Dean Thompson, you're the toughest critiquer in the group, never sugar coating your feedback, usually focusing on the negative, because someone's got to do it. But the night at the workshop, after I read my chapter, *The Lady On the Bus*, moved by my prose, you looked at me and said, "you have a gift". Even if I get all one-star reviews on Amazon, that alone validated this book.

Jeff Raimer, Stan Denman, John Langlet, Frank Chapchuk, Donna Hornick, Jim Mitchell, Sheryl Thompson, Robbie Hudson, Dia Fauss, Larry Guera, Ryan Krems, Juanita DeRyan, Kyle Vandivort, and Cindy Garland, your tireless technical support, critique, proofreading, and encouragement kept me going at different stages of the multi-year process. Ryan Krems, thanks also for your help in giving me a web presence. Wayne Parham, thanks for your help with rural Ebonics spellin', although I think twenty-five years working as an engineering bigshot has diminished your expertise.

Thanks to my once-agent, Alice Martell, who fawned over this book and tried hard, albeit unsuccessfully, to sell this project to Taylor, Harper Collins, Ballantine, Penguin, Random House, Simon & Schuster, Holt Macmillan, and almost every major press in New York City. Their flattering rejection emails all had the same theme:

"A memoir from an unpublished non-celebrity is just too big a risk for us to take on right now."

Thanks to Carrie and my girls, Lindsay and Leanna, for inspiring me every day. And, special thanks to all the characters in this book for being a part of my story.

Note to My Readers

This book once earned me representation with a reputable NYC literary agent, but she was ultimately unable to sell the title to a publisher. When my contract with her expired, I reconnected with several other agents whom had also offered representation or expressed interest one year earlier. Unfortunately, they saw this as a "recycled project".

With no agent, I marketed directly to several small publishers one of whom was interested in publishing a PG version of *One Way Ticket to Anywhere*. I felt doing so would detract from the authenticity of characters and certain scenes in this story. Full chapters would have been totally cut. I mean...really...there's nothing PG about an alcoholic's rage or the thoughts of a seventeen-year-old boy. So why pretend there is? You're about to read a book without restraint. Because this work is self published, the manuscript was reviewed for typos and technical errors by friends, not by a professional staff of editors. If you find any errors in grammar, punctuation, spelling, word usage, or other technical aspect of this work, your pointing them out to me is greatly appreciated. I will consider incorporating your feedback into future revisions of the book. If you'd like to point out a technical error or have any comments at all about the book, just send an email to richochoa@gmail.com. I will respond directly. You don't get that accessibility to the author with *Random House*. Also, because I'm not paying a full-service publisher, you probably paid less for this book.

The reach of a book depends on word of mouth referrals and positive reviews. If the book entertains you or moves you, please tell your friends and tell the world by giving it a positive online review on Amazon or Barnes and Noble. If you are bored by this story and lose interest after two chapters, no need to write a review. Let's just keep it a secret.

Introduction

Don't be confused by references within the text to multiple last names for the author. I am Ochoa, Schnabl, and Hanson. This is part of the story and I explain how that came about as part of the narrative.

Many of the character's names have been changed and a few characters are composites. There are also some characters whose names are authentic. I kept them unchanged because I think they are portrayed positively, so please don't sue me; it's my way of thanking you for being a part of my story.

I have fairly detailed memories of my childhood. That said, of course I don't remember the exact dialog used in a conversation when I was five years old. This is a memoir, not a court transcript nor a history book. You'll enjoy the book more if you don't ask yourself, "How can he possibly remember that?" Memoirists must take some writer's liberties when they develop the scenes which support the key events that they do remember. In doing so, I've tried hard to not misrepresent the fundamental storylines in this book. Although some of the blanks were filled in by parents and grandparents, the perspective and points of view represented in the book are mine, and I am human, and humans are inherently subjective and may remember events somewhat differently than other humans. In this book, I attempt to stay as objective as possible. Still, if my mother, father, sister, friends, or any other character depicted were asked to write about an event in this book, the story would come from a different perspective and likely be interpreted differently. However, you did not pay five bucks to read their stories but you have for mine, so you get my version.

I'm Gonna Die

    Sometime in 1970, we were getting ready to go to the drive-in movies when my mother got a phone call. I don't think I felt anything after she got off the phone and told me "Big Grandpa" had died. If any emotions stirred within me, it was relief that the old man whose standard greeting toward me was to twist my ear so hard that it hurt, and then stick the tip of his thumb between two fingers and say, "got your ear" wouldn't be doing that to me anymore.

    I thought my mother was overreacting a bit by cancelling the movies and all, it's not like we were planning to bring him with us or anything like that. Why couldn't we still go to the movies?

    I asked my mother what made him die.

"He had a heart attack, honey."

"What's a heart attack?"

"His heart stopped beating; then he died."

"Could *you* die?"

"Not anytime soon."

"But you might someday?"

"Yes, someday."

"You mean you *might* die someday, or you *will* die someday?"

"Hon, we all die."

"Whaddayamean?"

"Richard, everybody dies someday."

"Everybody?" I asked, slowly considering the broad scope of the word *everybody* and the way she drove the point home with her serious look and by addressing me by name.

"Yes, everybody."

Surely *I* was exempt from this cruel fate. What she meant to say was, "everybody except *you*." I was afraid to ask the question, but I did anyway. "Even me?"

She was speechless for a long time. It seemed like forever... Every silent second brought me closer to the unspoken truth. Finally, the most devastating words of my childhood. "Yes even you."

"You mean...*I'm* gonna die someday?" I needed to hear it twice to make sure there was no misunderstanding.

"When? When am I gonna die?"

"Nobody knows for sure but it's probably a long time away. Don't worry about it right now, Hon."

Probably? I knew that word. I knew it well; *probably* meant no guarantees. *Probably* meant I would probably have a heart attack like that old man who had no teeth and was always spitting nasty black tobacco juice into a red Folgers coffee can and twisting my ear. *Probably* meant I'd probably die very soon.

I walked away from my mother, pursuing solitude to ponder the enormity of what I just learned. In the backyard, I knelt in the dirt under my swing set, covered my face with my hands, and sobbed into my palms about my own impending death. It didn't matter how many superhero costumes or pajamas I wore, I was gonna die. *This ain't like a cartoon. Someday, I'm gonna die.*

The dirt on my hands absorbed the tears from my face, as I wondered why my mother even let me be born if she knew I was gonna die. At five, I was already asking myself the ultimate question about life: *What's my purpose here?*

The innate memory limitations of early childhood bring me to this starting point. This is the first scene, my first substantial memory I trust as absolute—the first event that doesn't fade into a few dots of truth connected by strands of supposition fabricated by the mature mind in an effort to create meaning from those dots. This is where my memoir begins.

Abducted

I must've been about five when I made a slight modification to my wooden jigsaw puzzle of the United States. Every state was represented by a separate piece of compressed particle board, except the five non-Maine, New England states, which on such inlaid puzzles were typically clumped together as one unit, a necessary concession the toy execs made—to strip the identities from the size-disadvantaged members of our great union in exchange for reducing their company's legal exposure to kids like me. Absent of their thoughtful gesture, surely I'd have choked on Rhode Island or wedged Vermont so deep into my ear that only a surgeon could remove it. And Delaware, poor Delaware, what a humiliating afterthought. Our first state reduced to a single blotch of paint that looked like a manufacturing defect dropped onto the edge of Maryland. But I didn't much care about those puny little states on the top right corner of the puzzle. I was focused on something bigger. I took the California piece of compressed particle board and mutilated it—smashed it with rocks, threw it repeatedly onto the pavement, and pounded it with a baseball bat. The result was a California that looked like it had been devastated by an earthquake. California was bad, and had to be punished. I knew only one thing about California. That's where my father lived.

My father abducted me when I was eight months old—stole me from my mother's Los Angeles home under the pretense of a visitation—and, for the next nine months, went into hiding with me in New York City and then Minneapolis, not once making direct contact with my mother. He occasionally called his sister to report that he and I were doing fine. Those reports, delivered to my mother by her once best friend, were the only status she ever received regarding her baby's welfare. Your son is doing fine. Nothing else.

My mother had already given up her first-born child for adoption at the age of seventeen. Three years later, my birth was her chance at redemption. She had a husband, and her husband had a job. Things were going to be different this time. But the Vegas marriage turned sour fast and ended abruptly in divorce. Then, one day my father picked me up from my mother's for a day at the zoo and returned nine months later. In the days before sensationalized national media outlets no one cared about a Father taking his own son. There were no *Amber Alerts*, no flyers posted around town; I didn't even make it onto a milk carton. My grandparents spent two thousand dollars—their life savings—to hire a private investigator. After their check cleared, he was harder to find than my father.

My mother and grandparents were powerless. The weeks turned to months and my mother began to lose hope. Then a call came from my father. "Meet me at the airport and you can have him back." When my mother was finally reunited with her child, the baby who couldn't walk or talk was running and speaking in full sentences. She missed my first steps and my first words. That's my mother's account of the story. I've never asked my father for his, nor has he offered.

I grew up listening to my mother and grandmother's horror stories of the abduction, how my evil father returned me with pneumonia, chronic asthma, and infected diaper pin holes in my hips. As the story goes, my father explained that the lady who watched me during the day was old and arthritic and probably had a hard time with diapers; then he disappeared for the next fourteen years, this time without me.

Mom and Grandma coached me on what to do if he tried to get me again. I was made to study my father's picture, and told to run and scream if I ever saw him. After nightly training rituals, I could recite my name, rank, and serial number at a much younger age than other kids. Although we'd relocated from California back to suburban Milwaukee, where my grandparents had raised my mother, and my father was in that faraway place living within a beaten puzzle piece, I fully expected to be taken again someday and grew up with a father phobia, hating and fearing a man I didn't remember.

Except for occasional complaints about his selfish ways, tidbits like he spent money intended for baby food and diapers on records and Hi-Fi stereo equipment, my mother spoke little of my father in any context other than the danger he presented to me. I was certain every stranger with black hair and a dark complexion lurking at the edge of the playground was my father preparing to take me away from my mother forever. For the first half of my childhood, that fear was always with me.

***

I'm walking home from kindergarten with two of my neighborhood classmates when a dark-haired man driving a red pickup truck with a camper in the bed offers us a ride home. I've been trained to recognize this situation. This is the moment I've been expecting and fearing. All my instincts tell me this man is my father who had returned with the intention of making that camper my childhood prison.

I am five-years-old and it's up to me to save myself.

I take off running and screaming as I've been coached, zigzagging through yards and bounding over white, picket fences, weaving a crooked path through my personal suburban obstacle course, trying to make myself harder to follow by the man who had stolen me before. I dare not look back, in fear I'd freeze in terror at the sight of my father bearing down on me. I stumble over an empty plastic baby pool, lose my balance and slide headlong across the grass. I scurry back to my feet, surprised that a huge hand had not yet horse-collared me, and run even faster, knowing he probably closed the gap during my fall. I'm exhausted, wheezing, and confused.

Why isn't he catching me?

Because I'm the fastest kid in my class, that's why.

Yeah, but he's a grown up, surely he could've caught me by now. Have a look...

While still running, I glance over my shoulder at the ground I've covered and there's no one in pursuit. I stop and scan the area like an alert soldier assessing an ambush threat. Still, nobody. Soon I'm in my own backyard, whereupon seeing no red truck outside, I dash into the safety of my house. One of my buddies is sitting at the kitchen table excitedly reporting to my anxious mother how I had fled the scene when his father offered us a ride. My father, though thousands of miles away, was always somewhere in my mind, chasing me.

***

Gradually my fear of my father abducting me diminished. No longer part of my fears, I gradually stopped thinking about him, altogether. For several years, I may not have thought about him at all. Then one night in May 1980, when I was sixteen, my mother, deeply under the influence of Jim Beam, called me into the living room—the Drinking Room.

"Richard (she only called me Richard when she'd been drinking), you're going to see your father."

She'd been in contact with my father. That alone was huge news. This was going to be an important conversation, and like almost every serious talk we had, it would occur while she was in her irrational, inebriated state.

This was the first time I'd heard my father mentioned as a present tense, real person. Until this moment, he'd always been someone from the past—the distant past, before my memories began—or maybe some kind of abstract entity, like a monster in the closet—a boogeyman. I always expected it would stay that way. My mother was opening a time capsule, and I was afraid of what was inside.

"My father? Whaddayamean?"

"I've done it for long enough." She tilted back the last ounce of her Jim and Coke, slurped, and popped the empty glass on the coffee table like a cowboy at a saloon. "It's *his* turn."

"What are you talking about? What do you mean, *his turn*? Am I coming back?"

She lifted her cigarette to her mouth, poked it between her lips further than a sober person would, engulfing almost the full length of the filter, closed her eyes, fluttered her eyelids, and drew passionately. Her Salem crackled softly as the tip glowed orange in the dim room. She paused as she absorbed every bit of precious tobacco, nicotine, and menthol. She exhaled through nose and mouth in my direction, her words modulated on the stream of smoke. "We'll see."

In a few days (when I finished my sophomore year), I'd *Go Greyhound* from my home in Lindale, Texas to introduce myself to my father and then spend at least the summer with him and his family in Sandpoint, Idaho.

"The whole summer? Why so long?" I asked. "What if I don't like him?"

"Don't worry, you'll like him; he's just like you."

I didn't take that as a compliment.

The bus stopped in Salt Lake City and a pretty girl took a seat in front of me. Too shy to speak, I tapped her arm and passed her a note:

Hi, my name is Rich. I'm going to Idaho. Where are you headed?

After a few note exchanges, I boldly moved up and sat next to Wendy. She liked me, laughed at my jokes, smiled and twirled her shiny blonde hair for hours.

Somewhere on I-84 near Mountain Home, Idaho, I realized her stop was only an hour away. Overcome with a sense of urgency, I tried to hold her hand.

She withdrew and asked me a confusing question. "Are you LDS?"

"LDS?" My mind raced for recognition of the acronym. I was clueless, but figured the correct answer was a prerequisite for taking the relationship to the next level. "You mean LSD?"

My luck had run out. While not holding my hand, she spent the last hour of our time together trying to convert me to Mormonism, before leaving my life forever in Boise.

***

There were some twenty people milling about the bus station as we pulled into my final destination. I tried to locate my father through the window, but wasn't sure what exactly to look for.

Among the men, which one is forty, has black hair, is 5'11", and resembles me?

Through the process of elimination, I reduced the list of candidates to two possible choices. One looked more like me than the other, but he seemed disinterested in the arrival of my bus. The one who resembled me less was shifting his head trying to see inside. He appeared anxious, and began walking parallel to me—me in the aisle in a slow-moving line to disembark the bus, him outside, dodging past a few people in his way.

This was definitely him.

As my foot hit the pavement, I looked at him. At first he looked right through me, like he was looking for someone else, then he saw my knowing expression and for a moment our eyes locked. This was my father. But then, as I moved toward him, he didn't come toward me; that faraway look returned, and his body language was unreceptive.

He must be quite nervous, I thought, as I approached him.

"I'm here."

His eyes twitched and nose wrinkled. His look expressed confusion.

Geez, he's got Tourettes.

Finally, he spoke. "Excuse me?"

"Uhmmm…" I hesitated and thought for a moment about how the events in one's life must have gone terribly wrong when a boy must ask the question I was about to. "Are you—?"

"Rich!" My name was being called, not by the man in front of me, whom I had already decided was both my father and odd, but by a voice from the distance, from a dark horse, a write-in candidate, a non-contender from nowhere.

"Rich!"

I turned to see who was calling my name. The man I'd spent years fearing as my abductor was hurrying toward me holding a lidded paper cup of coffee. He wore dark Levi's and a yellow T-shirt which commemorated his presence at some classic car show. His hair was jet black, like mine. He wore it slicked back like Johnny Cash, exaggerating his widow's peaks which framed a peninsula of full hair. He studied me for a moment and I him. Everybody had been telling me how much I looked like him, and now I saw for myself; I was looking into a time machine. I was looking at myself in 2005. When he hugged me, I stiffened. I felt nothing—no anger, regret, relief, love, comfort, bond—just nothing.

After telling him what a great forty-eight hour bus ride I had, we rode through Spokane in his mint condition '57 Chevy two-tone blue Bel Air two door hardtop. Outside, a thin layer of volcanic dust from the Mount St. Helens eruption was forming a blanket over the town. We made small talk about the volcano and my sports activities while many people outside wore scarves over their faces or held handkerchiefs over their mouths. Then we pulled up in front of a dilapidated house in a run-down neighborhood as he announced that he had to make a quick stop to try and collect from a customer who owed him money. Great, I thought. In addition to being a kidnapper, my father is also a drug dealer. He asked if I wanted to go in with him. I didn't really, but neither did I want to sit alone in his hot car in this ash-laden neighborhood. I followed my father into the smelly living room of an obese woman's house. I couldn't exactly place the smell, perhaps it was nursing home smell.

The big lady sat on her couch. She wore a muumuu (or maybe it was a sleepwear). The beige base of the gown was color-coordinated with the sofa, so in an odd sort of way she looked like a couch with a head sticking out.

My father got straight to the point. "Hey, remember I let you take that ten dollar Bobby Darin record for five dollars, and you said you'd pay me the other five later?"

"Yeah Richard, I'm sorry, but I can't pay ya today."

"Well, it has been two months, Joan…"

She shrugged. "Sorry."

"This is my son, Rich; he just came in from Texas. Just picked him up at the bus station. I really need the money to take him to lunch."

"I'm sorry Richard; I just don't got it right now."

"Okay, but I really need—"

"Like I said, if I had it, I'd give it ta ya, but I just don't got it."

Fifteen years of not seeing me, fifteen years of not providing one nickel of support, a childhood of constant fear, and what's the first thing he does with me? Use me as a tool to try and collect a debt.

"Oh…ah…so, you can't write a check?"

"I don't got no checking account, Richard."

"Oh, really? You don't have a checking account?"

"No."

"Wow, that's crazy, how do you pay bills? You shouldn't send cash through the mail you know…"

"I get money orders."

"Yeah, I used to do that too, but checks are so much easier. You don't have to go to the store all the time to buy money orders. And they charge fifty cents for money orders now at the bank, and seventy-five at the post office. You should get a checking account."

The head on the couch stared at him, said nothing.

He tried one more time. "So you don't have any money?"

"Jesus Christ Richard, I told you I don't got no money right now!"

"Oh, I'm sorry, when do you think you will?"

Oh my God, he must've driven my mother fucking nuts.

I examine the tattered furniture resting on the filthy carpet and grungy drapery hanging from crooked curtain rods, while trying to breathe through my mouth, because I've come to associate the smell not with a nursing home but with body odor or possibly urine, and I contemplate the situation. I want to scold him. *You've had fifteen years to prepare for our reunion, and you're depending on this lard-ass to come through with our lunch money? Nice move kidnapper. I have a few bucks, let's just get out of this putrid place and I'll buy us lunch!* But I keep my thoughts to myself, partly because I want to give him a chance, but also because the repercussion of such an outburst might be to immediately get back on that bus and return to Texas, and I didn't want to do that—my mother was back there.

My first impression of my father will always be of an age-progressed version of myself, asking the big lady who smelled like piss and never once stood from her sofa, "Can't you write me a check?"

I may look like him, but I will never be like him. I will never harass an obese lady sitting on her couch in her own smelly home for five dollars.

It was a variation of the same promise I had made to myself while on the bus ride to meet him: Even if I like him, I will never be like him. I will never abandon my child and leave him at the mercy of the world and a series of step-fathers. No matter what happens, no matter what the situation, no matter how bad the mother, I will be a better *man* than that; I will be a better Father than that. I would spend a lot of time that summer building a mental list of ways I would never be like him.

***

We arrive at his house where there are two thick photo albums, conspicuous by their solitary placement on the kitchen table in an otherwise cluttered home. We sit down at the table and he begins showing me pictures he took during the nine months we hid from my mother, the apathetic police, and the lousy private detective. He flips through pages of photos of me I've never seen before while talking about the period of time he had me as if he's reminiscing about a family vacation, with no apparent remorse for the anguish he inflicted on my mother and grandparents, or the trauma he may have subsequently caused me. I wait for the explanation, the emotion, the tearful apology. It doesn't come. It will never come.

He makes no mention of the events leading up to those nine months. No explanation of how it is he came to believe it'd be a good idea if he took me and hid for almost a year. Those nine months he had me were his only reference point now, his only real connection to me that made me his son. I think in his mind, those nine months made him my father. In my mind, those nine months would prevent him from ever being that.

I look at one particular black and white photo that spooks me. I'm at the 1964 New York City World's Fair, standing alone in some kind of drab outfit, high-water pants accenting my white socks and Buster Browns. There's not another human in the picture. The sky, overcast and foreboding, frames the skyscrapers behind me and they loom over me like giant monsters. The wind pulls my hair over a barely discernible side-part and my face is hollow with lack of expression. But here's the eerie part: I get this weird sensation. It's like the-me-in-the-picture is desperately looking for help, someone...yes, the kid is waiting for the-me-here-today to come rescue him. And today-me knows I'm the only one who can do it. I look into my own eyes like I'm looking at a file photo of a child I do not know; a photo that had just popped up on a television newscast with a bold caption stretched across the bottom of the screen—**MISSING CHILD.** This boy's safety depends on me. I must find that boy. I gotta get a message to that kid: Hang on little man, you will be okay. I *promise* you will be okay.

I snap out of the semi-trance and study my father's face for just a moment as he turns a page in the photo album; just long enough to contemplate the fact that I am here, in my abductor's house, but just short enough to avoid his realizing that I'm freaked out.

"...And here's you with the sweet old lady who watched you during the day when I was at work..."

That's her! The old hag who stuck me with diaper pins.

The abduction is not in the past, it's happening right now, right before my eyes in the pages of this photo album, just as my mother had described it, no... predicted it. I'm watching it but am helpless to stop it. I want to punch him, punch my father right in the side of the face before I see the next picture. And while my father is stunned from my punch, I will run to the basement where there's an old lady poking the little boy in these pictures with diaper pins, and I will lead him to safety. And all the terror and anxiety will be gone, like it never happened.

But he is nice, my father. Polite. Funny. Good-looking, like me. He is like me in many ways. He seems pretty reasonable. He hugged me and bought me lunch and paid for my bus ticket up here.

How could *this* man have done *that*?

Maybe I should ask him?

No, maybe later, after I get to know him.

I'm reminded of a feeling that I haven't had in many years. That same paranoia I used to live with every day. I'd forgotten what that feels like.

This doesn't seem right. Why am I here?

I tell myself my feelings are absurd. *It's okay, that's the past. I'm as big as he is.*

He can't hurt me anymore.

I was wrong about that.

Chocolate Milk

It didn't matter that I was five, I didn't want anyone bossing me around or telling me what to do. I was a big boy and wanted some control over my life, so I talked a playmate into walking from the playground outside our apartment building to the Waukesha business district, even though it was miles away. My mom was taking a nap so I figured we'd walk to town, check out the scene, and walk back before she woke up.

An hour or so later, with parched throats, we came across a diner I'd been to before. Neither of us was big enough to push the heavy door open, so we hung around until somebody passed through then piggybacked in. We climbed onto our own spin-able barstools at the counter. Mom always made us sit in a booth; she never let us sit at the counter, right there where all the action is. The two of us spun ourselves dizzy until a waitress came over.

Certain my charm would supersede our need for cash, I ordered large chocolate milks for both of us. Mom always made me drink white milk, but since she wasn't there, I figured I'd try to get away with chocolate. *How could she possibly find out?* Our very own waitress complied with our request, cheerfully serving us each gallon-sized glasses of chocolate milk, and a dose of small talk.

"So, where do you guys live?"

My buddy had been struck mute by the bright lights and big city. He had that I-wanna-wrap-my-arms-around-my-mommy's-leg-and-hide-behind-her look. If we were going to carry on with grown-ups, I knew I'd have to do all the talking. "In those gray apartments by the big slide," I said.

She smiled and nodded. I was convinced she knew exactly where to find me if struck by the urge to push a five year old on a swing. "Do you guys want some gum?"

"Yeah!"

"My treat," the young waitress said as she plopped down a pack of Trident on the counter.

Her treat? Can we take the gum home or not? Whose gum is this, ours or hers?

I was so excited to chew gum, perhaps it was my first time doing so. The TV said, "four out of five dentists surveyed recommend Trident for their patients who chew gum." I felt like a grown-up. I'd decided when and where to go, where to sit, what to drink, all on my own. I even had an adult serving me. I loved the independence of making these decisions for myself. I was powerful, in charge at the scene, and showing my little buddy how to live. *Stick with me kid, I'll take you places.*

One old lady, in her thirties, came and sat on the barstool next to me. She had an inexplicable lack of desire to spin on her barstool. Instead she joined the waitress in quizzing me. If their question was easy enough, I responded with an answer; if I thought the answer might get me in trouble, I'd just spin on the barstool and say "I don't know," or "I guess." There seemed to be a lot of fuss being made over us by the other diners and I didn't understand why we were getting so much attention. The small crowd around us was making me a bit nervous; what if someone recognized me and told my mother? I wanted to keep the whole thing low key; you know, just knock back a couple tall ones and chew some gum with my playground buddy while chatting with the waitress. A policeman came into the diner and took the lady's place on the barstool next to me. By this point, I'd grown a bit weary of explaining to people where my gray house was and how it is my friend and I came to be in the diner, drinking chocolate milk and following dentists' advice while spinning on these barstools. I explained it one more time to the officer, "We're here for the chocolate milk..."

I remember thinking how nice this policeman was. He had a gun and bullets on his belt, and as an officer of the law, I thought he'd be well within his rights to shoot us in our heads for leaving our play area and drinking chocolate milk, killing us both as we sat there on the spinning barstools—splattering our brains all over the counter in the process. But instead of shooting us, he offered to give us a ride in his real live police car!

I had fully expected for us to drink some milk, chew some gum, and walk home, arriving just before my mother awoke from her nap that I was hoping would last four hours. A ride increased the chances of my mom not even knowing I'd been gone, so I accepted the ride on behalf of my little buddy, believing I actually had a say in the matter. I was hoping we'd get diverted to a crime-in-progress on the way home. Maybe the policeman would pull over and use his long black club to beat a bad guy who'd stolen an old lady's purse. Nothing that exciting happened, so I settled for getting to turn the siren on for a few seconds. I directed the officer to my apartment complex, but when we got there, my plan began to fall apart. Instead of dropping us off at the curb, the officer insisted, over my objections, on taking me all the way to my door and speaking to my mother. I realized I'd been trapped. This policeman was not my friend; he was a tattletale. I knew a meeting between he and my mother wasn't in my best interest—he had too much dirt on me. My mind raced with ideas for avoiding punishment. *Maybe I'll tell my mother the policeman is lying. That he just came up to the playground and grabbed me because he wants to get a medal for returning a lost boy.* I realized my buddy was too weak to stick with me on that story, so I gave up on that idea. Still sitting in the squad car, I knew I had to take charge of this situation, just like I had in the diner.

"Uhmm...my mom's not home."

"Where is she?"

"She's at work."

"Well, let's just check to see if maybe she got off early."

"Actually, I think she's sleeping right now, and she's really mean to whoever wakes her up from her naps..."

"I think she'll be nice to me."

"I don't think so, she's not nice to anybody," I replied, trying to instill the fear of Mom into him.

But this guy was not gonna give up. Obviously, my best chance was to make a run for it. I'd outrun the policeman and lose him in the woods across the street. Then, after he tired of looking for me, I'd re-emerge from the forest and walk into my apartment as if I'd been playing on the monkey bars all afternoon.

As he let me out of the car, I prepared to make my break and leave my friend to his own devices. I studied the officer and waited for just the right moment to take off. *I'll go when he's distracted with my friend.* I figured a little head start was all I'd need. Then I noticed his gun, again. The policeman had been very nice so far in that he had not shot us, but I was certain if I ran from him now I'd take a bullet right between my shoulder blades and meet with the death that I'd recently come to fear. So I reconsidered my options and showed him to my apartment.

When we reached the door, one last time I tried to assure him that I was okay now and no longer required his assistance. Out of desperation, I tried to level with him. "Mister, if you tell my mom, she will whip me." This may have been the first real truth I'd told all day.

He knocked anyway. Mom came to the door. She was frantic. Sure enough, she was nice to the officer—I'd never seen her so submissive before.

When she was spanking me, I screamed so loud she put one hand over my mouth while the other tended to business. I bit her hand. She responded by hitting me harder. Her striking hand got either tired or sore, so she retrieved a wooden spoon, and whipped me with that until it snapped in half. This began a long history of wooden spoons breaking across my backside.

Tomorrow was another day, and I went to bed seeing nothing wrong with my behavior. I knew the freedom, and the gum, I had tasted this day was just the start. I didn't take well to parental oppression, and I knew many more similar adventures were waiting for me; I simply had to be brave enough to pursue them. I hated being a little kid, living at the whim of my mother's decisions, doing the boring stuff that she made me do: sitting at the beauty shop, watching her stupid TV shows, being dragged into women's restrooms while shopping for ugly wigs and hideous dresses that seemed to come straight off the set of *Love American Style*. I wanted to be a grown-up. I wanted to be big and strong so if my father ever tried to take me, I could beat him up.

***

Unable to get chocolate milk at home, I often resorted to cold calling, knocking randomly on doors, asking whoever answered if they had any I could drink. While dressed in my Batman outfit, I knocked and waited. An old lady (*old* like really old, not in her thirties) came to the door.
I asked very politely, "Hi, do you have any chocolate milk?"
"Chocolate milk? What for?"
"To drink."
"Where's your mother?"
She lectured me about how it wasn't her responsibility to feed the neighborhood kids. If I wanted chocolate milk, I'd have to get it from my mother, she told me. It was like the old lady was flaunting her chocolate milk. *Na nanny boo boo, I got chocolate milk and you can't have any.*

She closed the door on me before I had a chance to respond. I was outraged by her scolding and by the arrogance of her dismissal. *My mother? What's wrong with this lady? If I could get chocolate milk from my mother, I wouldn't be asking her.* I'd taken the trouble of dressing in my Batman costume, and felt I should be rewarded—kinda like Halloween. I knocked on her door again. When she opened it, I immediately punched her in the stomach and yelled, "Kapoooowww", like I'd seen pop-up in animated dialog boxes during the fight scenes on the *Batman and Robin* television show. Then I ran down the stairs landing on every third one, singing the Batman theme loudly as my cape flowed behind me:

♫♫*Da na na na na*
Na na na na na na
Batmaaaaan! ♫♫

Soon, I'd be released from that grounding, and stand upon the hood of a parked car, raise a brick over my head and with both hands throw it down onto the windshield with all my might, just to see what would happen. A broken windshield and another broken wooden spoon...

Bouncing Baby Sister

I enjoyed getting up on weekend mornings to watch cartoons while everyone else slept in. In the days of four channels, the most significant cartoon time was Saturday mornings. The Sunday morning lineup consisted mostly of church programming and shows like *Meet the Press*, which featured old men, dressed in suits, using their vocabulary words in sentences. But there were just enough kid's shows to keep me in front of the TV on Sunday mornings as well. I'd drag my pillow and blankets off my bed and make morning camp on the living room floor. Then I'd make myself a few bowls of cereal, and drift off into an animation-induced bliss while the rest of the house slept.

One Sunday morning, *Davey and Goliath* was interrupted by an important message. An Indian cried about litter. The next commercial reminded me I had a *Stretch Armstrong* in the basement, so I ran downstairs to retrieve it. Returning to my pallet, resilient man tool in tow, I heard Christopher Glenn babble about what's *In the News*. I tried to pull the limbs off the beefy brute, but as always, was unsuccessful in stretching the unflappable slug to its snapping point. I decided to retrieve a box of cereal from the kitchen.

My attention was split between three activities: watching the claymation Morman sermonette, digging the free toy out of a box of cereal—one of those little cars that you wind up by rubbing its wheels against the floor—and keeping an eye on my one-year-old sister, Ginger. On this morning, my mother had assigned me the task of looking after her, before returning to sleep off whatever she had drank the night before. Despite being four years older, watching my sister was something I'd already proved I was not qualified to do. I wasn't even capable of watching myself, let alone a baby.

My arm was elbow deep in the Frankenberries, having trapped the toy car with my fingertips against the bottom of the box while disbursing a volume of pink dyed oats equal to the volume of my lower arm on the living room carpet, when I heard a series of thumps coming from the basement—as if someone had thrown something down the steps. I knew what that noise was—Ginger. She was the reason I had been constantly scolded by my mother to keep the basement door shut. I ran to the top of the stairs, stood in the open doorway, and looked down. Ginger was lying quiet and motionless at the bottom of the staircase. I ran down the stairs, placing my hands under her armpits lifted her limp body, and carried her up the steps while studying her face and making baby noises at her, trying in vain to draw some response. When I laid her on the floor in the living room, I noticed she had a gray bulge the size of half a golf ball protruding from her forehead. She was still unresponsive. I began to panic in the realization that my negligence had caused my sister's death.

Distraught over her death, and the enormity of the punishment I'd get for causing it, my mind grasped for stories that would exonerate me. *This can't be my fault!* I needed to make up a lie so good, so detailed that even I would believe it. A tall, black man wearing a blue shirt opened the front door, came in and hit Ginger in the head with a pipe, and then ran away. No, they'd never believe that... A rock, yes, that's it, a rock came flying in through the window and hit her in the head. I'd need evidence. I'd have to produce a broken window and a big rock. That could be arranged...

From the television, something Davey's Father said caught my ear. The clay dad, with his big, blue, round eyes, brown helmet hair, and an undying faith in God's love, was lecturing Davey in his typical youth minister voice. The non-confrontational approach was far different than the get-your-shit-out-of-the-goddamned-driveway-or-next-time-I'll-run-the goddamn-things-over lectures I was accustomed to getting from my step-father. "God loves all of us

Davey, and he's watching over us all the time, even when you do the wrong thing." At that moment, Ginger began to stir. Then she started crying. She was alive. Ginger was alive! She may never be as smart as me because of brain damage but it'd take years for anyone to figure that out, and by then nobody would ever know it was my fault.

    I was convinced God was talking directly to me through Davey's Father's three position mouth. I felt like I had saved Ginger, and I'd been a good big brother. I recall how important I thought it was to be a good brother and knowing that it was the right way to be. I remember this event probably as much for those custodial feelings as for the incident itself. I wish I could write a lot of stories about how I protected my little sister, stories that would make me a more endearing character. I wish I could say that when my friends threw handfuls of pebbles at her as she played dolls on the driveway, I defended her, instead of having to admit I joined them. And when she was the target of my mother's wrath, possibly even for something that I'd done, I wish I could claim I came to her defense, standing boldly between my mother's rage and my little sister. Instead, mostly I remember the thoughts of self preservation, the at-least-it's-not-me feeling. Sadly, this story—my rescuing her from the bottom of that stairwell—is the last time in my childhood I remember protecting her. The adult-me wonders what happened to that little kid, who on that Sunday morning, wanted to be a good big brother? Where did I lose it?

A Scarred Childhood

It was time for God to introduce me to the concept of payback.

I'm riding a tricycle in the apartment play area when this little girl I know approaches. She wants to play with me, take turns riding the tricycle that I'm perfectly happy not sharing.

She asks nicely for a turn. "Hey Rich, can I ride that bike for a little while?"

"Nooooo!" I exclaim, as I peddle away.

"Okay, then I'll just ride that one…over there," she announces while pointing in the direction of a second tricycle.

She begins to trot toward the other bike. I turn my head to have a look. It's no ordinary bike. This is a brand new, fire engine red tricycle decked out with a squeeze-horn, handle bar streamers, and pastel spoke sleeves. But most of all, it sports a little red wagon as a towable accessory. *I could ride that bike and pull other kids in the wagon.* The girl is almost halfway to the prize bike when I change my mind. I don't care if she rides this old bike; I want to ride the one with the red wagon.

There's an Aesop fable in which a dog with a piece of meat is crossing over a bridge. He looks down and sees his reflection in the water below. Instead of enjoying the meal he already has, he prepares to attack what he thinks is another dog carrying meat so that he might have both pieces. He opens his mouth to bark, but when he does, his dinner falls from his mouth and is washed away in the water.

I jump off my tricycle and start running. I have to beat her to that bike. Even with her head start, her foot speed is no match for mine. She's running with her arms down and her palms facing the ground—like a girl. I pass her just in time to claim my prize, but in my haste to arrive first, I neglect to decelerate. I'm headed for the bike and can't stop. My legs become entangled and I'm soaring spread eagle toward the little red wagon. I commemorate my arrival by planting my forehead into the rim of the wagon. Undeterred by the collision, I get up and claim my prize. My head hurts from the crash, but pain is secondary at this moment. Everything is secondary to enjoying the moment of my hard-earned reward.

"Rich, you're bleeding," the girl cries out in a horrified tone.

Don't trust her. She's a girl; you know they can't be trusted. She's just trying to trick you into getting off the bike. Maybe I should make her get in the wagon, take a corner real fast and see if she tumps over.

"I'm sure," I respond sarcastically, raising my hand to my forehead to touch the point of impact. I swipe the wound with my fingertips and look at my hand. Blood streams down my fingertips toward my palm. Soon, the vision in one of my eyes is distorted by the blood pouring into it from my forehead. I look down and see drops of blood on the pavement—blood is everywhere. Suddenly, I no longer care about bikes; not when I'm in danger of bleeding to death. I scream for Mommy and run toward my apartment. Not wanting to be in trouble for my selfish behavior, I explain how the girl had pushed me into the wagon, and insist she be punished for causing my injury. The stitches feel like a third eyelash. For a week, I pretend I have an eye in the middle of my forehead.

While I still had the stitches, my mother, during a tantrum, threw a shoe at my step-father. He dodged it and the shoe struck me squarely in the eye. At four, I was too young to understand what could provoke my mother into a shouting fit and cause her to throw a shoe at my eye. The perspective of years tells me that this was likely an alcohol-related accident. The doctor put a bandage over my injured eye and took the stitches out of my head.

Ramming my head into a red wagon was not an isolated event. My childhood was a series of reckless activities and the scars on my body serve as an outline for the childhood years of my memoir.

I knew a stovetop was used to heat food, but what exactly would it do to my finger? It burned the flesh on the middle finger of my right hand so badly I still remember the smell. I didn't even have the sense to preserve my dominant hand by experimenting on the other. When I started following NFL football a couple of years later, I imagined the horseshoe shaped scar on my finger was a divine sign that I was destined to play for the Baltimore Colts. Fans of the Colts probably already know that never happened. If God was sending a message with that scar, he overestimated my ability to properly interpret it. The experiments continued.

Would it hurt if I put my foot under the tire of my grandparent's slow-moving Volkswagen Bug? Yes—it hurt. I escaped serious injury only because Grandpa was driving on soft grass.

We lived in one house in Mukwonago, Wisconsin, at which the school bus stop was across a small lake from my house. The lake froze solid for months during the cold winters, allowing me to take a shortcut across the ice, saving myself five minutes of walking time in the frigid weather. As winter eased and temperatures climbed, my mother warned me the ice was too thin to walk across. I continued to do so for another week, proving to myself that I must be smarter than her. One day, after the thin ice fractured beneath me, soaking both legs up to my knees and nearly turning me into a human Popsicle, I hypothesized, "Running on thin ice must be safer than walking on it." So, the next day I sprinted across the lake. The ice cracked beneath me but I didn't fall in, proving to myself that, literally speaking, my mother's statement was correct, the ice was too thin to *walk* across, but running was okay. Somehow I made it through that winter. Fortunately we moved before the next one, thus I avoided certain drowning.

Mom knew I was a risk taker and often exaggerated a threat in hopes of keeping me away from danger. After she spread a film of ant poison on a sheet of Saran Wrap, and placed it on the pantry floor directly under the cereal shelf, she called me to the pantry and pointed at the jelly-like substance. "This is to kill ants, don't ever touch this. This poison is so powerful that if it comes in contact with your skin, it will kill you!"

"But couldn't a doctor save you?"

"No, you will die instantly, just don't ever touch it."

To my seven-year-old mind, the idea of spreading such a lethal substance in a high traffic area just to get rid of a few piss ants was a bad decision. Even to me, the king of all risk takers, the small reward didn't seem to justify such a high risk. My fear of that poison was so great I didn't even go near the pantry for several weeks. I asked Mom to remove it for the sake of me and my three-year-old sister. She wouldn't comply.

One morning, I woke up first and decided to help myself to a bowl of cereal. I had completely forgotten about the poison, so I opened the pantry door and took a step toward a box of *Life*—the cereal that Mikey liked—but stepped in the deadly Saran Wrap. I quickly lifted my leg but the gooey poison caused the Saran Wrap to stick to the bottom of my foot. My scream carried the horror of a boy who was expecting to drop dead within seconds. This was my death. *Everybody dies,* and now it was my turn. I was sure my foot was about to disintegrate before my eyes. After that, it'd be a matter of time before I bled to death from my sizzling stump.

My mother came running down the stairs wearing only a bedspread. When she arrived at the scene of my imminent death, I was hopping around on one leg while kicking the other desperately in the air in an effort to shake the Saran Wrap loose, believing it was already too late to save my own life.

"The poison! I touched the poison, Mom."

My mother nonchalantly pulled the wrap off my foot with one hand as she held the bed linens over her breasts with the other.

"I'm gonna die!" I cried in full throttle panic.

"Richard, stop it. It won't really kill you unless you eat it."

I didn't believe her, because I'd seen enough war movies to know they always tell the guy who's about to die that he's gonna be okay. *Does it hurt to die?*

In those old movies, false reassurance is always the last thing the dying man hears before his head tilts sideways signifying his death. There's compassion in having the man's death capture him by surprise as he lies there expecting a lifesaving shot of just the right doctor's medicine. Nobody ever tells a dying soldier, "Dude, it's bad. Ain't no way you're pulling through this one."

Skeptical of her reassurance, I tried to catch my breath through my sobs as she hugged me. The flesh on my foot was not disintegrating into bloody bubbles. "How long will it take before I die?"

"You're not gonna die. I promise."

"But, you said touching it would kill you!"

"I just said that to keep you away from it."

Everybody has a few moments in their life in which they thought they were going to meet their maker. My moment is unique in that it involves gooey Saran Wrap on my foot.

Another dramatic near-death episode occurred when I was seven. One night at a family get-together, an uncle told me that when the last word of the Bible is read, the world will come to an end. I was mortified. Granted, the Bible is a huge book but with all the people this world, I was certain one of them was on the last chapter at that very moment, catapulting the earth toward Armageddon. Distraught over my own imminent death, not to mention the annihilation of the human race at the hands of some wise-ass speed reader, I went to my older cousin's room and repeated the terrifying news.

"That's bullshit, Rich."

"No, Danny, Uncle Gary said so."

He retrieved a Bible from a bookshelf in his room. Then, he sat on the corner of his bed and began reading the last few paragraphs of *Revelation*.

MY GOD! What's he doing! I wasn't sure of the rules. Did he have to read *everything* prior to this for God to kill us all, or can he jump right in at the very end and launch the Doomsday machine?

Horrified by his disregard for the human race, I started screaming with all my lungs, desperate for a grown-up to come rushing into the room and intervene. But we were upstairs, there was loud music playing downstairs. Everyone down there was blitzed anyway. Loud-talking and dulled senses were the norm. *Nobody is hearing me.*

And he read, "God will add to him the plagues that are written in this book."

"No Dannyyyy! Cut it out! Stop it!" My words broken with fear and sobbing.

And he read, "Surely I am coming quickly."

Oh crap. This can't be about to happen. There was no time to run for help and return, perhaps with my uncle who knew what was at stake. Before I got back, everything and everyone I knew would be vaporized. The fate of mankind lay in the balance, so I wrestled with my cousin, trying to rip the Bible from his big hands before his teenaged defiance killed all three billion of us. *Please God, give me strength to save the world and I will do anything you want for the rest of my life!* Danny, so much bigger and stronger than me, was easily able to fend me off with one arm as he held the good book with his other hand and continued to read the last verses of Revelation. "The grace of our Lord Jesus Christ be with you all. Ahmen."

Please God, he cheated! He only read the last page. That doesn't count, don't blow us all up! I hope you noticed he cheated!

I bit my cousin's hand, which would surely be my last act on earth seconds before the planet exploded into a great big mushroom cloud. God heard my prayer and answered it. The world did not end and I lived to deal with trivial matters such as accepting the fact my uncle was a liar, and hoping my favorite cousin would forgive me for the deep imprint my incisors left on the meaty palm slab under his thumb.

Discovering your parents and other adults lie about everything from ant poison to the Bible had a profound effect on me. I became cynical at a young age and soon began to doubt everything. At an extended family picnic, my cousins and step-cousins were moping around the pool after eating their lunch, believing what their parents had told them—that they would surely cramp up and sink to a horrible death at the bottom of the pool if they tried to swim within thirty minutes of eating. *There's no way a hot dog and a few potato chips are gonna sink me.* Wanting to dispel this idiotic notion, I cannonballed into the pool and swam around in the deep end as the other kids watched in bug-eyed astonishment. They would have been no more impressed with my brashness had I been dodging gunfire. My mother came over and persuaded me out of the water by digging her fingernails into my arm. She led me over to the picnic table, collecting more DNA with every tug, where, with her free hand, she grabbed a wooden spoon from the German potato salad. Then she took me behind a car where she broke the spoon over my ass on the first swat.

Sometimes adults don't lie about that kind of stuff, and separating the truth from the fiction can be risky. I noticed tweezers sitting on the bathroom counter right below an electrical outlet. *Is this just another in a long string of lies?* In case you've never performed the experiment yourself, FOR THE LOVE OF GOD – DON'T. When I poked the tweezer tips in the side-by-side holes, an invisible force jolted deep within my arm and shoulder and threw me against the toilet as all the lights in the house went out. Turns out Mom was telling the truth on that one.

Skepticism defined my childhood. I didn't rely on hearsay; I wanted to find out everything for myself. When Mom told me looking straight into the sun would burn my eyeballs, I thought she meant my eyes would catch on fire. That had to be a lie. *If my eyes were on fire would I be able to see the fire?* I sat on the front porch ready for the experiment. Just in case she was right, I had a big glass of water beside me to douse the first flames. My eyes burned, but didn't catch on fire. I saw spots for days—sometimes I wonder if I still see those spots.

I truly believe my surviving childhood was a divine miracle. The grace of our Lord Jesus Christ *was* with me. Ahmen.

The Pee Desk

I was one of those unfortunate children whose ears stuck way out. It wasn't until fourth grade that I started concealing them with long hair. Until then, I was often teased about looking like a monkey in my school pictures. When I go back and look at those photos, I realize I did look like a monkey.

On the morning of first-grade picture day, I hatched a plan. Using clear scotch tape, I tried different techniques of taping my ears against my head. I tried different angles, but the tape just wouldn't stick. My hair was in the way. Finally, I ran a long piece of tape from one ear, around the back of my head to the other, similar to those dental headgear straps that unfortunate kids wore as accessories with their braces. In a ridiculous attempt to obscure the band of tape running around the back of my head, I fluffed up my hair so it partially layered over the tape—akin to a middle-aged man with a bad comb-over. I looked at my reflection in the mirror. *Yes! That's it. This will not be like Kindergarten. I will not look like a chimp in this year's picture.*

With my ears pinned back, I got on the school bus and went straight to the back seat, where I spent most of the ride obsessively pressing the tape solidly onto each ear by pinching it between my thumbs and forefingers. I went to class hoping that nobody would notice, after all, the tape was supposed to be "transparent."

Before class even started, some kids were laughing at me. The girl sitting behind me told me I looked stupid. *What do I do now?*

How much longer until we take the pictures? Should I take the tape off? By the time class had started, I felt like the whole room was snickering. Humiliated and distressed, I peed my pants. I'm not talking about a couple ounces sneaking out and creating a questionable spot in my shiny purple pants the size of an *O* in a handmade *Okay* gesture. When I say I peed in my pants, I mean I emptied my bladder, creating a puddle on my desk seat, and a flowing waterfall which fed a small man-made lake on the tile floor. One boy felt compelled to raise his hand bringing it to the attention of the teacher. "That kid peed," he said, pointing at me. *Wait till recess loud-mouth. I'm gonna beat the snot out of you.*

Our teacher suggested to the class that this was not funny, then pulled the tape off my head and moved me to an empty desk, much to the amusement of twenty six year olds. Then she called the office on the intercom and asked for a custodian visit.

Moments later, a janitor poked his head through the door and interrupted class, "Mrs. McKinney, you called? What's the problem?"

"Uhmm…Ahh… we had a little accident over here," she said, trying to use a tone like it was no big deal, while gesturing toward me with the typical female underhanded point, complete with the classic 90 degree elbow bend.

"An accident you say, what kind of accident?" he grunted with all the couth of a small town drug store clerk calling for a price check on Viagra over the store's loudspeaker. He mopped up my pee while Mrs. McKinney tried in vain to keep the class's attention; but whatever she said was not nearly as fascinating as watching the janitor mop up my puddle of urine and spray the desk with disinfectant.

"Mrs. McKinney, what's he spraying on the desk?" asked one idiotic kid.

"The spray kills germs," she said, as if my piss would make everyone sick.

Wait till recess you stupid little runt, when I get through with tattletale, I'm beating you up next.

For a long time, nobody would sit in that desk, hereafter referred to by my classmates as the "pee desk." A new kid came to class one day, and Mrs. McKinney directed him to sit in the pee desk. Twenty kids gasped and surveyed each other for reactions—eyebrows raised, eyes bugged, everyone spellbound as they watched the new kid walk toward his assigned seat. The moment the boy's butt touched the seat, everybody started cracking up. Befuddled, he looked around the class, wondering what could possibly be so funny. I wished he had peed himself in panic, as I had done, to take some focus off me. No such luck. At recess, someone apparently told him about that desk's history, because afterwards he was sitting in a different desk. Mrs. McKinney solved the problem by rearranging the desks, creating uncertainty and a class debate about who was sitting in the pee desk.

One thing about my elementary school years that I want to be clear about: I was a bad-ass—always the toughest kid in the class. I didn't back down from anyone. Not that I went looking for fights, but they seemed to come my way. It didn't matter how much bigger the kid was. By beating up older kids who made fun of me, I was able to take back some sliver of the self-esteem that they took from me. Usually, I'd establish my alpha male status within the first week of being at a new school. When you're still peeing in your pants at seven, you'd better be tough. And I was. I walked around with a chip on my shoulder. *Yeah, I peed in my pants...ya wanna make something of it?*

***

I was playing marbles with a second grade classmate one morning before class, when a sixth grade bully ran up and kicked a plastic butter tub of my friend's marbles, blasting them across the asphalt basketball court. My friend was too scared to even object, when his collection of marbles, including *cat eyes* and several translucent oversized marbles we called *boulders*, skittered in fifty different directions. Well on his way to a life of pacifism, he just buried his face in his hands and started crying, which was just the response the bully was hoping for. I had a far different reaction. As the marble kicking punk was walking away laughing, and backslapping with his buddy, I ran up behind him at full speed, leapt into the air and did a Kung Fu kick into his lower back. The big kid went skidding across the blacktop on his stomach, leaving some elbow and chin flesh on the pavement. Before he knew what hit him, I was on top of him rabbit punching the back of his head, bouncing his face against the hard asphalt. He started crying out, "Stop! Stop! I give!" With those magic words, I was obliged to honor the playground code of conduct. I'd just accepted his unconditional surrender, when his buddy came up from behind and grabbed me. Aggressive gestures directed at a kid already engaged in a fight with someone else was a clear breech of playground fight etiquette. I spun around and landed a solid elbow to his jaw. He dropped to his knees, clutched his chin, and stared at me in awe. Perhaps he was in shock. The fight was over.

Shortly after class started, I was summoned to the office. When I walked into the Principal's office, the bullies—each of them over a head taller than I—were sitting next to each other in little plastic school chairs, holding ice packs on their bloody lips. Marble kicker still had granular traces of blacktop grit pressed into his cheeks.

I was accustomed to being there in the principal's office; I'd made regular visits at the behest of my teachers. Every time, it was the same thing: my teacher complaining to some out-of-touch old fogie about my impulsive behavior. Even though my visits were routine, the whole Principal's office scene made me anxious. Principal's lectures seemed to last forever.

What are you gonna do to me this time? Just get to the punishment old man, what's the bottom line here? Are you gonna take away my recess? Call my mom? Detention? Write sentences?

I will not beat the hell out of bullies who kick my marbles.

I will not beat the hell out of bullies who kick my marbles.

Five times? What? Just get on with it; punish me and let's get this over with...

On this morning, after beating up those two bullies, I pretended to listen to the Principal, but his words were Charlie Brown's teacher noises in my brain. I replayed the fight in my mind, as the Principal droned on. "Blah, blah, blah." *Look at them with their fat lips. Huh!* Drifting off into a daydream, imagining myself as the leading man in my favorite TV show, *Kung Fu,* a smile took over my face. There was an abrupt silence. The Principal had finished his lecture. He looked at me with raised eyebrows, indicating he was waiting on my response. *What did he just ask me?* I probed my subconscious to see if I could at least rerun his last sentence in my mind. *Nope. Time for the default response.*

"I don't know," I said, looking down at my feet. *I don't know* was pretty versatile, it could be used in response to almost any interrogative. But in fact, I did know. I knew pretty much everything.

My Favorite Song

It's the first week of my freshman year at Lindale High School, and KTYL, the most popular radio station in Tyler, Texas, is giving a presentation at our school. The whole student body and faculty—six hundred people—gather in the auditorium for the assembly.

On stage, some DJs tell us about careers in broadcasting, the music industry, how they rub elbows with rock stars whose concerts they promote. They pitch some upcoming events they're sponsoring. One talks about interviewing Van Halen on her morning show. *Yes, spinning records sounds like a pretty solid career choice. It might be a good followup plan after I win the 1988 Olympic Decathlon.* As they talk, I envision myself in a successful DJ lifestyle. Maybe I'll work in New York and party with the guys from AC/DC and Styx.

They finish filling my mind with grand illusions about a media career, then they announce they want to close their presentation with a contest—pop culture trivia questions. "Okay everyone, the game is simple. We ask a question and the first student in the audience to raise their hand gets a chance to answer."

Get the question right, win a ball cap, a bumper sticker, T-shirt, or a Frisbee branded with the station's call letters.

The DJ begins. "Who sang with Elton John in the song, *Don't Go Breaking—*"

My hand shoots up, but it's too late; somebody else wins the coveted T-shirt. It goes like this for about three questions. *I need a more aggressive strategy. I'll raise my hand on the first syllable of the next question.*

"Okay, this last one should be easy," the DJ says.

I assume the ready position.

"What—"

I throw my hand high into the air, spring to my feet, maybe even leave the earth, make *Horshack* noises, hoping to catch the eye of the speaker.

"—is your favorite song?"

The hot DJ, who looks like a college girl, sees me. She points to me while others are still thinking about raising their hands. "The young man in the blue T-shirt and the...the...ahhh...green corduroy pants..."

All eyes are now focused on the over-excited freshman who'd outsmarted everyone. I'm the only one standing in the audience. All ears anxious to hear my answer. The victory of being selected quickly turns to panic. My mind repeats the question and for the first time actually processes it. *What's my favorite song? What kind of stupid question is that?* My brain races for an answer, but nothing is there, nothing at all, I can't think of a single song. My earlier thoughts of AC/DC and Styx abandon me. Hundreds of kids still have their hands up. The DJ grows impatient. "Green corduroys, what's your answer?" I'd better come up with something in the next second or two, or I'll lose my chance for a T-shirt and look like an idiot. The only thing worse than giving a stupid answer would be not giving one at all. How foolish would I look if I sat back down having not uttered a peep? People would laugh at me.

There is no wrong answer, just say something...anything. Anything at all will get you that T-shirt. What's that song where they say, "Hey teachers, leave them kids alone?" Hell, I always forget the name of that song. It should be named "Hey Teachers, leave them kids alone," but it's not. It's got some stupid one-word title of an inanimate object or something...SHIT! Why can't I remember the title? Forget it dumbass, you know you always forget the name of that song. Think of something else...

Finally an image—actually it's a series of images—comes into focus. I see Helen Reddy dressed in a long sleek *Barney*-purple pantsuit.

Her outfit has bell-bottomed legs with rhinestones, and rhinestones on her sleeves to match. Or maybe they aren't rhinestones; maybe they're diamonds. Maybe she got so rich off that song—the song that's now playing like a broken record in my mind—that she can afford to perform with hundreds of diamonds glued to her purple outfit. She's singing on *The Tonight Show*, or *The Dick Cavett Show, or The-I-can't-remember-what-show*, but it was a long time ago. I was about ten when I watched it. Helen Reddy—kinda cute—not hot, like Jeannie (from *I Dream of Jeannie*), but cute in her own strong, matronly, small-but-perky-breast-and-no-curves kind of way. And she sings:

♪ ♪ *I am strong (strong)*
I am invincible (invincible)
I am woman ♪ ♪

Helen Reddy's face and breasts build a force field around my mind. Nothing else can enter. Yes, I hear her roar, in numbers too great to ignore. My brain, so hopelessly locked into those sounds and images from five years before, tries to trick my mouth into blurting out the name of the song and launching a Capella into the anthem for women's rights.

♪♪ *I am woman watch me grow*
See me standing toe to toe
As I spread my lovin' arms across the land ♪ ♪

But I'm a fourteen-year-old boy and *I am Woman* is not the right answer to this question. I don't know what that right response is, but I will not utter those three words. I am smarter than that.

Searching for a song—any song—any song but *that* song.

Finally, another TV memory comes to me. It's more Helen Reddy, but at least she's not in that purple outfit singing that song, so it's a breakthrough in that regard. She's at the *Grammys*, wearing a yellow dress, accepting an award for that song, and she's thanking God because "*she* makes everything possible." She's calling God a *she*? But she's cute here too, giving her Grammy acceptance speech. I like her shoulder-length hair—not too long, not too short either. The tips of her hair caress the sides of her neck. I want to push that hair aside, expose her nape, and kiss—

Her hair, it's like…like…Toni Tennille's! Finally, another artist has broken Helen Reddy's once impenetrable shield around my brain and a better song comes to mind. Relief pours over me like medicine. I've thought of someone else—someone who has never called God a *she*. I'm excited—excited that I have something to say. Still standing, about to address almost everyone I know who have all assembled here, at this place and time, for the sole purpose of hearing me answer this question, I excitedly exclaim, *"Love Will Keep Us Together!"*

The deafening laughter hits me like a train. A highly contagious dynamic follows. Each person in the auditorium is laughing louder than they ever have. I never knew laughter could be so loud. *Nothing could possibly be more embarrassing.* I try to find a safe place, but instead I'm back in the pee desk, waiting for the janitor to come and clean up my puddle of piss. And every boy and girl in class is laughing at me, the girls laughing louder than the boys. And it feels like I've lived my whole life in that pee desk.

The DJ motions for me to come and claim my prize.

I think of every shameful thing I've ever done. As I reluctantly walk toward the stage, I'm sure they are all reading my mind. Every time I've picked my nose. Every time I've touched myself. They are seeing it all. The crowd is passing around naked pictures of me; and in those pictures it is shriveled and small, barely discernible, and each of them laughs at my withered manhood with complete and heartfelt amusement. The girls laugh louder than the boys. They all revel in my humiliation.

The previous prize winners had jogged up to the cusp of the stage where they caught a prize tossed down to them, after which they unceremoniously returned to their seats as the next question was asked. Now I'm at the lip of the stage, one of the DJs extends his hand, pulls me up to join him, then guides me toward the smoking hot blonde who has the microphone in one hand and my prize in the other. She hands me a t-shirt, grabs my wrist and raises my arm as if I've just knocked out Muhammad Ali in a title bout, and hollers into the microphone these five words: *"Love Will keep*

Us Together!" Before the initial jubilation even subsides, she's whipping the student body into a heightened state of frenzy.

I glance out into the audience and see a mob of bloodthirsty sadists, a sea of carnivores throwing their heads back and forth. I notice two guys high fiving. I even see two or three guys who have thrown themselves out of their chairs and are literally rolling in the aisles.

This is a nightmare—no, a daymare—of epic proportions. I'm standing on the stage totally naked, just as I was moments before in the pictures that all have seen. But now, it's not pictures, I'm flesh-and-blood-naked, and the most important part of me is withdrawn like a turtle's head tucked inside its shell, just as in the pictures.

As I hurry back toward my seat with my stupid T-shirt, a group of seniors bombard me with paper wads, pens, and pencils, as the DJs announce the presentation is over. The crowd files out amid a jovial buzz. I hear words and sound bites jumping above the laughter: Captain and Tennille, gay, geek, freaking homo, Love Will Keep Us Together...

How will I ever live this down? How will I ever be able to endure four years at this school? How will I ever possibly get a girlfriend? The next four years of my life will be hell. I'll never make it to graduation. People are pushing and tugging on me as we bottleneck through auditorium doors. With my head bowed in utter embarrassment, I notice my green corduroys. *Thank God I wasn't really naked. Of course there were no pictures, and they weren't reading my mind...*

But the laughter persists.

We'll see who's laughing when I win an Olympic gold medal.

Man of the House

My mother was living a life of divorces, marriages, alcoholism, and suffering from cycles of depression. I didn't understand how deeply those factors penetrated my life. Some things were obvious. I knew Mom didn't speak as clearly at night as she did during the day, her words slurred, lectures rambled on without a point. I knew every time I started a new school, I probably wouldn't be there long because I'd never been at any school very long. Nothing was permanent, not my house, friends, school, or even my mother's mate. The only constants: my mother's drinking, my grandparents, and my bratty little sister who knew less about what's going on than I did.

Carl Schnabl was my first step-father. Even though he was technically my step-father, I thought of Carl as my father, since I couldn't remember a time before he was there. I called him *Dad*, even though I knew my real father was a bad man who stole me. Carl and my mother started dating around the time my real father abducted me.

Soon after I rammed my forehead into the wagon and my mom threw that slipper into my eye, we moved out of an apartment and into a nice house. On the back of Carl's relentless work ethic in building trades: framing houses, working concrete, drywall, and roofing, we had the American dream—a nice house with shag carpet, avocado-colored appliances and a green station wagon. Across the street from our house was a great big hill. The top of the hill was covered with trees. My friends and I liked to hike to that woods and build forts, hit one another with sticks, beat each other up, throw rocks at anything that moved, including each other, and most of all, climb trees. One day, I'd climbed halfway up a tall tree—I would say I was fifty feet up, but you know how everything seems bigger when you're a kid, so it was probably more like ten—when I lost my grip. I was rotating toward a head-first impact. This probably should've been the end. There'd be no talented and beautiful daughters, no bitter ex-wife who believes she's entitled to not only the formal dining room table that I made with my own hands, but also the belt sander and table saw I used to make it, no memoir. If God hadn't had other plans for me, right now you'd be reading some overrated David Sedaris essays, or maybe a totally different woe-is-me story that I wrote by holding a pen in my mouth. One of my legs caught between two twisted branches. My torso kept rotating. The tree branches gripped my ankle, first like the hand of God, then like a vise. I was hanging upside down, suspended by my ankle. I screamed. I cried. I squirmed and tried to grab another branch with my arms so I could pull myself up and work my leg loose. But I needed four strong arms (like most boys my age, I had only two scrawny ones). The harder I tried, the tighter the tree squeezed. I was stuck.

"Go get my dad!" I cried to my friends.

One boy ran down the hill, while another stood beneath me trying to calm me down. Hanging upside down from the tree, I saw my running friend fall down (or up), get back to his feet and then disappear over the ridge.

Carl was 5'5", but ten minutes later, when he came running over the ridge beside my friend, he looked like a giant. He climbed the tree and like Samson pushing against pillars, spread the branches apart and pushed my leg out. My dad had saved me. *That's what Fathers were supposed to do, not take their kid and hide him from his mother for a year.*

***

Carl owned the first porn I ever stumbled upon. He left Ginger and I in his white '68 Chevy pickup while he ran into the filling station—

probably to buy cigarettes. Always fidgeting, I opened the glove box and an endless stream of hardcore porn came flowing out. Well-worn miniature picture books and magazines covered our laps and the passenger side floor mat. I took a curious moment to consider the content, and then panicked when I realized I'd better not get caught looking at these pictures—pictures of men whipping women, of naked women kissing each other, and pictures of policewomen handcuffing men, apparently arresting them for being naked. I had a thousand unanswered questions, but above all I wondered why men were sticking their wieners into the faces of adult women who were dressed as cheerleaders. I quickly gathered all the liberated porn and tried to cram it back into the small space from which it came. But it was no use—the glove box was not built to hold so much porn. One thick piece was designed to be unfolded into a poster and folded up like a road map. When Carl returned to the truck, I had that thing completely unfolded big as a map of Texas, while frantically poking at one of the creases.

I thought I was gonna be in trouble; instead Carl took a defensive position, trying to justify his possession of the fine art. In retrospect, this makes sense, but at the time, I thought I was in for a major whipping. Funny how a kid's mind works; how he can be conditioned to think everything that goes wrong is his fault.

"I caught one of my workers on the jobsite 'whacking off' with this trash in a porta-potty. I had to take it away from him so he'd get back to work."

I had no idea what *whacking off* was; I assumed it was construction worker slang for *wiping off*, so for several years I assumed most construction workers wiped their asses with glossy pages of hardcore porn, which seemed a little stiff and not very absorbent to suit me, *but, hey, those guys are pretty tough, so I guess they don't mind.*

***

Carl and my mother broke up less than a year after moving into a quad-level, custom house in *Hidden Lakes*. We kids didn't see much of Carl, mainly because he worked so much construction overtime to pay for such a big house in a neighborhood of white-collared moderate wealth.

When Carl was home, he liked to play with us more than Mom did. We fished from the back yard, just the two of us, where he'd trounce me in long distance casting competitions, and then rub it in. "You will never beat the cast master, young grasshopper." The first time he took me to a sporting goods store, he let me pick out a tackle box. On subsequent visits, he always let me get a new lure. Shiny and colorful, I always had a hard time deciding, but would be sure to pick a heavy one, hoping it would improve the length of my cast. He taught me the alphabet, and we raced slot cars on a track we built in the basement. I had a tendency to hold the throttle lever down completely for max speed. My car invariably jumped the track on the tight turns and flew across the room before slamming into a wall. Fed up with constantly retrieving and repairing cars, Carl put a pin in the throttle handle, preventing my car from going airborne. When we raced each other, he'd lap me and laugh at me when I cried about how unfair it was. Twenty years later, he'd beat Ginger and me in a game of miniature golf by trimming eight strokes off his actual score by discounting all the three foot "gimmies" he missed. That was Carl. He had a great sense of humor. One which perhaps is difficult for a small child to enjoy.

After he and Mom split, Carl saw us kids a handful of times during the next year, before he too disappeared without prior notice for the rest of my childhood. I had no clue the last visit we had with him would be the last time I'd ever call anybody *Dad*, and that Ginger was about to join my fate—having *her* father unceremoniously disappear for her entire childhood, as mine had eight years before.

I recall sitting on the front porch in front of our big house on the lake with my fishing pole and tackle box, adding a new lure or bobber or something to my line, getting ready to go out back and fish by myself. My mom walked out and said, "You probably should hide that fishing stuff somewhere, he might come by today and decide to take it." *Oh my God! Would my dad really take my tackle box and all my lures? I'm not sure I want him to come back if he's gonna take my tackle box.* Whether by design or accident, with that simple statement, my mother had aligned me against Carl.

Carl is mean. He wants to take my tackle box away. Mom is good. She wants me to keep it. Carl never had a chance to defend himself. Never got the chance to say what he probably would have had he known what I was thinking, "I would never take your tackle box, Rich. I want you to have that tackle box forever, because you and I stocked it together, and when you use it, think of the great times we had fishing together, and know that I'd like to be there with you." *Mom good. Carl bad.* That's how a child's mind works. I can't remember what became of that tackle box, but I know Carl never came for it. He sent Ginger a birthday card from Florida and then twelve years of nothing. Eventually, Ginger and I re-established relationships with Carl. By then, I was twenty, and he was no longer *Dad*; he was *Carl*.

Because I didn't meet my biological father until I was sixteen, I never felt comfortable calling him *Dad* either. And I couldn't bring myself to address him by his first name, either. Mr. Ochoa would have been too formal. I'm in my forties now, and I still don't know what to call him. Haven't we all had someone in our lives that we never felt comfortable addressing by either name or title, and for some reason it makes sense that they remain un-addressable to us? Your girlfriend's father, a grandfather you never met until you were an adult, a little league coach who you knew damn well wasn't a real coach, so *coach* didn't seem right and you were too chummy to call him *Mr. Bradley*, and too young to use his first name, even though he once said you could, a Chinese lady at work whose name begins with *X,* who gave little consideration to your English tongue when deciding to not take an American name like *Mary* when she immigrated, or your Vietnamese neighbor, Phuc Loung. Well, for me, that un-addressable person is my father. For almost thirty years I've managed some semblance of a relationship with him without ever addressing him as anything other than "Hey." Even today, if I want to call him, I contrive some greeting that purposely circumvents my need to address him.

"Hey, I hear you're getting some snow up there."
"Huh? Who's this?"
"This is Rich."
"Oh, hi, how's it going, Rich?"

Nowhere is it more obviously awkward to deal with an un-addressable than when one engages in a team sport. We played a touch football game in the park a few years back at a family-and-friends outing. I was playing quarterback and had just thrown a pass to my father. In his late fifties, he was a little slower running the out pattern than I'd anticipated. He had yet to make his turn and the ball was nearly halfway to him. If he didn't turn, not only would the pass be incomplete, but it might knock him out, since the ball was a line drive headed straight for his head off my strong arm. I had to get his attention with one or two syllables, but didn't have a name for him. So I yelled, "Hey!" My father turned instantly, responding as if he had heard his own name, snatched the ball and tucked it under one arm, holding it like a girl, with the tips of the ball pointing up and down, as he ran for a touchdown.

"Hey, nice catch," I said as we exchanged a high five afterwards. *Hey*. Yeah, it seemed to fit as well as anything.

I wondered what it would've been like to have that as a child, to play football with your dad in the park, to be like my friends who were always doing stuff with their dads. To have your dad help you build a tree fort. The football game in the park occurred twenty-five years too late. It's like that really hot girl in high school that never had the time for you and then shows interest at your twenty-year reunion. But she's let herself go, she's not who she was, neither are you, and it's just too late. The years have stolen your feelings. There's nothing left. That day in the park, I realized the years had stolen my father. Our touchdown hook-up was a meaningless score at the end of a blowout. It looked nice on the stat sheet but the game was already over.

***

One cold winter Saturday it occurred to me that I hadn't seen Carl for a couple of days, and asked Mom where he was.

"Where's Dad?"

"You know, Carl's not really your dad..."

"Yeah, I know...but where is he?"

"He's moved out, Rich," her voice had a hint of sadness.

"Well...when's he coming back?"

"He's not coming back."
"Whaddayamean? Why not?"
"Carl and I are splitting up."
"Well...where is he? I want to see him."
"I don't know where he is."
"Will he come back to see me?"
"We'll see."

And that was it for an explanation. The man who I knew as my father—the one I counted on to protect me from my real father, the man who rescued me from the vise-like grip of that twisted tree—may or may not come back to see me. *We'll see.* The same response my mother gave when I asked for candy at the grocery store—*we'll see.* I began to cry.

"Rich, now that he's gone I'll need you to look after me and Ginger. You're going to be the *man of the house.* Me and Ginger are depending on you..."

I remember with such clarity that moment. Distraught about my dad's departure, at the same time overcome with pride over my promotion. This was a serious responsibility for an eight year old and I wasn't sure if I was man enough to succeed at it. I was asking my mother for some specific duties that went along with my new role of *man of the house*, when our conversation was interrupted. A man named Doug pulled up in the driveway in his baby-blue Buick convertible with white leather seats. I knew who Doug was; I'd seen him at two or three parties at our place. He and his wife Beth were friends of my parents. He got out of his car, gave my mother a hug and a quick kiss on the lips, regarded me—"How ya doing slugger?"—and walked into my house like he owned the place. *What the heck's going on? Hey Mom, there's a guy we barely know that just walked into our house, but don't worry, my first course of action as man of this house will be to throw his ass out.* My tenure as *man of the house* had lasted as long as it had taken for Doug to walk from his Buick to our front door. I had a new step-father, and this one was 100 Proof.

Doug was three years younger than my mother—a twenty-six-year-old hippie who worked in the same real-estate office as Mom. Doug left his wife to move in with us. Meanwhile, Carl started seeing Beth, which angered my mother. At my age, I wasn't concerned with who started seeing whom first; it was a simple Wife swap, or from my perspective, a Father swap.

At first, Doug made an effort to spend time with Ginger and me. One night we all played Monopoly. As Mom and Doug's liquor flowed, the game began to lose order as my opponents started sharing each other's money and rolling the dice into the green houses and red hotels, scattering them with all the veracity of a killer hurricane. Mom knew integrity of competition was important to me, and that annoyed her. Ignoring my requests for them to roll the dice into a separate box, which I'd set up beside the game board, she and my next stepfather slammed game pieces with dice for the sole purpose of watching me reconfigure the game board after their turns. But I was happy the four of us were doing something as a family. That Monopoly game would be our last board game together. And, the first time Doug and I played catch with the Frisbee was also the last. During those first few months with Doug, there were a lot of first and lasts. At the beginning of Doug's reign, my mother seemed to give us kids a bit more attention, but her intentions didn't have staying power.

I was in a vacant lot across from our house, throwing a baseball up and then batting it as far as I could, pretending to be Hank Aaron breaking Babe Ruth's home run record. Exceeding my expectations, I slammed it beyond the short grass and watched as it bounced into the tall weeds on the first hop. My mother came outside and saw me across the street knocking down the brush, searching for something.

"Whatchya doing?" she yelled in a pleasing tone.

"Looking for my ball."

She walked across the street and joined me. Side by side we kicked down weeds, looking for my baseball. *Why is she out here? She's never done anything like this before. Surely she has something more important to do than help me find this baseball.* For a few minutes, I was happy to have her with me. With her help, I just knew we'd find my ball. Then I realized, this was my Darrell Porter autographed ball. He was a catcher for the Milwaukee Brewers and often came into the IHOP where Grandma worked. She had gone through a bit of effort to get that signature. My mother had told me not to play with that ball. *God, please don't let HER find that ball. If she does, don't let her see the signature.* After ten minutes she gave up. "We'll get you another one," she said, and went back inside. I was glad I hadn't wasted any more of her time, but was also relieved she hadn't found out I'd been playing with *that* ball. I finally found it an hour later. But somehow those ten minutes she spent made me feel like we'd found it together. Everything had worked out. I didn't get in trouble and my mom had helped me. I was so excited, I ran inside to tell her that I'd found my ball, shutting the front door hard behind me on my way in. *Where is she?*

"Quit slamming that goddamned door! I'm trying to sleep!" she yelled from her upstairs bedroom. I remember thinking I'd tell her later, when she was in a better mood. I don't think I ever did.

After those first and lasts with Doug, soon it would be only the drinking—every single night, both of them, drinking. One night, a few months into Doug's reign, my mother called Ginger and I into the living room toward the end of happy hour.

"I want you two to call him 'Dad'," she said. Doug looked at her like he supported what she was asking.

Ginger tried it for a little while, but the idea fizzled out when I didn't go along with it. I wasn't even certain if Mom remembered making the request. Sorry *Hey*, Carl, Doug, everybody else who later married my mother, and my father-in-law, nobody ever was, nor will be, my "Dad."

***

I knew there was something wrong with my mother's rationale when she and Doug went on a spy mission one evening. As Ginger and I sat in the back seat, they drove to Beth's house—the one she had shared with Doug—until a few days ago. They took pictures of Carl's truck in the driveway. Then they tiptoed up to the window and snapped some pictures of whatever was going on inside. They scurried back and when they got inside the car, Mom was talking about what a sonofabitch Carl was, while Doug was going on about what a tramp Beth was.

Apparently, they believed their conversation was above my head, but I knew about sex. My mother had explained it to me about once a year during her frequent rummed-up rants, beginning when I was in first grade. There I was—still wetting the bed and just having outgrown eating crayons—and my inebriated mother is slurring an explanation as to what possesses a man and a woman to come to a mutual agreement that it would be a good idea for him to stick his wiener up inside her as an expression of love.

I was horrified at the visualization of this revolting act. How could a woman ever forgive a man who would do something like that to her? "But, you and Dad [Carl] don't do that, do you?" I asked, believing what she was describing to me was surely some sort of deviant behavior practiced only by a few sick people, kinda like cannibalism or something—certainly not behavior happening in the room next to mine. "Doesn't it hurt?" I questioned, dumbstruck by her admission of practicing this despicable behavior.

I didn't get the thirty-second overview; I got everything, right down to bleeding vaginas. I still recall the look of exasperation on her face when I asked questions—questions that made it painfully clear that I didn't get the reason for this outrageous activity, nor understand why she didn't simply put an end to the abuse. I mistook her frustration for sad resignation that she was doomed to spend the rest of her life having to endure such cruelty from men.

She talked about sperm, which I deduced to be just the grown up, proper word for pee. Pee was the only thing I'd ever seen come out of there, so for the next five years I just assumed the man peed to make the woman pregnant. The thought of a woman consenting repeatedly to this practice made me want to throw-up. I promised myself I'd never engage in such disgusting behavior. I would make my wife very happy because I would never do that to her! How ironic that the initial thoughts of a six-year-old boy regarding sex are close to how some women really feel.

At that age, I made no distinction between drunk-mom and sober-mom, so I was confused as to why I kept getting the same lecture over and over: "Richard," her brain and mouth and tongue numbed by booze, "Do you know where babies come from?"

Yeah, Mom, you told me this twice before. In later years, I came to understand that sober-mom recalled little of what drunk-mom did or said.

At the time of the paparazzi expedition, as she and Doug talked adult-code, it didn't occur to her that she had already given me the encryption key to easily decipher their unsecured conversation. I couldn't understand why my dad [Carl] wanted to make a baby with Doug's wife. I thought he was *my* dad.

I never understood Mom and Doug's motivation that night they took those pictures. Perhaps she was trying to gain leverage in the upcoming divorce settlement. Probably she was drunk that night.

It's hard to for me to say how my mother's drinking evolved because I don't know how much of my recognition of the problem was due to heightened awareness because of my advancing age, and how much was due to a possible increase in her intake. Later, she would claim she began drinking only because Doug drank. Doug literally forced her to drink, she claimed. But when I first met my real father's mother who had last seen my mother eight years before Doug came into the picture, one of the first questions she asked was, "How is your mother? Is she still drinking?" And, I remember many pre-Doug occasions when she was drunk. I'm sure booze was in her when she threw that shoe into my eye. She drank daily, years before Doug and in years since.

She will read this—read of things she did that weren't clear to her the next day, but clear to me many years later. She will not like what she reads. She will need a drink.

Will You Be My Friend?

When Carl left, he took more than himself. My new stepfather, Doug, had a blasé approach toward earning money; and without Carl's sixty-hour work weeks, our family couldn't afford to stay in the big house in Hidden Lakes. So, at the end of my third grade, just in time for a lonely summer, we moved to a smaller home in New Berlin. I explored the new neighborhood every day but there were never any kids outside.

I missed all my old friends, including my best friend, Tim. The two of us were bound by our passion for football. We played it every school recess, talked about the Packers at lunch, swapped our NFL clothing, and traded football cards on the long bus rides home. We traded the same cards to one another for so long that they had each at some point belonged to the other, except one coveted card—Tim's John Brockington rookie. Tim would never let it go, no matter what I offered. One day, after pondering it all day, I got on the bus and made a final offer.

"Tim, I'll give you all my cards, for your John Brockington."

He looked down at the card, then at me, contemplating the deal for a moment before he decided. "No way, Jose."

That bus trip went very much like every other, even though we both knew it was our last ride together. This was my final day at school. I was moving away from Mukwonago, away from Clarendon Avenue Elementary.

"Hey Tim, maybe after I move, this summer my mom'll drive me over to your house and we can play all day."

"Yeah Rich, that would be cool. We could play electric football!"

"Alright, I'll ask her!"

Just before Tim got up at his stop, he unceremoniously handed me his Brockington. "Here, you can have it until you come over this summer."

I was stunned. This, by far, was the most generous act ever directed toward me. He got off the bus and then chased it a few strides while waving. I stuck my head out the window as the bus picked up speed. "Bye Tim, See you this summer!"

So I wouldn't forget to give him the card back when I saw him again, I wrote in pen, in the sky, just to the left of John Brockington's head, *Tim*.

I never saw Tim again. At nine, I didn't understand childhood friendships at that age rarely transcend time and distance. Today, that John Brockington card is my longest held possession.

Despite having a football card of my favorite player, the summer was turning out to be a real drag. It was so bad that I was looking forward to the start of school. I was moping around the house all day, playing with my baseball and football cards, wondering how the Professor could be smart enough to build a radio from a coconut but never thought to fix the hole in the boat so he and his friends could get off the island, when my mother suggested, "Maybe you should knock on doors and ask people if they have kids who want to play."

I thought this was the stupidest idea ever. But instead of sitting around waiting for Pong to be invented, I followed her advice, fully expecting to return home in an hour or so and complain. "Mom, I knocked on every door in this neighborhood, and there's nobody to play with. I told you we shouldn't have moved! We should've stayed at the old house; I had friends there. You should've just stayed with Dad [Carl]."

After dumb looks and quick dismissals from the occupants of the first five houses, finally a cute girl answered the door. She wore a tight T-shirt with no bra, and she'd just begun to bloom. I was dumbstruck in her presence. Her face looked my age, but her body said she was two or three years older. At a pit stop between the little girl she no longer was and the sexy teenager she was about to become, this lovely creature had lips that screamed to be kissed. But I was just trying to summon enough nerve to speak. I hadn't considered playing with girls, they weren't even on my radar that morning, or probably ever before. But, if this girl-woman grabbed my wrist and asked me to come in and play dolls, I would've happily done so. I was prepared to do whatever she wanted. I tried to tell her little breasts the nature of my business, how we could hang out, play football, board games, catch grasshoppers, tear their legs off, take them to the pond and feed them to frogs, dress up in each other's underwear, whatever, but I was nervous she might think I liked her. "So…uhm…do you have any brothers that like sports?"

She gave me directions to a house where two boys lived. I was walking away from her place, when she yelled from an upstairs window. "His aim is ready!"

Aim? What Aim? Is he gonna shoot me? "Say what?" I hollered back.

She cupped her hands around her mouth. "His name is Eddie!"

I imitated her megaphone hands. "Oh…Okay, thanks!" *Eddie and me will definitely be coming back here.*

A man wearing a crisp golf shirt and a welcoming smile opened the door at Eddie's house. He had a styled haircut and was clean shaven. There was a twinkle of kindness in his eyes.

"Hi, my name is Rich and I'm looking for somebody to play with. I heard two boys live here."

His smile broadened, he extended his hand and introduced himself. "Nice to meet you Rich, I'm Don Stube. I've got two boys who I'm sure would like to meet you. Come on in."

I knew about stranger danger, but the warmth in his voice and smile and the way he shook my hand in an introduction ritual normally reserved for grown-ups, this man was no stranger. He looked and acted like a man I could trust. Tall, fit, strong jawline, and good-looking, Mr. Stube was far different than Doug, who, with his long, scraggly hair and a beard, would have answered our door wearing frayed cutoff jeans and a tank top, with a cigarette dangling from his mouth and a cocktail in his hand. Mr. Stube invited me to sit down on a chair at the kitchen table. I didn't hear any commotion coming from other rooms. Still in the kitchen, he called for his boys. "Eddie! Danny!" There didn't seem to be anyone else in the house. "Hold on a second, Rich." He disappeared for a minute and returned with two boys near my age. Mr. Stube was an all-American dad—Ward Cleaver—and I was about to play catch with Wally and Beaver. Afterwards, June would serve me, my new best friend, Eddie, and his little brother, Danny, fresh-baked chocolate chip cookies and ice-cold milk.

Oddly, my new friends knew nothing about the girl who set us up. I described her in great detail.

"She knew your name, Ed!"

"Yeah, right, you're such a liar."

"Ed, I'm not kidding, she knew you. I thought she might be your girlfriend or something."

Eddie and Danny wanted to see her, this legendary beauty in her full pubescent glory. After a week of playing in the street in front of her house, waiting to catch a glimpse of her coming or going, my friends doubted her existence. Time for plan B: We got up the nerve to ring her doorbell. The idea was to ask her if she wanted to help us build a tree fort. We stood three abreast on her porch, on the altar of puberty, about to be graced with a phenomenal beauty. The power of three, accomplishing together what none of us had the courage to do alone. Eddie was especially nervous because this girl knew him, and he didn't know if that was good or bad. I acted cool and bold to compensate for my buddies. I knew it'd be up to me to do all the talking. But as soon as I heard the doorbell ring, our plans evaporated in the vapor of my panic. I was way out of my league. I took off running—running from those little titties because they scared the hell out of me. They were loaded with ammo and she could aim them at me and shoot holes in my body. My friends followed in full sprint behind me. I never saw that girl again; my friends never saw the girl at all. My fear of girls, and the mysteries inside them would last many years. We built one heckuva tree fort, the three of us, with occasional technical support from Mr. Stube, but the whole time I wished she was with us—with me.

***

Eddie had a BB gun, but the only game he allowed us to hunt was grasshoppers. Sometimes if we were hunting near a street and a car passed, I'd check to see if Eddie was paying attention as I toted the gun. If he wasn't, I'd shoot at the car. The first time I did this, he heard the puff noise, then turned around and chastised me for wasting ammo, shooting at nothing. From then on, every time I shot at a passing car I masked the noise with a series of loud coughs. Sometimes I even pulled the trigger with my thumb as the gun sat on my shoulder, the barrel pointing behind me. He never knew I was shooting at cars until one driver stopped to chase us. Fortunately, we were both fast runners and disappeared into the woods easily.

Eddie was very popular at school among boys, girls, and teachers. Besides being smart, he was a good athlete, like me. He liked my jokes and seemed to appreciate my obnoxious side, yet he had a sincerity I hadn't yet developed. He had mature judgment for a nine year old and was measured and analytical in his decision making, while I was spontaneous and often reckless. He knew shooting someone's car with a BB gun would mess up their paint job and cause them stress. He didn't want to do that. He was concerned about other people and had thoughts that didn't cross my mind. I just thought about how challenging it was to try to shoot a moving target. He was my first friend who did what his parents told him, even when they weren't looking, and that blew my mind. I'd never known a kid who thought so deeply about the consequences of his actions. He was the first friend I had who wasn't impulsive.

"Come on Ed, your parents won't know, so explain to me again why we shouldn't take that tennis racquet out of our neighbor's open garage and use it to hit rocks high into the air over those houses?"

"It could hit somebody."

"Hit somebody? Come on Ed, I doubt the rock would hit someone."

"What if it hit a pregnant lady?"

"Don't be ridiculous Ed, what are the odds that it would hit a pregnant lady? All the pregnant ladies are inside or at hospitals."

"I'm just saying, it could hit anyone, an old man maybe."

"No old men live round here Ed, and besides if it hit an old man, it'd probably be just in the foot or the arm, and he'd be okay anyway. I mean he wouldn't be hurt very bad; he probably wouldn't even cry."

"Or, you might break someone's window."

"Yeah...that would be neat."

"It wouldn't be neat for them..."

In those subtle exchanges that all boys have with their friends, Eddie was rubbing off on me, his influence greater than my parents'; he was trimming the edge off my impulsiveness. And I saw a little bit of me reflected in him. I taught him to loosen up and live a little bit.

On the first day of fourth grade, we were riding the school bus home. I noticed Eddie had a brand new *I Dream of Jeannie* lunchbox. I loved Jeannie. In fact, within a matter of minutes I would be plopping down in front of the TV to watch her.

"Wow! Let me see your lunchbox!"

He pulled it closer toward himself and cradled it with his other hand as if he were trying to hide it from me.

"Ed, what's wrong with you? I said let me see your lunchbox."

He held it out, offering me a look, but his hands were covering Jeannie. He was acting weird. I pulled it from his grip before he had a chance to put up a fight.

I held the wonderful lunchbox in my own hands and looked down at it. Placed right over the focal point, running straight across Jeannie's chest, was a small piece of masking tape, maybe only an inch long. Written on the tape, in black marker, in two lines was his name:

Ed
Stube

"What's this? You put your name right over her tits?" I peeled the tape off and took a good look at what I'd been waiting to see, but Jeannie's breasts were blemished—the paint completely scratched off, leaving two dime-size areas of shiny unpainted tin. At first, I thought I'd messed up his lunchbox by pulling off the tape, but there was no paint residue from Jeannie's red genie top on the masking tape.

"What happened to it, Ed?"

"Whaddayamean?"

"It's all scratched up. Her tits are gone. What happened?"

"I don't know, I guess it got scraped against something."

His little brother, Dan, sitting behind us on the bus, spoke up. "He's a liar! He tried to rub her shirt off so he could see her titties."

"What? Ed, did YOU do THAT?"

He didn't respond, but his body language told on him. He bowed his head and looked ashamed.

"I can't believe you're so stupid," I said, laughing. "Did you really think they'd paint titties under her shirt?"

I couldn't believe a ten-year-old A-student could be ignorant enough to ruin such a stunning lunchbox like that. I visualized Eddie sitting in his bedroom, door closed, heart beating with the excitement of undressing Jeannie by scratching on the lunchbox with his finger nail. I was struck by the realization that his stupidity ran much deeper than I first imagined. Eddie had not rubbed out just one of Jeannie's breasts, but he actually applied his misguided handiwork to both of them! At some point in the process, having already scrapped her blouse into bare tin, instead of fleshy breast, Eddie still thought it a possibility that the other breast would be different. So, like a lottery junkie rubbing that gray crud off a scratch-off card, he scratched at the second one. As if the lunchbox guys had said when setting up the production line, "Hey, let's make her naked under her clothes on one side, but not the other…"

Until the lunchbox, I'd always assumed Eddie was much smarter than me. He made better grades and his artwork and science projects won blue ribbons. But, all his good grades would be forever tainted in my eyes because of the lunchbox debacle, and whenever my mother held up Eddie as a role model of how I should behave, in my mind I always compared my offenses to his lame attempt to sneak a peek as Jeannie's titties. "Okay, maybe I did accidentally hit Ginger in the chin with a shovel requiring six stitches, but at least I'm not foolish enough to destroy a Jeannie lunchbox because I think some lunchbox artist painted naked breasts under a woman's blouse."

It's not that I didn't admire his intentions; I wanted to take a peek at Jeannie's breasts as much as the next kid. I wanted Jeannie. I didn't know exactly for what, but I knew I wanted her for something. I wished I could summon her to appear in my bedroom, watch her wiggle her nose, and hear her say "yes master?"

***

I should confess that even as Eddie was trying to undress Jeannie with his fingernail, I had my share of irrational misconceptions. We were assigned to give an oral book report to the class. I choose a book about UFOs. To fourth graders, UFOs, the Lochness Monster, Bigfoot, and the Bermuda Triangle where the most fascinating subjects of the day; and most book reports were on one of those four mysteries. I didn't actually read the UFO book, so I had no idea what was inside. With so many books on the subject, I just assumed their existence was well documented. For my presentation, I made everything up. To add my touch of flair, I added visuals: pictures of spaceships I'd drawn with crayons on small poster boards.

I got up in front of the class and showed the pictures and talked about alien spacecraft I'd drawn. One drawing looked like a great big silver pinball bearing with two support legs. "This spaceship landed in Japan and is in the Tokyo Museum of Science." In the middle of the circle there was a door, depicted simply as a rectangle that wasn't colored silver. In the doorway, a stick-figured green alien with an over-sized yellow head and slanted black eyes (as if landing in Tokyo would cause the alien pilot to have Asian features), waved to my classmates with his three-fingered hand. With its thin, green body, yellow head, and slanted eyes, my alien looked like an emaciated Japanese wearing a Green Bay Packer uniform. "Physicists think this ship travels faster than the speed of light, but no human pilot is willing to try and fly it because a human's reaction time isn't as fast as the aliens' who landed there…"

More fabricated artwork and explanations. "This UFO is in a museum in Paris, France. Scientists believe it came from a much closer planet than the Tokyo craft because it only travels at the speed of sound…and this one was tossed to the ground and smashed up in a Kansas tornado…and this flying saucer here, it has ribbed panels to make it aerodynamic. It landed near downtown Moscow, but the Russians won't let any Americans study it, so not much is known about it except a couple of pictures that a double agent snuck out of Russia…"

After class, Mrs. Adams challenged me to read the book a little closer, to which I confidently replied that I had read it pretty good the first time. I didn't understand why she gave the most entertaining presentation a C.

***

Eddie became the first fourth grader in Prospect Hill Elementary School history to win the Presidential Physical Fitness Award. To win the award, a student had to place in the 90th percentile in each of ten different athletic events. The award criteria were intentionally set high, so that less than two percent of kids nationwide would achieve it. Back in those days, trophies and awards meant something. Participation trophies for every member of the last place soccer team were unheard of. If you (or your team) sucked, you got jack shit.

When explaining the rules for the competition, the gym teacher, Mr. Wilson, mistakenly stated the minimum standard for chin-ups was six. I did my six chins then quit, seeing no point in pushing myself further. Eddie did as many as he could, maybe eight or nine. In the end, I'd achieved the minimum standard in nine of the ten events, breaking the fourth grade school record in the 660 Yard Run, and tying for the fastest 50 Yard Dash time of the year. After all our scores were recorded, Wilson announced to our gym class that Eddie was the only winner of the Presidential Award, and then apologized to me for his misinformation resulting in me winning only a consolation certificate, which didn't even have a copy of President Nixon's signature. I was bitter and resented Eddie's winning. He was gracious and tried to console me. I responded by berating him, pointing out that I beat him in most of the events.

The next day, Wilson read guidelines from the *official* rule book. "Students are allowed two attempts at the chinning event."

This gave me another opportunity to perform the required seven chin-ups. The class gathered around me and cheered me on with each successful chin. When I got my chin over the bar for the seventh time, Wilson shouted, "YES!" My friends cheered. I let go of the bar and landed on my butt on the tires below. Eddie was the first one to grab my hand and pull me up, patting me on the back with a big smile. I'd just joined him as the first two fourth grade Presidential Award winners in Prospect Hill School history. He was happy to have the company. That was the difference between me and Ed. I knew I wanted to be more like him, but didn't know how to do it. What would it be like to be a *good* kid?

I'm not saying I was completely transformed, but around this time I began considering how my behavior impacted others. Even at a young age, friends have a great influence on each other, and having one that cared about other people had a profound affect on me. I lived down the street from Eddie for only two years before moving out of state, but it seems like we grew up together for our whole childhood. We managed the impossible, something my previous best friend and I had not, to sustain a childhood friendship through time and distance into adulthood. Eddie and I are closing in on two generations since the day I knocked on his door looking for a friend. Knock on a door, ask someone to be your friend, and he becomes exactly that for the rest of your life. Fortunately for me, making friends was one of those things that would become easy. I had no idea how important friend-making skills were about to become.

A few years back, two thirty-five-year-old men visited Prospect Hill Elementary School. I had lived everywhere since we went to school there together. Ed still lived nearby. He wanted to show me something. There was a trophy case in an alcove outside the gym. In the case, there was a plaque commemorating the first two fourth-graders at that school to win the *Presidential Physical Fitness Award*—1973, Rich Schnabl and Eddie Stube. I reminded Ed my name was only there because the gym teacher gave me a second chance. Ed didn't even remember my special treatment. "All I remember, Rich, is that you were head and shoulders above the rest of us. And everybody knew it, including you."

"You should be the only one on that award, Ed."

"No way man, it'd be lonely on that plaque by myself." We looked at our names on the award in a glass trophy case. The mirror behind the plaque reflected an image of two ten-year-old boys. Ed could have been talking about our reflections, our names on the plaque, or perhaps he was clever enough to mean both when he said, "Right there beside me Rich, that's the way it should be."

California Is the Place You Wanna Be

When I was in fifth grade, Doug inherited some money from an uncle. We also had some equity in the house in New Berlin, Wisconsin, so my parents decided to cash out and move to California. Neither had a job lined up, or any family in California, they just wanted the California lifestyle. We packed a U-Haul and left Wisconsin during the school year and drove to California to look for a place to live. Mom and Doug discovered houses in LA were out of our price range, so we headed into the desert, where rent was cheaper—it's not like we had to be close to the office. We rented a small house in the Mojave Desert. Sometimes I'd wake up in the morning and hear Paul Harvey announce that during the previous day I had endured the hottest temperatures in the country. The house had a pool in the back yard which was surrounded by a red, cinder block fence. The idea of drinking rum around the pool was so alluring that Mom and Doug decided to not work in order to pursue this passion full time. When they got cabin fever, they'd take us on camping trips.

We saw everything California had to offer: Disneyland, beaches, mountains, deserts, Hollywood, tar pits, and Robert Redford. Between the trips, Ginger and I attended class. After nine months of sitting by the pool, drinking, smoking, listening to hippie music, towing a silver Airstream camper behind our white '73 Kingswood Estate station wagon, with wood grain side paneling, over the snowy mountains of Yosemite, up and down the hills of downtown San Francisco, along the Pacific Coast Highway, and over dirt roads in Baja, Mom and Doug ran out of money. So Mom did what she always does when she gets into a bind—she called her mother.

Grandma and Grandpa had recently moved from Wisconsin to Tyler, Texas. Why Texas? Grandma had twenty-five years as an IHOP waitress in Milwaukee. The owner was selling his Milwaukee restaurant and opening a new IHOP in Texas. He asked her to relocate to do the same job she could've kept in Wisconsin. He knew her loyalty. So when he added extra incentives, like a fifty-cents-an-hour raise, a thousand dollars for moving expenses and a job offer for Grandpa to be a host, my grandparents were Texas bound.

I liked to watch Grandpa work. "This way please," he'd say with a wide smile to anyone who walked into that IHOP for breakfast between 1976 and 1981. I liked to watch him bowl in his league, a sixty-year-old man, wearing a denim shirt with *Just Frank* embroidered above the front pocket. "Just Frank," because Texans weren't too good at pronouncing his last name, Kratowicz. I'd cheer as he clumsily high fived the black cooks and busboys after a strike. With his 150 average, I thought he was possibly the greatest bowler ever. I was proud of him. He was so engaging, so pleasant—nothing like the blank stares and confusion that would become him in later years.

People stood in the parking lot to eat at Tyler's most popular breakfast place. Grandpa and Grandma became the face of the restaurant. Most regular customers thought they owned the place and many came as much to visit with them as they did for the pancakes. "We want to sit in Vi's section," the regulars would say. "We don't care how long the wait is."

Even though Grandpa made only five dollars an hour, and Grandma averaged around eight, including tips, Grandma always tucked away money in case of an emergency, and "emergency" typically meant Mom had gotten herself into a financial mess.

So when Mom asked, Grandma sent enough money for our second transcontinental move in nine months, this time to join them in Texas, with the promise of an IHOP waitress job for my mother. I didn't get it. Sure they made good pancakes, but what was so great about IHOP that everyone in my family was willing to move across the country to work there?

Instead of selling the Airstream, Mom and Ginger towed it behind the station wagon, while Doug and I rode in the U-Haul. Unfortunately we had the two people with a sense of direction in the same vehicle and the two who did not traveling together in the other.

We stopped for breakfast in Albuquerque. Mom finished her breakfast, lit a cigarette and blew a river of smoke toward the ceiling. A twisting column of smoke snaked upward from her cigarette tip and a cancer cloud formed over our table. She flicked her ashes into her half-eaten scrambled eggs as Doug ragged on her for driving too slow. Mom had a stomach-turning habit I found so repulsive that on this morning, as she was about to take her last drag; I decided to finally speak up. "Mom, could you please not crush out your cigarette on your plate?" She held the back of her hand at me and curled her forefinger, motioning me toward her. I leaned over the table; she met me half way. *She's gonna tell me a secret, or scold me for my disrespect, or maybe she's gonna thank me for reminding her to mind her manners.* When her face was three inches from mine, she blew a big puff of smoke into my face. This would become her method of response any time I exhibited disapproving body language for her smoking. If I dare wave smoke out of my face, adjust my head position for cleaner air, make a face, roll my eyes, shake my head, or move further away from her when she smoked, I was subjected to a Salem facial.

She took one more drag. The red-black tip fizzled. "Watch this." Two distinct puffs accompanied each syllable.

She doused the butt in a pond of catsup and swirled it in slimy puddles of egg yoke until it was unrecognizable, leaving a smoldering plate of red and yellows swirls. *Somebody's gonna eat off that plate again. Gross!* Nobody was ever successful in telling Mom what to do. Asking her to do something was a sure way for it not to happen.

When breakfast was over, Mom and Ginger made a wrong turn and started heading west on I-40 instead of east. Certain that Doug was just ahead of her, she frantically drove the station wagon/Airstream 80 miles an hour while cursing Doug for driving off and leaving her. Twenty miles later, when she saw a sign for Phoenix, she realized she was going the wrong way. Doug and I hung out on the overpass by the café we had just eaten at for nearly an hour, until we watched Mom go screaming by in the correct direction on the interstate below. We hopped in the U-Haul, which barely had the power to fetch the silver bullet Airstream thirty minutes later. When we finally caught up with them, we all pulled over. Mom and Ginger were bawling their heads off when they got out of the car. Doug griped at Mom for being so ignorant. The family was reunited, and the next day we arrived in Tyler. We stayed with Grandma and Grandpa, in their trailer, for a few days, until we found a rent house. Doug parlayed his business degree into a job as a laborer at a truck terminal, Mom took the IHOP job, and within a few months we were house hunting again.

Pet Cows and Dogfights

In the fall of '75, Mom and Doug decided to buy a farm in Lindale, Texas. As a sixth-grader, Lindale would be my seventh school district. That farmhouse would become the first place I'd call home longer than two years.

The farm suited my mother well. She hated the oppression inherent in government and society in general. The farm was her escape, a chance for her to pursue what she'd always wanted—self-reliance. Her ultimate goal was to eliminate our dependency on the outside world. Besides, she loved animals, and the seventeen acres gave us a chance to accumulate an impressive collection of scraggly cats and mangy dogs, each blanketed in ticks and fleas. The ticks would gorge themselves on so much dog blood that they morphed into replicas of ripened blueberries. On one mutt's mange-infested head, the cluster of bloated ticks was so dense the dog appeared to be wearing a purple-gray beanie. Ticks and fleas ruled the house. I was constantly pulling them out of my legs, underarms, neck, even scrotum. I won't give details regarding Ginger's battles against ticks. Poor girl.

The combination of dog dander and cigarette smoke had me in a continuous state of allergic irritation. My eyes and nose were always itchy and I'd sneeze uncontrollably all day long—every day, hundreds of sneezes, snot everywhere—no reprieve. But I wasn't living with the Brady Bunch; they weren't going to give Tiger away because he made me sneeze. On the contrary, Doug was on the lookout for a big manly dog to rule over the kingdom of motley mutts—maybe a St. Bernard...

Our old farm house had never been upgraded with central air or heat, and that didn't help my allergies much. Our heat sources consisted of four gas heaters, and two wood stoves. Those gas heaters must've been engineered before lawyers. To ignite them, one had to put their face near the combustion area, hold a lit match with one hand, and open the gas valve with the other. To exacerbate the matter, ceramic grates guarded the burners, which meant the match could be held no closer than three inches from the gas orifices. As the match burned down the stick, it got further from the fuel source and closer to your fingers. This dynamic meant you'd hear and smell the gas flow for about five seconds before the thing finally lit with a whoosh, discharging a gas fireball into the air toward your face which hopefully would dissipate before it singed your eyebrows. The worse part about these heaters is that they weren't safe to run while sleeping. Before we went to bed in the evening, all gas heaters were extinguished, making for some really cold nights. On winter mornings, each of us woke to the sight of our own breath. The scorching hot summers were only slightly better. We had one window unit air conditioner in the house, strategically placed in Mom and Doug's bedroom. Fortunately, for them, they could run their air conditioner safely all night.

***

Our first cow, a Black Angus named Bart, was treated more like a family pet than a means of self-reliance. I fed that steer for three years past the point it was ready for slaughter before we finally had it processed. It was always breaking its way through our flimsy barbed-wire fence. "Rich, go get your sister and chase Bart back in," Doug would say. So we'd try to force Bart back through the same gap in the barbed-wire that he'd used to get out. When Doug was drunk, he'd often rave about what a prize bull Bart was. So big and powerful, no ordinary bull, but a true champion-grade animal. "We should have him stud." he'd say. "He could make us some money." But to me, Bart looked very much like every other Black Angus in Texas.

Ginger and I were eating beef stew one night when our mother walked into the kitchen to refill her drink. She was blitzed and thought it'd be a great time to not only tell us we were eating Bart at that moment, but also to review the Bart-based dishes that we'd already eaten over the last week—Bart spaghetti, Bart Chili, Bart Burgers... Ginger and I were shocked by this revelation, because Doug had told us that Bart had been sold at auction. Mom continued about how self-sufficient we were, explaining that Bart was not the pet that we had been treating him as, and that it's okay to eat him. "Even Jesus ate meat."

I stopped eating the Bart stew. Ginger took it worse than I, becoming physically ill. She had a hard time digesting the fact that the cow she enjoyed feeding and petting was in her stomach, mouth, and in the bowl in front of her. Doug came into the kitchen and started chewing mom's ass for telling us kids the truth about dinner. She tried to defend herself, and the argument escalated from there. Ginger was in the bathroom sick, two drunks were screaming at each other in the kitchen about a dead cow, so I retreated to my room to listen to the Texas Rangers on the radio. A typical evening on the farm.

We had one male Australian Shepherd mutt, named Willie. That dog had no sense and no fear. He'd bite the wheels of any car as it pulled into our driveway. He'd also chase our car for as long as he could when we left the house. Every time we left home, I'd look out of the back window and watch Willie running as fast as he could to keep up with the car until the gap became too great, at which point he would pull up and stare at us with a defeated look.

One day Doug finally brought home his dream dog—a huge ill-tempered black lab named Ben. As soon as the one hundred pound Ben got out of the car, little Willie was all over him. The fight was fierce but we managed to get the dogs separated. Willie, one third the size of big Ben would rather die than turn over his position as alpha male over his harem of mangy tick-infested females. So for weeks, we rotated the male dogs in and out of the house. One dog was brought in one door while the other dog was ushered out on the other side of the house. The inbound dog would have a pissing fit over the scent of the other male, and it wasn't long before the whole house smelled like urine. Doug would get talkative drunk every night and fawn over what a magnificent dog Ben was, and how lucky we were to have such a powerful animal to protect us... Protect us? All our cats were turning up dead since Ben arrived. Ben hated children and often growled at Ginger and me when we made eye contact with him. He even snapped at my leg once when I did nothing more than walk past him.

We already had a temperamental female, German Shepherd in the house that had bitten me twice and had once thrown itself on a small child like Lawrence Taylor threw himself at quarterbacks. So the last thing our house needed was this mammoth beast—Ben. I was scared shitless of that dog and rarely ventured out of my room when Ben was in the house. If I needed to leave my room, I'd crack the bedroom door and call Willie's name. If Willie came, I knew it was safe. If Willie didn't come, I called out to have Doug watch Ben while I left my room. Doug grew tired of my cowardly attitude real fast and soon he refused to protect me from that brute.

One late night after everyone had gone to bed, I needed to use the toilet. I cracked the door and saw the glare of Ben's eyes in the kitchen and saw him move toward the door. I shut it tight, ensuring it had latch, and then looked around my room for something I could pee into. All I came up with was the shroud of a *Glade Wild Flowers* scented air freshener. I quickly filled the 8-ounce makeshift cup to capacity but had to pinch off the flow before I was close to finishing. I stood in my room holding a plastic air freshener cap full of piss in one hand while pinching my pride and joy with the other. Leaving the room was not a viable option before, so it certainly wasn't one now that I only had one free hand to fend off Cujo. I had no option. *To hell with it; there's so much dog piss in this house what's the big deal if I mark **my** territory?* They'd made me a hostage in my own house. I was quite literally "pissed". If you ever find yourself in a similar situation let me recommend drawing a large "s" pattern in the carpet to avoid concentrated puddling. It's your best chance to get away with it without your mom finding out.

The alternating dog practice was not an optimal system for a household of drunken adults and forgetful teens accustomed to letting animals enter and exit as they pleased. So it was no surprise when I was awakened by the sounds of a dogfight and my mother's scream outside my bedroom door. I sprung out of my bed and rushed to the kitchen to see Willie's upper snout buried in Ben's mouth. Willie had Ben's lower jaw clamped inside his mouth. Doug was trying to pry Ben's mouth open while my mother was frantically pulling on Willie's collar. "Grab his balls," Doug yelled at me, as I arrived on the scene.

I'd been awake for about four seconds. My eyes hadn't adjusted to the light, and my brain had no idea what balls Doug was talking about or why he wanted them. My foggy mind processed this: Our German Shepherd, who was not in this particular fight, loved her ball so much that she'd leave her food to chase it and bite anyone who tried to take it from her. In fact, one of my dog bites occurred when I tried to pick up her ball. I figured Doug was going to try and distract Ben by getting him to chase a ball. *What a stupid idea, that savage is not going to release its death grip to chase a toy, Doug is either stupid drunk or he's cracking under stress.* I ignored his demand and continued to help my mother try to pull Willie out of the Ben's locked jaws.

"Grab his balls Rich!" Doug screamed again. This time Doug pointed with his eyes at Ben's testicles. I hesitated for a moment, wondering if in his frenzied state, Ben would go for my throat. I knew if we didn't get these dogs separated, Willie was gonna be dead. I thought about the chance to squeeze Ben's package until the contents turned mush. And I knew what I had to do. It was time to be a man. And if being a man meant ripping the nutsack off a vicious beast then I needed to step up. When I look back at my life, one of my biggest regrets is that I let my mom beat me to the prize. Ben's aggressive growls turned to meek yelps as he let go of Willie for a moment to turn and address the matter of my mother's fingernails ripping at his doghood. Doug grabbed Willie, pulled him into the bathroom, and shut the door. Both dogs were chewed up pretty good, their mouths drooling saliva and blood. Willie hobbled around for days on three legs. Us people suffered nothing more than minor scratches and adrenaline rushes. We kept Ben for another three weeks until after another brutal dogfight, Doug finally agreed to get rid of the magnificent creature while he still had his balls.

I think we were all lucky Willie stood up to Ben. If he hadn't, I believe Ben would've eventually mauled either Ginger or me.

The End of the World as We Know It

The declining economic climate of the mid-seventies convinced my mother we were on the cusp of the greatest depression ever. She believed our so-called farm would be our salvation. We had seventeen acres, and she wanted us to become "self-sufficient." After cocktails, she'd wake us kids up and tell us how the world was about to change. She's sitting on the edge of my bed, and I'm wondering what is so urgent that she has awakened me:

"Richard, do you know what's gonna happen soon? The depression is about to hit. We are due. It happens every fifty years you know. It's gonna be bad, Richard. Money won't be worth the paper it's printed on. But first, there'll be a run on the banks, leaving them without cash. Everybody will want their money at the same time, and the banks won't have it.

The economy will collapse. Doug will lose his job at the C&H. There'll be violence at the banks. To try and stay afloat, banks will foreclose on people's houses as soon as they're one day late on their house payment. People will burn worthless paper money during the winter to stay warm because the nation's power grid will go down. Without currency, everything will be done on the barter system. Soon, most people you know will be starving, searching the dumpsters for food…"

The whole concept was intimidating to a child. My classmates will be eating from dumpsters?

She'd leave and I'd try to fall back asleep while contemplating how shitty my life is about to get: Lindale bank tellers will invade our house with the aid of police. My parents would be handcuffed, taken off to jail for not making a house payment on time, the bank employees would come inside with suitcases full of worthless cash. They'd spend the evening sitting around our woodstove burning stacks of bills and toasting their new house over a candlelit dinner of Bart stew and eggs from our chickens. We will end up homeless, eating my mother's canned beets.

Mom made an effort, one that she truly believed in, to increase her worth in a barter society. I envisioned myself in the school cafeteria, candles lighting every table, Mrs. Hicks demanding a roll of toilet paper, twenty feet of rope, or a quart of goats milk, in exchange for my school lunch. *Maybe my folks will give a cow to the University of Texas for a semester's tuition.*

Gas lines were bad; she said it was because the world was running out of gas and oil. "You and Ginger can forget the idea of ever having your own cars—we're heading back to the days of bicycles and horses." Even people who were lucky enough to keep their jobs wouldn't be able to get back and forth to work, so they'd be fired too. Life as we knew it would cease. Society would be thrown into chaos, and only those who prepared themselves would make it through. She studied *Mother Earth News* magazine so she could position us for the imminent depression. We would be among the lucky ones she claimed; we were prepared. We had our garden, fruit and Pecan trees, animals, and stockpiles of canned fruit and vegetables, dehydrated beef jerky, gas, guns, ammo, booze, and cigarettes.

It didn't matter to me that my mother was a high school dropout, or even that she was usually sauced when she talked about these things; from my perspective, these were facts about the way things were going to be, not wild predictions. In my early teens, I hadn't come to realize how impaired alcohol made her, so I fully believed her prophecies. My grandparents and great-grandmother compounded my anxiety, telling me stories of how bad it was in *The Great Depression.* My grandfather sold papers all day in downtown Milwaukee for 8 or 9 cents. My grandmother worked in the fields from sunup to sundown on the family farm. With stories of past hardships surrounding me, each night I expected Walter Cronkite to throw it to a Jimmy Carter press conference in which the president would announce that he is declaring a state of depression. "As of midnight tonight, businesses will no longer be accepting cash. Until further notice, we are now on the barter system. We regret the inconvenience that this may cause. I urge all Americans to plant gardens and fruit trees as soon as possible and Godspeed to y'all."

    The adult-me has a sense of respect for the energy that my mother put into her beliefs, and even give her credit for making me aware of real issues, like our resources not being infinite. In those respects, because of her, I was much wiser and enlightened than my classmates. I understood something few of them did. Lindale was a spec on the world, it was not *the* world. Mom tended to a vegetable garden every year and even in the oppressive Texas summers spent many summer hours in the hot kitchen, canning vegetables and drying fruit for the family's future consumption. Even the teenage-me had respect for her hard work, but I loathed when she dragged me into her endeavors. I wanted to hang out with friends, see a movie, or play sports. Instead, we kids would spend weekends peeling pears, picking strawberries, cracking pecans, or gathering firewood. I wasn't opposed to performing an occasional chore to contribute, but there was never an end in sight. She came up with a monster list of weekly chores that had to be done; some, like harvesting fruit or feeding the animals, were in support of her agenda to reduce our dependence on the outside world. Other chores, like scrubbing the painted wood planks on the wrap-around porch every week, were just insane. When the list was finished, and we thought we might get to finally play that new *Pong* game, or bounce around on our Hippity Hops, she'd track us down, and add more work. "Shine the brass."

***

My mother had a lot of abstract beliefs and opinions. "Jesus was Adam reincarnated." She professed her belief in this theory after a few rum and Cokes. "Richard, the first sinner should be the one to suffer for all the sins."

During her rants she'd ramble about reincarnation, talking to the dead, holograms living among us, government conspiracies, and the return of Adam (Jesus). She often refers to the event of death as *crossing over*, because that's what some guy who has a TV show calls it.

"There's a subterranean colony of humanoid creatures consisting of the crossbred offspring of aliens and humans, living at the earth's core, Richard. And living among us are lizard-like aliens who are able to morph themselves to appear as people. These lizards also have the ability to exert mind control over us. Many politicians, including the president and other influential world leaders are actually lizard people masquerading as human beings, or they are controlled by lizards. They've been here for years, Richard. Howard Hughes was a lizard. You know he went crazy, don't you. You know who Howard Hughes is don't you, Richard? There's people right now that are working to expose these aliens, but every time they get close, they're killed. Besides that, the government controls the media. It's certainly something to think about Rich..."

Mom distrusted government and big business so much she refused to put money into banks, stocks or any other investments that wouldn't have value as barter. When I asked her to save some money for my college, she said that would be foolish. Everyone would be making runs on the bank and our money would be gone. She became disenfranchised with society and any entity that tried to impose their will or beliefs on her.

When the school district wouldn't admit Ginger and me without proof of immunizations, she scolded the school administrators for interfering with her right to parent as she sees fit.

"Look lady, it's the state law. I'm just doing my job," they told her.

She asked for a copy of that law, and the school provided it. She sat Ginger and me down for a talk. "If anyone ever asks, you're a Christian Scientist, can you remember that? Christian Scientist," she reiterated. "As Christian Scientists, we don't believe in medical intervention. Instead we just pray to not get sick. If that fails, and we get sick, then we pray to get better. If that doesn't work then we die because it was simply time for the Lord to take us. Prayer is our medicine. "Do you guys understand this? You don't have to believe it, all you have to do is say it, otherwise you'll have to get shots."

The next day, she got us admitted based on a religious exemption. Although I was fine with the fact that I wouldn't be getting any shots, I made sure my friends and coaches knew that I wanted them to save me in a life or death situation, instead of joining hands in a prayer circle.

My mother's insistence on pushing her beliefs has always been a source of conflict, but never more so than regarding my education. She never put faith in formal education. As an adult, raising a family in the 90's, I pursued an electrical engineering degree while working as a copy machine repairman. It took ten years to earn the degree while attending school part time. During those years, she tried to persuade me that instead of spending so much time and money on school, I should focus my energy on opening my own business. She sent me a book that could guide me in starting a tech-based business. "People are making good money as VCR repairmen or phone jack installers, Richard." I explained that I'd double my pay when I got an engineering degree. She came from a blue-collar background, and since she didn't understand what an engineer did, to her, it wasn't a very good idea. To support her position against formal education, she pointed out that she knew of a young man who had a degree in geology and works at the photo-mat, or another that has a business degree working as a cashier at the grocery store. "What good did college do them?" She asked. "You should open a fireworks stand, Rich…"

The Olympics

I was fascinated with the Olympics, and fed that passion by decorating—from floor to ceiling—every inch of one of my bedroom walls with an Olympic collage. My Olympic wall was a collection of photos, articles, and headlines. Materials—glue, tape, magazines, newspapers, thumbtacks, twenty poster boards, even library picture books—were unknowingly donated to the project by Lindale Junior High School. I found a school library book which listed every track and field medal winner dating back to the 1896 Athens Games. I cut those lists from the book and included them in the tribute. In case anybody ever needed to know, I could tell them that somehow distance runners from the little country of Finland had won six of the last fourteen Olympic Gold Medals in the 10,000 Meter Run.

The publishers of one book couldn't imagine the consternation they'd later cause me when they elected to place photos of Jim Thorpe and Jessie Owens on opposite faces of the same page. *How can I show my reverence to the Indian or to the black man without disrespecting the other? There must be a way.* I poked a small hole in the top of the page, ran a piece of yarn through it and tacked it to the ceiling above the foot of my bed. Jessie and Jim gently swayed and twirled above me as I slept. World record holders Lee Evans and Bob Beamon would soon join them. Nadia had a dedicated photo arrangement right beside my bed. In one photo her legs were bent so far back, the soles of her feet framed her pretty face. *I wonder if she might like me if she knew me?* Mary Decker was there too.

In my 1976 version of *Tivo*, I recorded a lot of audio from the Montreal games on the shoebox-sized cassette tape recorder placed next to the TV speaker. Echoes of announcer's calls of Edwin Mosses, Alberta Juanterina, and Sugar Ray Leonard would bounce around inside my head for years.

Another section of my wall was dedicated to the great Decathletes. I was obsessed with the Decathlon. My dream was to win an Olympic Gold in that event. Naturally, I was a big Bruce Jenner fan. When he took his victory lap, waving the American flag, I had one prevailing thought—*why can't that be me someday?* I would be the one to continue the tradition of great American Decathletes. I did the math and set my sights on the Decathlon gold medal in the '88 games, when I would be 25.

Before the '76 Olympics, I had Bruce Jenner all to myself. I might have been the only one in my town who knew who he was. Then came the hype in mainstream magazines, the *Up Close and Personal* feature on Jenner during ABCs Olympic coverage, featuring his hot wife, Christy, the Olympic Gold medal, the Tonight Show, books, Wheaties. Eventually I had to share my hero and his new girly nose with the rest of the world and eventually lost him to Hollywood reality shows and the Kardashians.

***

My interest in the Olympics actually began with the '72 games in Munich. Jim McKay reported that guerillas had murdered some athletes in the Olympic village, and had taken others hostage. The horrific events reminded me of a science lesson about how the Russians had once put a chimpanzee into space. I'd also recently seen Planet of the Apes, a movie depicting highly educated, evolved apes who'd overtaken humans as the dominant species on earth. Eddie and I had once discussed the possibility of such a thing actually happening. We concluded if mankind were too complacent, apes could indeed evolve to take over the world. Why not? They were already piloting rocket ships.

You can laugh if you want, but when the news reports talked about guerillas killing Israeli athletes, I'm sure I wasn't the only eight year old who thought a pack of apes came out of the jungle into Olympic village on a murderous rampage. Reports weren't clear on how many, but they were out of control, barricading themselves into a room with a group of athletes. Had the authorities considered dropping a bunch of bananas outside the window and then shooting the evil apes when they came out to take the bait?

As I lay in bed, trying to fall asleep, I listened to the latest news reports on my radio, and then to a talk show about the standoff. My world was turned upside down. *What's to keep a pack of gorillas from breaking into our house tonight, and killing us all?* What if the Olympic attack was a call-to-arms for apes all over the world to go into kid's rooms and kill them in the first stage of a monkey conspiracy to forge above man on earth's evolutionary totem pole? I stared intensely at the open doorway to my room. *They're coming. What if they're coming to get me?* I grabbed my baseball bat, gripped it under my covers. *I'm not going down without a fight. If they come for me, I will act like I'm asleep and then bash their heads in.*

Pole Vaulting

On the first day of seventh grade track season, Coach Johnson asked for volunteers to carry the pole vault equipment to the pit. For years I'd wanted to be a pole vaulter—I'd have to pole vault to be a decathlete—finally this was my chance. Neither of our coaches had knowledge of proper technique. Each offered their own advice: Coach Bradley, when giving us the poles, pointed out the end with tape, not the end with the knob, should be gripped. Coach Johnson said, "Schnabl, I like you. Don't crack your head open out there." That was the extent of our pole vault training. Tracy Coomer and I carried the poles and crossbar. We got to the pit and put the crossbar on the lowest height, which was 7 feet.

I'd seen Bruce vault and read about technique, this made me the most accomplished pole vault authority in our class. Coomer and I made a few reasonable attempts at clearing the bar. We knew one would have to plant the pole in the box and actually hold on for some time, despite the jolt it exerted on one's shoulders; and we could at least do that. Our near success inspired every nincompoop in the class to rush over and get in line for the sole purpose of wasting the time of us serious vaulters. Soon, thirty guys waited in line for their chance to make asses of themselves.

After enough people got lumps on their heads, or busted their butts slipping into the plant box, the pole vault queue diminished. As a tune up for the first official track meet, we had an intramural practice meet. Since no one could clear 7 feet, which was as low as the equipment allowed for, the coaches brought the high jump standards over and set the bar at 6 feet. Coomer cleared it on his first attempt, and everyone who saw it, including me, was amazed. Finally, someone had cleared the bar! I went next and matched his feat. We were jubilant, hugged each other, and I was on my way to being Bruce Jenner. I felt like a real stud. I could pole vault six feet, one foot higher than my classmate, James Kunkel, could high jump.

I Bet Bruce Jenner Didn't Have This Problem

Some of my most vivid childhood memories are those associated with Christmas. Grandparents, aunts, step-grandparents, and great-grandparents all came to our place for the sole purpose of stacking presents three feet high on the living room floor. To me, this was the real meaning of Christmas. It was a time of hope, love, and wonder. I *hoped* I would get a lot of cool toys, *loved* the relatives that got me the neat stuff, and *wondered* why the heck a grown-up thought I wanted socks and underwear for Christmas.

For Christmas 1976, four months after Bruce Jenner's gold medal, I asked for a shot put, discus, javelin, and pole vaulting pole. My plan was to turn my pasture into an Olympic training ground. On Christmas Eve there were two gigantic gift boxes under the tree, one for me and one for Ginger. And mine was twice as big as hers; the box was almost as tall as I was! We had to wait until all the other gifts were opened, and then we'd each open our special gifts together. The anticipation was maddening as each gift unwrapping brought us closer to the grand finale. There must've been two hundred gifts and, according to Mom's rules, everyone had to fawn over every single meaningless gift before the next could be opened. For me, time cannot move fast enough. *Yeah, Yeah...nice flannel shirt Grandpa. More house slippers for Grandma? Doesn't she like the ones we got her last year? Who's next? Let's get this thing moving! Come on you slowpokes! I wanna go outside in the freezing rain and throw my new shot put around a few times tonight.*

I couldn't wait to open that huge box and start my decathlon training. The layout of my training center was already mapped on a poster and hung on my Olympic wall. The throwing events would be in one flat corner of the pasture. I'd already gathered some little wired flags that the electric company used down the street to warn potential ditch diggers of the presence of underground wires. They'd be used as markers in the landing area of the throwing events to indicate distance. The pole vault/high jump pit would be near the big pecan tree close to the road, so passers-by could watch me jump. I'd build my own hurdles and mow a running strip in the pasture. My plans were in place; all I needed was gear.

We were down to one gift between me and the big moment. Mom called Ralph's name as the recipient. *No not Ralph!* Ralph (Doug's Father) was the most frustrating gift unwrapper ever. First he acted surprised that he got a gift. He inspected the wrapping paper and complimented the giver on everything from the colors, theme, and overall presentation. *Good Lord Ralph, it's the same damn wrapping paper as the last two gifts you opened. Enough about the wrapping paper already.* After searching for his pocket knife he'd misplaced somewhere under a mountain of wrapping paper, he methodically selected just the right blade for detaching the bow without damaging it. Then he passed the decapitated bow to his wife, so she could hold it as far as humanly possibly from her seventy-year-old eyes, shake her head in reverence and cry in disbelief about what breathtaking bows K-Mart sold in their *assorted 50-count* package. After the bow worshipping, Ralph used his seventy-five-year-old eyes to hunt down every piece of tape on the package, each of which he carefully sliced with a different blade than the one used for bow removing, being careful during this process to not disfigure the wrapping paper. When the gift was unwrapped, he addressed the matter of any loose tape fragments by folding them back 180 degrees so he could attach them to the white, underside of the wrapping paper. *For the love of Baby Jesus Ralph, if you don't move your ass, I swear to God I'm coming over there and ripping that fucking box open right this instant.* Only after all the tape was tamed did he fold the wrapping paper into a neat square and hand it to his wife, so, it too, could be used next year. Finally, after he watched his wife lovingly tuck the wrapping paper safely into a box that contained their collection of reusables, he began the slow process of opening the box, which seemed to take longer than it had for him to unwrap it.

Ten minutes after the gift was presented, Ralph finally finished discussing how thoughtful the French coaster set was. Finally, Ginger and I were allowed to start tearing into our boxes at the same time. With one swipe she tore the wrapping from one side of her box, revealing a picture of its contents. She'd gotten a stereo, complete with an eight-track and record player. As she squealed with joy, I was still clueless regarding my gift. I didn't remove the wrapping around the box, just around the top, the minimum required to separate the flaps on the top of the box and access whatever was inside. I didn't want to discover the contents of my gift by looking at a box; I wanted to be surprised by what was inside.

The first thing I found was a yellow sphere that had the look and feel of a child's plastic bowling ball. The ball had some kind of removable cap with raised letters that read *Fill with water only*. The next thing I grabbed was another plastic object; this one the diameter of a salad plate and shaped like a small flying saucer. It had a similar cap.

What was this stuff? Then I reached down and grabbed the longest piece in the box. It was a red plastic spear, with a hand grip in the middle. It looked like toddler toys. I tore the wrapping off the box to see what this product was supposed to be. *There must be a mistake.* This is a *Playskool* track and field set. It says in big red letters on the box, *Ages 2-6*.

My mom's been screwed; they sent her the wrong thing.

"Do you like it?" she inquired with an odd smile.

I was speechless. *What's going on? Is she really so ignorant to think I could use this gear to train for the Olympics? How could I make it to the cover of a Wheaties box training with a high jump kit that maxed out at three feet? Should I act gracious, and thank her, thereby not hurting her feelings and save her from looking stupid? Is it possible that she ordered out of a catalog and got the order number wrong?* I sat next to the Christmas tree, deflated, looking down at the little hurdles that didn't even come knee high, at the plastic shot put that was better suited as a whiffle ball, and at the toy discus, barely bigger than the palm of my hand.

I tried to show politeness in my voice. "I think...this stuff's for little kids."

She took a deep drag on her cigarette as the tension mounted. The extended family waited for her response. Her head kinda bobbed in circular motions like she had that disease that Audrey Hepburn had in her later years. She was lit like a roman candle.

The smoke flowing out of her mouth and nostrils carried her cold-hearted reply. "Richard... it's a joke."

Stunned, tears welled in my eyes. "Is that it?"

Okay, it's a joke: Haha, real funny Mom, but now I'm expecting the punchline. Surely she'd finish this joke by leaving the room and coming back with a shot put or discus, maybe even both. How much could an eight-pound ball of pig iron possibly cost?

Seeing I wasn't amused about the way my special gift stacked up against my sister's, she chastised my show of disappointment in her slow drunken cadence, "Come on Richard—you poor abused child—I thought you were mature enough to enjoy a good joke...

Disbelief on my face.

"I guess I was wrong," she said.

"I guess so," I replied. And that was the extent of my verbal retaliation. Everything else, I held inside.

I looked around the room to see if anyone else was laughing. Grandparents, step-grandparents, step-aunts, most of them looked at me for a moment and then turned their heads away. My grandmother shook her head. I don't know if she was shaking her head at my mother's ill-conceived joke or at my reaction to it.

She crushed my Olympic dream by giving me toddler toys for Christmas, and then was insulted because I wasn't laughing about it with her.

I wanted to take that plastic discus and shove it up her ass sideways and smash Ginger's godamned stereo to bits with my brand new plastic javelin.

Less than four years. The day I turn 18, I'm walking out of this hell and never looking the fuck back. How bout that for a joke, Mom? That'll teach you a lesson. One day you'll be sorry for treating me like this, and you can sit back and smoke and drink your fucking brains out the rest of your life thinking about it.

On that Christmas Eve, 1976, I had no idea how prophetic those thoughts really were, except that day—the day I would be on my own—was a lot closer than I imagined.

I always enjoyed Christmas mornings because I'd inventory my new gifts and indulge in them all day long. This Christmas, for the first time, there were no entertaining gifts. For a thirteen-year-old boy, the novelty of admiring four new shirts and a stack of green-striped tube socks wears off pretty fast. I left the plastic track and field set in the living room, went to my bedroom, closed the door, and put a shoe box in the corner. I sat on my bed and flicked baseball cards, including Nolan Ryan, Robin Yount, and Johnny Bench rookie cards, which could have provided me with financial security later in life, across the room into a shoebox. From my sister's bedroom, a song I liked by 10cc blared from her new stereo:

♪ ♪ *Like walking in the rain and the snow*
When there's nowhere to go
And you're feelin' like a part of you is dying ♪ ♪

That's me. I had nowhere to go, and on that night, for the first time in my life I was overcome with a sense of betrayal and loneliness. My mother, who was supposed to love me, had gone out of her way to cause me pain. This wasn't a case of apathy or impairment; it was first-degree premeditated cruelty. Even then, as it was happening, I knew I'd never forget this night and that feeling of betrayal. I had no idea this was the same pain, the same feeling of loss, that would come with broken relationships later in life—the pain of a breakup with someone who you still love, but doesn't love you, and they offer no reasonable explanation why. I didn't forget the pain of that Christmas. Years later, I came to understand that on Christmas Eve of my thirteenth year, my mother and I broke up.

Selling Roses

    During my early teen years, I looked for alternatives to spending weekends doing chores around the farm. At 5:00 a.m. on Saturday mornings, a truck would come for me. I'd jump into the shell-covered bed and ride around the pre-dawn countryside waiting patiently while the boss knocked on doors of other desperate kids who'd expressed (or were rumored to have expressed) an interest earlier in the week in selling Tyler Roses. Given the timing of the recruiting mission, it's not surprising that one sleepy man answered his door with a shotgun pointed at the boss. His son didn't go with us that day, and that kid was never asked again to sell roses. But the incident created a business opportunity for me. The boss offered me a quarter for every door I knocked on while he sat in the truck. I was happy to earn an extra dollar before we even started selling. After the truck was loaded with the sales team, we were taken to the nursery where we joined a collection of other pickup trucks, and a crowd of nearly one hundred kids, mostly older delinquents with worse attitudes than me, many of whom enjoyed thumping my big ears, which my long scraggly hair did not completely hide.

    At the nursery, we kids loaded the trucks with buckets of roses, umbrellas, and signs, while the redneck drivers stood around smoking cigarettes and arguing with each other over who would get the best behaved kids (as if there really were any). Somewhere around sunrise, the lineup card was settled and the three toughest kids assigned to each truck would get into the cab with the driver.

The other five or six would climb into the back, step over the product and wedge ourselves facedown onto a mountain of umbrellas and signs, which were stacked on a four-by-four sheet of plywood braced above the truck bed. Sixteen square feet of surface area, three feet of headspace, five people, two-hour drive to Dallas. The signs read:
Tyler Roses
$1.00 Doz

The adult drivers had no respect for the innocence of children. They talked to thirteen year olds using foul language I'd never heard before. I had to ask some of the older kids what some of the words meant. I'd never seen kids my age so comfortable swearing while conversing with adults. The liberating feeling of cursing anytime became part of the appeal of selling roses. "Hey Schnabl," one of the bosses called while pointing at a different truck than the one I had just helped load. "Why don't you and your buddies break up your circle jerk and help load that truck?"

"Hey Cooper," I'd respond, calling a fifty-year-old man by his last name. "Why don't you go fuck yourself with a stick?" Cooper loved the sarcastic insults and I quickly became one of his favorites. *The power of cursing anytime I want. This is why I fucking come here. It sure isn't the bullshit pay.*

I wondered what my mother would do if I talked to her that way. "Why don't you feed the damn pigs yourself, bitch?"
What could she do to me? Really?
Okay, nevermind. Bad idea.

I learned a lot in the back of those rose trucks: Rod Stewart had to get his stomach pumped. Sperm and urine were two very different things, which ties into Rod Stewart getting his stomach pumped. Whacking off had nothing to do with wiping one's ass. A *bitch* is actually a female dog and an *ass* is a donkey, and when used in the right context, you could shock your whole sixth-grade class by casually using those words in formal classroom discussions, and your teacher couldn't do a motherfucking thing about it.

Once in Dallas, we were dropped off one-by-one with an umbrella, a sign, and two buckets of roses. If I'd planned well, I'd also have a sack lunch consisting of a PB&J sandwich, a piece of fruit, and a handful of cookies. If I was lucky, an army of fire ants would not swarm my lunch before I had the chance to eat it. At one point, I also had a water jug, but it lasted only a handful of Saturdays, until it was lost or stolen. Out of the one dollar per dozen, twenty cents was our share. That, plus any tips I might rack up, and maybe a dollar for accepting the risk of getting shot or attacked by dogs when knocking on people's doors in the middle of the night, usually amounted to a net in single digits. A twelve-dollar take was extraordinary.

Normally I'd sell my first dozen at around nine. After four hours of riding, knocking, loading, standing, and suggesting to grown men new and innovative uses for broomsticks, I finally had money in my pocket. I was so eager to make that first sale because by then I was always very hungry; so I'd immediately run into a nearby convenience store to get something to eat—maybe a Coke and a Honey Bun. *If the boss picked me up right now and cashed me out, I'd owe him money! This sucks. I'm never coming again.*

Some days my food and drink expenses took over half my earnings. Many times after settling, I'd come home with six bucks and a pack of baseball cards. Eventually, I found a way to get paid for my labor of loading the buckets. I'd sneak into the cutting shed, grab some sheets of wax paper and stuff them into my lunch bag. As soon as I sold a few dozen, I'd unwrap eleven packs one by one, pulling a single rose from each pack. Then I'd roll my own bundle. Doing this gave me a full one hundred percent commission on two or three sales. This could turn a seven-dollar day into a ten-dollar day. I knew it was dishonest, but I justified it in my mind that it was payment for loading the roses. I ran into the big boss at a Lindale football game when I was about thirty. I fessed up and offered him twenty bucks that I figured I'd cheated him out of fifteen years before. He accepted it with a smile; I think he needed the money more than he did when I stole it—I guess I did him a favor by holding that twenty bucks.

A kid can get pretty bored standing on a street corner for twelve hours. My job was to make eye contact with potential customers in the cars that stopped at the light, maybe get a sympathy sale, get them to think, "Aw, look at that poor little Mexican kid, the roses are only a buck, what the hell..." This technique rarely worked. Sometimes just to mess with people, I'd stare at someone for the full duration of a red light. This drew various reactions, usually a look-straight-ahead-and-somehow-fidget response, their job being to act like they didn't see me. So I'd wait it out, staring. Maybe I'd get a no-thank-you-headshake or a hand lift off the steering wheel to acknowledge my existence. *Okay, I'm not invisible.* That would be enough for me to move on.

I'd do anything to occupy my mind to pass the time. Over the years, I bought several transistor radios so I could listen to music or sports. The radios would last no more than four or five Saturdays before they were lost, stolen, or crunched in the back of the pickup. I even had one lifted from my loose grip as I slept on the plywood loft on the way home. A days pay—gone.

"Hey, which one of you motherfuckers took my radio?" Five black kids shouted a chorus of *fuck-you-mans* and threatened to throw me out of the back of the pickup onto I-20. I knew four of them were justifiably insulted.

I especially liked listening to the University of Texas college football games. There was one Dallas rose-selling spot situated on the southeast corner of Scyene and Jim Miller. Despite being located at a busy intersection, this corner was part of a big lot, covered with beautiful green grass. I was selling at that spot when UT played Oklahoma in October of 1977. I listened to the excited announcer describe how Earl Campbell, who was my hometown hero, was solidifying his Heisman Trophy season by abusing Oklahoma defenders, who usually ended up withering on the ground in his wake clutching a handful of his tear-away jersey.

I was so pumped by big Earl's performance, and roses were selling so poorly, that I left the rose stand and with a pack of roses in my hand wandered over to that patch of grass, and played a one-against-none football game. Using the wax pack of roses as the pigskin, I pantomimed my imagined role in a football game I'd one day star in. With one eye minding my rose stand, I took the handoff, bounced off a tree trunk at the line of scrimmage, stutter stepped around an imaginary defender, burst through the hole, put a spin move on the linebacker, plowed into the safety, and carried imaginary tacklers downfield ten yards, until I lunged forward, landing on the ground while extending the roses toward the make-believe goal line. I came up just short, which required me to finish the drive off on the next play with a leaping summersault into the end zone. Passers-by must have thought I was either on a bad acid trip or else being chased by bees as they watched me juke the trees, stiff-arm the air, spin like a ballet dancer, and throw myself awkwardly onto the ground, all the while holding a pack of roses, and imagining defenders clutching at air or holding onto me for dear life. One older lady parked her car and walked over to check on me. I called timeout and pretended that I was talking to the coach about strategy, and quickly dismissed her as if *she* were crazy.

I carried 30 times for 450 yards, and six touchdowns. I also returned a punt and a kickoff for a touchdown. My punt return was nothing short of spectacular, as I reversed field twice, broke tackles from every member of the coverage team and stumbled wearily into the end zone with the punter riding me like a horse. I especially liked to punish wimpy kickers and punters for having the audacity to try and stop me. On my kickoff return, I tight-roped down the sideline and bulldozed over the kicker before high stepping across the goal line. About the time I was starting my end-zone celebration I noticed the bossman's red Ford Pickup parked at my rose stand. I wasn't sure how much he had seen but when I jogged over to the stand he wasn't very pleased. "Whatinthehell ya doing over there? Dickin' the dog? You only sold four goddamn dozen?"

I noticed little red dots of blood oozing from my rose-pricked fingers. I held the most grisly pack of flowers one could imagine in my hand. Only half of the dozen stems had flowers left on the end, and the blooms that remained were bruised and battered. Apparently the boss didn't see enough of my antics to know I had been using the pack in my hand as a football, so I was able to discreetly hide the beleaguered flowers from him.

He refilled my water jug and took about ten dozen from me to redistribute to someone who hadn't spent the afternoon playing in the Rose Bowl.

I spent the next thirty minutes engaged in a more discreet athletic fantasy. I'm taking penalty kicks in the World Cup final. A golf ball sized rock perched atop the curb is the soccer ball. In my mind's eye, the gap between the passenger side front and rear wheels of a not-too-fancy car waiting at a stoplight serves as the goal. The fidgety driver, focused on avoiding eye contact with the kid selling flowers is the goalkeeper. I eyeball the keeper and make a quick go/no-go assessment. If the keeper is not looking at me, and not badass enough to stomp me into a country mudhole if my shot goes high and clunks off their Buick serving as the crossbar, I take my best shot. My toe punch is generally about 70 percent accurate, depending on such factors as angle, how many street lanes between me and the goal, and whether or not there are any defenders (cars) in the way. *No problem if I miss wide, but I don't want to miss high.* As a precautionary measure, my follow-through always includes a quick 90-degree left face and bringing the roses to the "show position," which presents my body to another vehicle instead of the one about to be struck by a bouncing rock. This makes me appear slightly less guilty. If I hear a clunk, I puff my chest out just a little bit and hold my arms out wide like I'm too muscle-bound for them to hang limp at my side. As much as I'd like to study the reaction of the snobby driver who refused to acknowledge me moments before, I avoid even glancing in the direction of the goalie.

I spend the rest of the afternoon pondering why I came. I decide I don't need eight bucks this bad and resolve this will be the last time I spend a day frying my sunburned ass in this piece of hell masquerading as an east Dallas street corner. But I come back next week to make another nine dollars and to chase my all-time consecutive goals record.

At settlement time, the boss notices the quality of my only unsold pack. "Jesus Christ Schnabl, what in fuck's name happened to those? Did you throw it out inta the street or some shit? What the fuck? Over?"

"They were fine when I sold 'em boss, but then this guy brought 'em back an hour later demanding his dollar back. Said he'd kick my ass if I didn't give him his money."

"You gotta be shitting me! I can't believe it, that cocksucking sonofabitch."

"Yeah, I know boss. What a bunch of bullshit. That asshole."

After all the kids had been picked up, a boxed dinner from *Church's Fried Chicken* was our bonus—two piece with cole slaw, fries and a dinky-sized drink.

Cole slaw? I hated cole slaw; everyone hated cole slaw, but I was so hungry I ate it anyway.

The parking lot at *Church's* served as the challenging ground for getting a seat in the front of the truck for the long drive home. Wanna challenge someone for the front seat? Beat him up and you get it. Sometimes guys who'd been picked up first tried to lock themselves in the cab at *Church's*, attempting to secure their positions.

Eventually, guys riding in the back started becoming wise to this practice, and we'd often jump out as soon as the truck entered the chicken house parking lot, despite the fact that it was still moving. We'd scamper to the driver side door and form a human door stop when the boss left the truck to buy our chicken. A fight would invariably break out in or around the truck. Nothing among this crowd could be solved diplomatically. It didn't matter what was fair, or whose turn it was. Who was bad-ass enough to bully his way into the cab and push others out? That's all that mattered. My goal was to work my way up to bad-ass status.

In ninth grade, I thought I'd achieved that level. Richard Cooper was a skinny, black, seventh-grade kid who talked more unsolicited trash to me than any of his bigger, older friends. I'd paid my dues for three years. By now, I was one of the older kids, and I wasn't inclined to take much shit from this punk. We squared off in the restaurant parking lot and bounced each other off the truck once or twice before the struggle migrated away from the vehicle. He was quick, so he landed a couple of punches, none of which really packed much power.

Since I was bigger and stronger, I turned the duel into a wrestling match. Like the form I used to make a football tackle, I lunged forward and hit him square in his waist with my right shoulder, nudged my head against his right hip, and wrapped him up with my arms. After securing my grip, I bent my knees, leaned backwards, and hoisted his bony body onto my shoulder, and stood erect. He was flailing his legs and pounded me in the back with his fists. Imagine a soldier trying to carry a fallen GI off the battlefield by throwing him over his shoulder. This was the position in which I held Richard Cooper. The kid only weighed about ninety pounds, and I was probably about one-thirty, so I wasn't even straining.

Although I clearly had the upper hand at this point, I didn't really have a plan of what I would do with this punk I was carrying on my shoulder. I looked around for something to smash him into. The only thing I saw was the Church's Chicken building. I carried him to the face of the building that lent full view of the dining room inside. On this side of the building, the brick came to a height of three feet, at which point it transitioned to huge glass windows. I glanced inside and saw a crowded dining room full of people eating. With my right arm, I pulled Richard's legs down toward my chest and began repeatedly ramming his ass into the window, which was the only thing separating us from the chicken eaters inside. The glass shuddered with each iteration.

My eyes caught a glimpse of the startled chicken eaters whose meal I'd just interrupted. They were scrambling away from their tables against the window. *They think this glass could break. Hey, that would be awesome! Just like a ferocious, backboard-shattering Daryl Dawkins dunk. I'm gonna back up and take a running start and piledrive his ass, with me attached, through the window.* I noticed a teenage boy inside the chicken house dash back to his table, pull a drumstick off his plate in anticipation of shrapnel landing on his dinner, then retreat deeper into dining room from which he came. Nobody was trying to save their cole slaw.

I envisioned us landing on a table with glass showering down around us, like a scene from *Smokey and the Bandit* or something. Not only would I secure a front seat for the rest of my illustrious rose-selling career, but when this story made its way back to school, nobody would ever mess with me again. *Man, don't fuck with Schnabl, that motherfucker is crazy, he once threw a kid through a chicken house window up in Dallas.*

I was preparing for the big slam when I heard Richard whimpering and begging. I knew I had him defeated, and that knowledge allowed more rational ideas to take over my thought process. I tossed him to the pavement like a rag doll and for good measure punched him in the face a couple of times. I had this idea that I was manhandling him like the Incredible Hulk. When there was no fight left in him, I talked some smack, probably something like "Next time, I'll kill you motherfucka." He acknowledged my superiority, and the fight was over.

I took my rightful spot in the front of the truck and he crawled in the back crying. On the ride home, I peered through the cab window into the back. Richard was sitting next to the tailgate on an overturned bucket, disgraced, sulking, smoking cigarettes. But he began treating me with respect after that night. I returned the cordial treatment, and in two years we'd actually become not only friends, but training partners.

Having quit smoking, as a mere freshman, Richard Cooper became the top distance runner in the district. As a senior, I was so far behind the sophomore talent-wise, that I shifted from the longer races that were his specialty, to the 800 meter run, specifically to avoid having to concede first place. In fact, not only did he become a multiple Texas High School State Champion, but he won a full scholarship to the University of Arkansas, where he majored in running. Richard competed in two Olympic trials and in 1988 was an alternate on the US Olympic team in the 3000 meter steeplechase. I could always beat the hell out of Richard Cooper; the problem was catching him first.

***

My better judgment spared Richard and I from being cut by glass that night, but a few weeks later, I wasn't so lucky. I was wearing shorts while selling at the corner or Gross and Hillcrest one summer afternoon, when I knelt down on a broken bottle hidden in the tall grass. When I tried to get up to walk, blood started squirting out of my knee. The stream of blood drew a six foot arc, but only when I bent my knee. So I walked stiff-legged to the restroom in a nearby laundromat. I sat down on the toilet and washed my knee with a handful of brown paper towels. I couldn't wash the blood as fast as it was squirting out. As long as I kept my leg straight and applied direct pressure to the puncture, it wasn't shooting blood. I realized that the squirting was occurring in pulses, at a cadence of about once per second, in rhythm with my heartbeat. By the time I left the restroom, it looked like a murder scene—blood splattering on all four walls, puddles on the floor and in the sink, blood-saturated paper towels overflowing in the trash can.

I grabbed every paper towel in the bathroom and hobbled back to the rose stand. I sat there applying continuous pressure with the paper towels for about an hour. I amused myself thinking about what we'd learned in seventh grade health class: The first step to stop bleeding is to apply direct pressure. "No shit," I thought. I didn't need a health class to know that.

I sold five or six dozen roses during that period of time, making myself a hard-earned buck in the process. My corner was littered with blood-soaked paper towels. Several kind people offered to take me to the hospital but I refused. In an age before pagers and mobile phones, there was no contingency plan of what to do in a situation like this. Like a good soldier, I didn't want to abandon my post, nor did I want to convert a Good Samaritan's Lincoln Town Car into a blood soaked triage center.

One of the ladies who offered to help returned five minutes after I had told her "no thanks." She told me that an ambulance was on its way. More than anything else I was upset that I wasn't able to handle this by myself. I tried to deny how serious this injury was, but deep down I knew it was bad. The ambulance took me to the hospital where the doctors worked on my knee. This was no routine cut; I had punctured a large artery just below my knee cap.

The lady who arranged for the ambulance stayed at my rose stand for an hour waiting for my boss to come by, so that she could tell him where I'd been taken. I don't know if she sold any roses, but if she did, I doubt the boss paid her a twenty percent commission. The boss showed up at the hospital, and we squared our finances while I was laying on the gurney waiting for the specialist to show up to do the stitching. The boss had eight kids he had to get home, all of which were standing in the doorway shifting their heads around so that they might get an unobstructed view of me. He called my parents and asked them to come to Dallas and pick me up, which was a two-hour drive (one way) for them. I'd cost myself a chicken dinner and my parents a night of heavy drinking, although I noticed they had a couple of cocktails on the drive home. I fully recovered in about a month and had a pretty nifty scar to show off. It was a tough way to make seven bucks.

Could Someone Give Me a Ride?

In seventh grade, I participated in all three school sports: football, basketball, and track. Practices and games were escapes from home life. The more time I spent in school activities, the less time I spent at home, with the drinking. Athletics became my life. For five years I participated in any sport I could, and with each successive season, Mom and Doug became increasingly displeased with the burden of my transportation needs.

After returning from a road game, kids needing to call their parents for a ride formed a line at the coach's desk. While waiting for my turn, I noticed how rude most of the other kids were to their parents. "Hey, come get me," was fairly typical. I dared not attempt that approach with my mother.

One night Coach Johnson complimented me. "Schnabl, I want to tell you something. I'm always impressed by the way you talk to your parents. I sit here and listen to the other kids *tell* their parents to come pick them up. But you show good manners in *asking* for a ride. I'm proud of you Schnabl—well done."

The truth was that I *asked* because it wasn't a foregone conclusion someone would come. There were nights we didn't get in until 11:00, which was an hour after Mom and Doug's last drink. Mom always insisted I rideshare, which I did whenever I could but there were very few athletes who lived in my direction, six miles west of town.

Waiting to make that phone call was an anxious time for me. Before it was my turn, I'd pray the call would be answered. *Please. Please answer.* After ten rings: *No, I don't wanna walk home again tonight. Not tonight!* Guys behind me are waiting their turn. Coach is staring at me, wondering what's taking my parents so long to answer. I go to the back of the line and try again five minutes later. I'm the last one in the coach's office. Ten rings. Coach studies my face. *I don't need your sympathy.* I speak into the receiver.

"Mom, Can you come pick me up please? Thanks."

But the phone at my house is still ringing as I hang it up. *I'm walking! Goddamn them. Why am I the only one who has parents like this? Why me?*

When I began playing high school sports, the need for rides increased. Football practices went until six in the evening, sometimes later. This shouldn't have been a problem because Doug passed the field on his way home from work between 5:45 and 6:00. But he had zero tolerance for practices that ran late. He couldn't wait to get home to his friends, Jack Daniels and Jim Beam. On those occasions he had to sit more than ten or fifteen minutes, he'd be agitated when I got into his truck. Then, after a few drinks he'd gripe to my mother about how inconvenient my practices were, and try to convince her to take away my sports.

One evening, after his self-medicating ritual, he issued a mandate to my mother that she passed on to me. "If you want a ride home, be ready to go at six sharp. At six, Doug leaves, with or without you."

This was the method Doug used to parent by proxy. He'd preach to my mother about the way things ought to be done and then send her off to implement his agenda. Rarely did I have confrontations with Doug directly, but my mother and I were always at odds regarding his rules she felt compelled to impose.

"I can't control what time Coach lets us out of practice, Mom."

"Life is full of choices. You can quit, find another ride, or tell the coach you need to leave practice early."

Hey Coach, I know you're about to make us all run until we puke, but my step-father is in the parking lot, and he can't afford to get a late start on his drinking tonight, so I need to leave now, right before the run. I'm really sorry about this. You understand, don't you, Coach? By the way, what are my chances of starting this week?

A few nights later, at 6:05, as we were lining up to run the last of ten windsprints to finish practice, I saw Doug's truck leave the parking lot. I dragged ass through the sprint.

"You were last Schnabl!" Coach Robinson yelled. "Dan Purvis beat you!"

He came toward me like he wanted to hit me, put his chest into my facemask. A fighting posture. "Do you wanna buy a ticket to the next game Schnabl?"

I responded with the tone of an Army recruit in basic training. "No sir!"

"I'm tired of letting you watch for free. You're not earning that seat on the bench, you worthless kraut! Give me another." *Forty yards as fast as I can, then a six-mile jog. I can do this.*

There Ain't No Free Lunch

During my first three years of high school, my Coach, Stan Davis, mentored me in basketball, football, pole vault, cross-country, algebra, church, and life. During those three years, he wasn't just my coach; he was more like my father. He sponsored a small group of students who started a *Fellowship of Christian Athletes* chapter, which I joined. It was no coincidence that I signed up for everything he led. Whether it was sports, academics, or my behavior, he was a constant source of feedback, positive and negative.

Often, we worked on my pole vault technique for an hour after everyone else had left the track. "There's a reason I'm out here with you, Schnabl, pushing you." He said it like a question.

"Money?" I joked.

We both laughed. He liked my quick wit, as long as I wasn't using it to disrupt his class.

"Because I want you to be a certain kind of man, Schnabl."

"Yessir. Thank you."

Even though Coach Davis was only in his early thirties, he was "old school." An unusual hybrid of ex-Marine and Sunday school teacher; he wore big glasses, oversized, over-colored ties with pants and jackets that could've functioned as chessboards. His angular jaw was always clean-shaven and his curly blond hair was smartly cropped, as though he were still on active duty. His fair skin didn't tan; it burned lobster-red. He was always nagging us guys to dress better and get our hair cut. "I've heard you say hair length dudn't matter. Okay, you're right, hair length dudn't matter; so get it cut. And, you've told me the clothes you wear dudn't matter either… Okay, if it dudn't matter, wear clean britches without holes in 'em." I respected Coach Davis' opinion on almost everything, but not so much on fashion and hairstyles.

During my gloryless football career, most of my action came as a defensive back. I was pretty good at pass coverage, but not much of a tackler. On running plays, I'd jump into the mob after the dirty work was done. After the ball carrier was down, it wasn't beyond me to burrow my way through a maze of limbs so after everyone else had un-piled, I'd be there on the ground, clutching an opponent whom someone else had tackled. Then, I'd get up and align myself so the press box announcer had a clear view of #19, sometimes even adjusting my jersey to ensure I'd be recognized over the public address system. Although I contributed only occasionally to my team's run defense, I once got my name called for being "in on the stop," on eight consecutive plays.

I began my sophomore season as second-string quarterback. Even though the starting quarterback, Bryan Johnson, was two inches taller and fifteen pounds heavier, I had a stronger and more accurate arm. BJ had about zero passing yards after the first two games. In the week leading up to our third game, there was talk among the coaches that I might get a chance to lead the team. Trailing 7-3, with five minutes left in the game, and BJ stinking it up as usual, Coach Davis called on me to quarterback our last series.

On the first play, the pass rush flushed me out of the pocket. I zigzagged backwards about twenty yards behind the line of scrimmage, into my own end zone. Then I turned upfield and ran thirty yards along the left sideline for a net gain of ten. With less than a minute left on the clock, and the ball at midfield, I ended another chaotic scramble by heaving the ball forty yards to a receiver who made a diving catch. We were at the one-yard line with time for one last play. Coach Davis called for a handoff to the tailback. I was devastated. My passing, running, and leadership had taken us from certain defeat to within a quarterback sneak of

101

winning. Now, with the game on the line, he wanted me to turn around and hand the ball to James Kunkel? *Bullshit!*

I took the snap, did my pivot step and began the motion of sticking the ball into the running back's gut. Then I pulled it out and tucked it under my arm. I cut behind Kunkel and turned him into my lead blocker by shoving him in the back toward a churning mass of football humanity. I closed my eyes, plowed into a wall and pushed bodies forward until I found myself falling forward into free space, across the goal line, and into the end zone—without the ball. *Shit, I just lost the game!* I looked up to see the referee, his arms extended upward. *Touchdown? How can that be?* According to his ruling, I'd lost the ball *after* having scored the winning touchdown. I'd led the team to a come-from-behind victory. Teammates, cheerleaders, everyone, except James Kunkel, were mobbing me.

Coach Davis, normally calm and soft-spoken, was furious. Even as the celebration continued around me, he put his nose on my facemask. While he reprimanded me, I turned away to avoid eye contact. He calmly clutched the cage in front of my face and persuaded my head back around, demanding my attention. "The quarterback must have the respect of his teammates. Tonight you were about to earn it. I was proud of you for that, but then, you blew it." Tears of a betrayed man welled in his eyes as he continued. "I woulda rather lost this game than to win like that."

I gave him my premeditated excuse. "Coach, my facemask got hung up on the center's butt pad—"

"That's bunk, Schnabl. I ain't blind. I can't trust you to be this team's quarterback."

He knew I'd kept the ball because I wanted to be the hero. Worse, he knew I was lying about it.

When I went to my locker before the next game, I had a new jersey number—76. Instead of suiting up, I entered his office. "Coach, I think there's been a mistake."

"There's no mistake, Schnabl."

"Coach, how can I play quarterback wearing #76?"

He raised his eyebrows and tilted his head without speaking. His expression said everything, but he spoke just to be clear. "You ain't my quarterback."

I never got to go back in at quarterback the rest of the season, even though BJ rarely completed a pass. More than anything, I wanted Coach Davis' approval. For the rest of the season I was mad as hell at him for not giving me another chance to earn it.

I spent the last six games hoping that BJ would screw up so much that Coach would have a change of heart and send me in. The combination of Coach Davis' stubbornness and BJ's poor play was maddening. To make matters worse, BJ was arrogant without basis, and I actually found myself wishing he'd get hurt. I didn't want him to break a leg or anything, maybe just get the wind knocked out of him and need to be carried off the field crying like a baby. He worked so hard to be cool, strutting around with an exaggerated swagger and his Izod shirt collar turned up.

When BJ first came to Lindale, in eighth grade, he was always talking about how he needed to be low-key "cuz there's people looking for me, ya know what I mean? I don't need the pub." He'd been in town only a short time when he offered me a ride home after an out-of-town basketball game. We were waiting together, BJ and me, at the designated spot where his cousin or his friend with a license, or somebody was to pick us up when a hot rod minus a muffler drove by. BJ looked nervous—contrived nervous. "I gotta split or these people are gonna fuck me up," He ran off into the night in full sprint and disappeared. I waited for half an hour, walked around calling his name, but he never answered. I had no money for a phone call, and my teammates and coaches had all gone home. This was the first time I walked/ran home six miles at night through the woods. And, I was scared shitless by howling wolves.

***

Coach Davis' teachings went far beyond sport. They were lessons in life. A devout Christian man, one of his favorite mini-sermons was taken from Zig Ziglar's book, *See You at the Top*. The most valuable lesson I've ever been taught: *There Ain't No Free Lunch*.

To some, the expression meant, "if it sounds too good to be true, it probably is." That, in itself, is sound advice. But Coach Davis taught a deeper meaning of that expression.

You are not entitled. If it's worth having, it is worth working for. Never expect things to be easy. Regardless of what you want in life, expect to have to work to achieve it. Pay your dues, reap the reward.

I didn't grasp the meaning of all this with an instant sense of enlightenment. Instead, I tucked this lesson, and many others, into a far corner of my mind. I had no idea that for years to come, I'd pull them out, dust them off, and rehash them. Some corner of my mind still takes me back there—back to his coach's office, the pole vault pit, the practice fields, the prayer meetings in the equipment room—back to his speeches, prefaced and summarized with cheesy clichés: Happiness is not about what happens to you but how you react to it. There ain't no *I* in *team*. Excuses are reasons losers give. Close only counts in horseshoes, bad breath, and body odor. If life gives you lemons, make lemonade…

When he preached his values to a large group, I often joined the other guys in snickering at his poor attempts at humor, his animated speech patterns, the funny way he cocked his head and stared at you when he was expecting a response, and his hideous selection of colorful clothes. But inside, I was getting the powerful messages embedded within his abstract methods.

After a road game loss, our football team sat in a dark hallway of a school in New London, Texas. Normally, we huddled in the end zone while Coach Davis talked, but on this night he had us assemble inside the school building. Morale was down. It was the low point of our season. *It was all BJ's fault.* Guys were complaining and pointing accusatory fingers as we settled into the cozy corridor for his speech. "You guys think it really matters who won this game?" He paused for effect. We looked around at each another. *What's his angle?* "Does anyone know why I brought you inside this school? Does anyone know what happened here forty-three years ago?"

The hallway was dark, my teammates were silhouettes, but I sensed a whole team's worth of dumb looks. We knew what had been happening the two hours out on the football field, but none of us had a clue of what he was talking about.

"In 1937, a gas leak ignited a huge explosion in this school. In an instant, the whole building was leveled. Look it up. All that was left were piles of bricks. Three hundred children and teachers died sitting in the same place you are sitting at this very moment. Many of the bodies couldn't be identified. Imagine everyone you go to school with—gone. Like that." He snapped his fingers, paused, and scanned the team's collective eyes looking for connections before continuing. He could tell I was interested. "Men, I bet almost every one of those guys you played against out there tonight has a story of how that explosion affected their family." Everyone stopped fidgeting with their gear.

His voice trembled and his forearms quivered. "Guys, **that** matters. Who won this football game dudn't matter. Every minute of your life is a gift from God. There are no guarantees, men. There is no guarantee any one of us will even see another football game. And you guys act like you wanna kill each other over who missed a block?"

He began to choke back tears. "I want to tell you something. Life is a series of opportunities, men, and how you approach these opportunities is what's called *attitude*. Your attitude determines if you succeed or fail in everything you do. What matters is not a football game, but your attitude in approaching it. Give it everything you got and rejoice in the chance you have to play this game. In every practice and on every play, you are building a pattern of behavior that'll become a habit in all aspects of your lives. Winning and losing has nothing to do with the final score. In a few years, you probably won't even remember who won this game. But if I get one of you young men to buy what I'm saying right now, I've won my game. Would you men join me in a moment of silence, please, for those three hundred people who died here forty-three years ago?"

I didn't want his speech to end. I wanted Coach to keep talking. I wanted to be made wiser. Before he was finished, I knew the most enduring thing that happened that night was not the game. For all the times my mother had told me sports were a waste of time, Coach Davis proved to me how wrong she was. Sports brought me to Coach Davis. I bowed my head. For thirty seconds I thought a little about burning children and grieving parents and about what I was going to do with my life and a lot about controlling my resentment toward the man who wouldn't let me play quarterback.

Coach Davis was right. Twenty-five years later, I don't remember a single play from that game, but I will never forget his post-game speech. "Every minute of your life is a gift from God."

Coach Davis won his game.

Yeah...About that Ride...Not Right Now

Coach Davis was also the head basketball coach at Lindale High School. Although I was disappointed when I didn't make the varsity as a sophomore, one day I was thankful for my status as star of the junior varsity.

Our school was hosting a JV tournament and one of our games started about a half-hour before school dismissed. As a special treat, any student who wanted to attend the game would be excused from their last class. Needless to say, the gym was crammed. There wasn't enough bleacher space to accommodate the crowd. Plastic cafeteria chairs lined the walls behind the basketball goals. For most home games, our JV team drew only parents, girlfriends, and close friends of the players. We came out of the locker room and six hundred fans greeted us with a standing ovation. This was my chance to put the Captain and Tennille thing behind me.

We were playing a school, Whitehouse, rich in basketball tradition. Their varsity team had recently won a state championship. Everyone knew they were the big kids on the basketball block.

I had a deliberate, but deadly, long-range set shot, putting more arc on the ball than most players, which added drama to my shots. After the tip-off landed in my hands, I took two dribbles and jacked up my renowned arcing twenty-footer. SWISH! Already predisposed to be in a good mood, having gotten out of class early, the crowd erupted. Hyped up on cheers and adrenaline, I stole the ensuing inbound pass and banked an easy lay-up despite being fouled. The gym was going crazy—crazy for me. At that moment, I knew what it felt like to be a rock star. I sank the free throw. Five points in the first eight seconds. Not bad. My mind did basic math as I jogged back down the court. *I'm on pace to score a thousand points.*

I forced shots I had no business taking; yet they were all going in. Passing? Nah—that was for my teammates. Their objective: Get me the ball. When we had the ball in the halfcourt offense, the crowd chanted my name. If someone else shot, the gym would grumble. I started calling for the ball every time down the court. I'd come off a pick, catch, shoot. Two points—automatic. Nobody remembered my favorite song; everyone was here to watch me play, and I did not disappoint. *This is big, as big to each of them as it is to me, all six hundred of us sharing a spiritual moment that transcends sport—an event that none present will ever forget. Twenty-years from now, people in Lindale will talk about this at their kid's games.*

"Remember that game when Schnabl—"

"Yeah, I remember, I've never seen anything like it to this day."

We headed to the locker room at halftime leading the basketball powerhouse 27-17. In only twelve minutes of playing time, I'd scored 21 points, which was already my career high for a game. I didn't know how many shots I'd missed, but it couldn't have been more than two or three. And, most of my ten baskets were from long distance, so had we had three-pointers, I would have had about thirty points. This far eclipsed my ninth grade district championship in the Mile Run as my greatest sports moment ever. For the first time in my life, I was what I'd always dreamed of being—a big time sports hero. *I will have this forever, and it will sustain me until my next great feat. Try to stop me Whitehouse. I dare you. You can't stop me; nobody can stop me, I'm Larry Fucking Bird.*

Maybe I'd be recognized at the end-of-the-year awards ceremony. After Mr. Pruitt awarded Melita Lang her hard-earned award for Outstanding Biology Student, Coach Davis would stroll to the podium and, with a big smile on his face, present me with a three-foot trophy for the most amazing athletic performance of the year. "I'm proud of him," he would say into the mic just before shaking my hand. "My only mistake was not putting him on the varsity."

I came out of the dressing room for the third quarter and headed down the short hall to the court with visions of grandeur. *I might go for 50. Why not? I'm on pace for 42. Why can't I pick it up a bit? After all, I did miss two shots in the first half. Had those gone in, I'd already have 25. Did you see Schnabl," they'll say to each other tomorrow in the halls. "He got 50! That son-of-a-bitch went for 50!"*

We're all pumped-up, slapping each other on the back. I heard one of my teammates remark giddily. "Whitehouse man, we're beating fucking Whitehouse." ***We're** beating Whitehouse? Huh, you mean **I'm** beating Whitehouse. You just focus on getting me the ball. I bet they're gonna give me a standing ovation.* This is gonna be awesome...

We trotted out onto the court and realized that while we were in the locker room something happened—something even more exciting to all my fans than the chance to see me go for 50. The bell had rung and school had been dismissed. The gym was empty. Six hundred had become twenty. No one clapped, no one cheered. It was like coming out onto the floor for a practice. *What's wrong with those people? Don't they even care who wins? Don't they care how many points I score? Where's their school spirit?*

Whitehouse double-teamed me the whole second half, even when I didn't have the ball. Their strategy was effective, and I rarely touched the ball in the second half. Even when I did got a shot off, my aim was bad and I ended up scoring only four more points. With five seconds left, and the score tied, I threw a bad pass that was intercepted, leading to a game-winning buzzer-beating basket by the visitors. I had hogged the ball so much, it may have been the only pass I had tried all day. I'd followed my best half of basketball in my life with my worst. Some of my teammates were down on me, for both my selfish play and my boneheaded pass, but, fortunately, almost no one in the student body saw me lose the game. In fact, for the rest of my years at Lindale, many misinformed students thought I was a basketball God, while the truth was: I wasn't even good enough to make the varsity team, at least not until the last game of the season.

The varsity team kind of fell apart on Coach Davis toward the end of that year. Before the last game, three seniors decided to quit the team just to spite Coach and his uncompromising methods. The dissension created some holes on the varsity roster. So, before the last game of the year, Coach called me to his office. "Schnabl, I'm bringing you up to the varsity for this last game. I want you to know I was gonna add you anyway, even before those guys quit. You've earned this chance. You've had a good season and, I've seen a lot of effort in practice lately. Congratulations." As he often did when he was pleased with me, he offered a handshake—a gesture I'd come to recognize as his utmost expression of praise. The promotion to varsity made me the self proclaimed best sophomore white basketball player at the school.

The attitude on the rest of the team was abysmal for this last game. Even one of the other JV call-ups quit the team just as we were about to take the court for warmups when he refused Coach's request to wear his warmup jacket. It seemed like everyone was challenging our coach's authority except me. I was just thrilled to suit out for a varsity game. For this last game, Coach Davis was down to six varsity players and us three JV call-ups. The nine of us were subjected to a halftime lesson that addressed the dissension and selfishness that had pervaded the team:

There were two tribes who lived in villages separated by a mountain range. One tribe had a defective gene in their ancestry. The gene caused all the people in the village to have fused elbows, making it impossible for them to feed themselves. What's more, that village was having a horrific drought and they were starving. The village on the other side of the small mountain was blessed. They did not have the genetic defect, so members of that tribe were physically capable of feeding themselves. They were also getting plenty of rain, and their harvest was bountiful. Even though there was plenty of food in that village, greedy neighbors fought each other over the surplus. Elders of the elbow-fused village had come over the mountain to see if their neighbors would be merciful and share some of their food and good fortune. But when they came upon the blessed village, the starving visitors found a bloodbath of death; the result of greediness over excessive food. They also found a stockpile of food which remained. Their own fused elbows were not a problem either. They had learned long ago that if you feed each other, you will be fed yourself. Two groups of people: one blessed by God, one seemingly cursed. The group that worked together and looked after each other survived; the group who were collectively greedy and thought only of themselves perished. But in a locker room knee deep in testosterone, me and the eight other guys rolled our eyes secretively at each other, our way of saying, "here is another silly fable from this losing coach with pants made from the same material as a couch I used to have, who will probably be fired after this season anyway." But just beneath the I'm-too-cool-for-his-children-stories attitude there was at least one kid who was filing these lessons away in his mental library for future checkout.

The game was in a town named Van, which was only fifteen minutes from Lindale. Our farmhouse was actually midway between the two towns, situated on an old country back road, a mile off the highway. So even though it was a road game, it was only a ten-minute drive for Mom and Doug to make a rare appearance at a game. I made one of my two free throws in that game and was elated to have made the varsity stat sheet for the season with one point. Not to be outdone, the less-talented BJ who was also a JV callup, scored 2 points.

Before the team got on the bus, my mother told me to ask my coach if I could ride home directly with her, allowing them to circumvent the hassle of driving all the way back to Lindale to retrieve me, only to turn around and drive the same way from which they came. Coach Davis denied my request without offering an explanation. I jogged back to the stands and told my mother the answer was "no" and asked her to pick me up at the gym in Lindale where the bus would take us. My mother was stinking drunk, so she was predictably quite defiant about her request being rejected. "I don't give a shit what your Coach says, you're coming with us."

"Mom, I can't do that. I'll get in trouble at school."

"What are they gonna do, kick you off the team? The season's over, now come with us."

"Mom, my coach said 'no'…"

"Don't worry about your coach; I'll handle your coach."

"Mom, they could kick me off the track team..." And with that, I quickly scampered off to get on the team bus. She and Doug went out to their car and followed our school bus down the highway at an alarmingly close distance. Coach Davis was driving the bus, while his assistant, Coach Anderson sat in the front seat. I could see Coach Davis getting agitated as he repeatedly looked in his rear view mirror to see how close he was being tailgated. In the back of the bus I could hear the obnoxious voice of Gatorbait, a scrawny black kid with a mouth bigger than JJ from *Good Times*. "That's Schnabl's crazy-ass mother, following us like that. Shit, what the hell is wrong with that bitch?"

As we got close to the road that was the turn off for my house, Doug started flashing his brights. An irritated Coach Davis pulled the bus off the road and onto the grass. He sent one of the other players out to tell Mom and Doug what I'd already told them; they would have to follow us to the school and pick me up there. I knew this would infuriate my mother. How dare he presume to make decisions regarding me that opposed her will. He had just finished a lousy season with a bunch of players who quit on him. I felt sorry for him. Rumors persisted that he'd be fired. He seemed down, maybe even hurt. I knew my parent's shenanigans were irritating him. When we got to the school, Mom decided she was gonna give Coach a piece of her mind. About half of us, including me and Coach Davis, had already made our way into the building by the time she pushed her way onto the bus salmon-style, through a line of disembarking basketball players.

Since I was already gone, I didn't witness the tirade. I was in the locker room and had just tossed my uniform in the laundry bin when a group of guys, including Gatorbait came in laughing their asses off. Gatorbait shouted across the locker room. "Schnabl, your mom tow Pokey a new asshole..." Pokey was a nickname for Coach Anderson. He was a quiet, reserved man who never seemed to get either upset or excited. He was as introverted as possible for a coach to be.

"What are you talking about?" I asked Gatorbait.

Gatorbait was loud, obnoxious and intent on becoming the next Richard Pryor. He launched into an impromptu mocking of my mother, giving a talented recital of my mother's rant he'd just witnessed on the bus complete with her slurred speech.

"You son of a bitch, who in the hell do you think you are? I'm his mother...do you understand that? You're just a goddamned coach....he's my son, not yours...I know what you're trying to do; you're trying to brainwash these kids. You don't have me fooled... I wanna know why you wouldn't let him come with me. You think I have nothing better to do than to follow your goddamned bus? You're just a coach..."

Jesus, Mom, the least you could do is curse out the right coach. Poor Coach Anderson, I need to find him and apologize.

At least to Coach Anderson, it would be a one-time thing. I lived in that world every day.

Cocktails

There was nothing my mother liked to do more than drink and talk. The mixture of cocktails and whatever biological chemicals were out of whack inside her created sort of an alcohol induced alter ego. One moment, she might be saying, "I love you kid." The next, she would spew allegations, render opinions and initiate the most inappropriate conversations. The president is not a real person. He's a hologram. Richard, have you started masturbating yet?" There was no way of knowing what she was going to do, or say next.

If there was no one around who'd listen, she might wake someone up. My mother came to my bedroom late one night and shook me awake to talk to me about drugs.

"Richard, you're taking drugs, aren't you?"

"What are you talking about?" I sat up in my bed and opened my eyes. "No. I'm not!"

"Richard, drugs are gonna ruin your life."

I've never, before, or since, used illegal drugs. Not one drag, drop, hit, or sniff, not a single —zero. Yet I'm being shaken awaken on a school night to be told drugs are gonna ruin me?

"Mom, I'm not taking drugs!"

"Quit lying. You can tell me. What is it? Pot?"

"What makes you think I'm on drugs?" I said to the human form sitting on my bed, in the dark.

"How I know doesn't matter, but I know you are."

I insisted she was mistaken and that her source, whatever it was, was incorrect. She continued to assert that her knowledge of my drug use was based on fact not speculation, and demanded an admission.

"Who told you that?" I asked.

Her shoulders and head swayed slightly as she struggled to maintain her uprightness. But this wasn't a two-way conversation, she wasn't going to tell me why she thought I was on drugs, instead she used the I'm-gonna-scare-my-kid-straight tactic. "About ten years ago...the pot had angel dust in it, Richard. It fucked me up like you wouldn't believe. I could've died. You need to know this. I could have died. You don't know what kind of shit those people put in drugs..."

How ironic. A drunk alcoholic with cigarette breath, who believes lizards, masquerading as people are living among us, has awakened me in the middle of the night to give me a heartfelt warning about how substance abuse was going to ruin my life.

Juxtaposed to that were the nights she woke me up to try and persuade me to drink with her. One night, I was already in bed when I was awakened by a shouting match. I heard the door close, Doug's footsteps on the wooden porch, and then the sound of his car driving off. As the rumble of his pickup truck faded into the distance, she came into my room. I pretended to be asleep. When she flipped on the lights, I buried my face in the pillow so she wouldn't see my eyelids twitch. She shook me anyway.

"Rich, get up..."

"Huh?"

"Get up, I wanna talk to you," she said in her slobber voice, like her tongue had swelled to twice its normal size.

She led me to the kitchen.

"Sit down," she demanded.

I sat at the kitchen table.

She grabbed a handful of ice out of the fridge and dropped it into a glass. She put the glass down in front of me, poured three ounces of Jim Beam in it and filled the rest with Coke.

"Have a drink, kid."

"I don't want a drink Mom. Thanks. I'm really tired."

"You big pussy, have a drink," she demanded.

"Mom, I don't want a drink; can I just go back to bed?"

She got in my face, interrupting my stare at the wall.

"I said have a goddamn drink you goddamned son-of-a-bitch."

"I told you, I don't want a drink." I got up to go to bed.

She grabbed my arm and tried to pull me back down into the seat. "You're a pussy, you hear me? A big pussy!"

I sat down, took a big gulp. "Okay Mom, I had a drink. I ain't no pussy. Now, I'm going to bed."

Alcohol gave her courage to say things that no sober person would. She was understandably upset that my father never paid court ordered child support. But instead of phoning him to have a productive discussion about it, she waited thirteen years before calling him late one night in a drunken stupor.

She covered a lot of ground in that conversation, blaming him for everything wrong with me. And, she got him to agree to take me for the upcoming summer after my sophomore year. *A bus ride to Idaho, to meet my father and his family. This will be an adventure.*

Are You My Dad?

I'm at the bus terminal trying to figure out which man in the crowd is my father. Then I'm at his house, looking at his photo album—looking at pictures of me—and listening to him talk about our time together. He's talking about the little boy in the pictures, and then he shows me that picture of me with that old lady who babysat and stuck me with diaper pins. *This is the man that took me from my mother, from my grandparents. This is the man that stole me. This is the man—the monster—that I grew up fearing.* It all comes rushing back, and for a moment, I see him as an abductor. I get this déjà vu, like there's a little boy in the basement, right below us, and the old lady babysitter is there too, and she's jabbing the kid with diaper pins, and he's crying. I wanna help, but it's too late. It's over. The danger is over. I am big, and he will not hurt me now.

I'd spent the better part of the previous four summers selling roses, picking blackberries, or doing chores on a scorching-hot Texas farm, isolated from my friends. Compared to summers on the farm, Idaho was a blast! I could ride a bike anywhere I wanted to go and with the help of being on a baseball team, I made new friends instantly. After I got over the initial weirdness of meeting my father, his wife, and my half-siblings for the first time, the summer was filled with sports, video games, bike riding, hanging out at the lake.

I had two first impressions of my father, which turned out to be remarkably accurate. One was that he was amazingly cheap (he knew the coffee prices at every cafe in town); the other was that, at forty, he could not move on—his mind was stuck in the 1950's. These two traits made him a master of initiating awkward conversations:

One day he asked me what I wanted to do. I told him I want to see *The Shining*. "I don't go to the movies that often. They're too expensive." I had a handful of quarters in my pocket so I told him I'd pay my own way. There's a cute teenage girl at the box office, selling us tickets. He orders his ticket; she asks for money. "Two bucks for a movie! You gotta be kidding me! Do you know I used to pay twenty-five cents to see a show? And on Monday nights, it was *fright night*—ten cents for horror movies! I saw a lot of Vincent Price movies for a dime. Do you know who Vincent Price is?" Supple blondie responds with a predictable blank stare, head shake, and a polite "no". *Please don't embarrass me any further. Let's just go in and watch the movie.* But he's not done. Astonished at the girl's ignorance, he brings me into the so-called conversation. "Rich, you know who Vincent Price is, don't you?" Cutie stares at me, not at all because she's interested in my answer. *I'm not with him.*

At the Tex-Mex restaurant, the whole family has been seated, served chips and water, and we're perusing the menu. "Three-fifty for two enchiladas and beans and rice? We're getting outta here."

I object. "But...we've already been served chips."

"Hey, if you're buying, we'll stay."

We're all walking toward the door when the college-aged hostess with a perfect smile and bubbly personality inquires about the odd timing of our mass exit. "Are you guys leaving?"

He stops, turns around and faces her, then speaks, not only to her, but in a volume and manner as if he's addressing everyone in the dining room. His voice booms like a politician demanding reform. "Yeah, you bet we're leaving. This place is too expensive! We're going to the Corner Café. They got two-dollar Tuesdays—lunch specials for two dollars." He waits for her rebuttal. It's sincere and accompanied with an empathetic smile. "I'm sorry; have a nice day."

He exits the cantina shaking his head in disbelief, waving a dismissive arm toward the staff. "You can keep your three-dollar Tacos." I trail the family like I don't belong (because I don't). As I get to the door, I turn and smile at the pretty hostess. She is smiling—almost laughing. I wonder if she's laughing with me, or at me. *I'm not with him. I hope you know—know that that is him. That is not me. I will never be like that. I will ride my bike back here one day and show you that I can afford this restaurant. And, I will apologize to you for my father's behavior. You will know—I am not like him. I may look like him, but I am not like him. I don't even know him. Really.*

My father's penny-pinching astounded me; I didn't understand why it was so extreme, but in retrospect, I realize he had one thing very much in common with my mother. Neither wanted to work for someone else. Unlike my mother, my father had been successful at this, having not worked a "real job" for the last ten years. He had derived most of his income from buying and reselling records from the 50's and 60's. Even though he had a store in town, most of his business was done through mail order or at swap meets. He made custom eight-track or cassette tapes for customers. His record collection was so extensive, and so well organized, that, in those days if someone wanted all their favorite old songs to be recorded onto a customized eight-track tape, he was the guy in town that could do that—a precursor to iTunes.

He also made a few bucks playing drums in oldies or Country & Western bands. Add to that an occasional DJ gig at weddings and private parties, and he eked out a living in the "music business." And then there were a few gumball machines he had placed around town, and the stuff they sold from their front yard. I guess there's something to be said for doing what you love, but his benefits and retirement package weren't too hot, neither was the level of financial support that he provided me. His wife, Mary, was matronly, old fashioned, and at the time, had never earned a wage in her life, which meant that with a bit of government assistance, my father somehow supported a family of five selling eight-tracks and gumballs. Then I came along, wanting to be fed every day, to see movies and to play video games.

My father seemed interested in making up for lost time. He took me roller skating with the family (on Family-night Thursdays when the whole family got in for five dollars), showed me the town, as we ran errands, just he and I. He even took me to one of his car club meetings for classic Chevys. He taught me the difference between a sedan and hardtop and explained why having four doors greatly diminished the value of a '57 Chevy relative to one with two doors. He taught me how to drive a three-on-the-tree shifter. He started tagging along with me on my runs, and, at a very fit forty, and a former runner himself, he was soon able to keep pace with me. He was a night owl, so we'd usually run at midnight, after the heat had abated, even if the haze from Mt. St. Helens had not. After our runs, we'd go to Denny's for coffee, and chat with our favorite waitress, who sometimes charged him for only one coffee. On some nights, we'd listen to his old records for hours and my songs for about ten seconds each. He taught me a lot about old music. We'd stay up for hours after his wife and kids had gone to bed. The late hours suited him, since he didn't have to open his oldies record store until 10 a.m.

Not long after getting there, I'd met some boys in the park who had just registered for summer baseball. I wanted to play, so I rode my bike to the record store to see my father.

"Do you think I could sign up to play baseball?"

"Sure."

He didn't understand I was asking not only for consent, but also for money.

"It's twenty dollars," I said.

"Twenty dollars?"

Yeah, I know, I know, you used to play baseball for free in a vacant lot. Whoever heard of charging a kid to play baseball? Well that's the way it is now.

"Yeah, but that includes the T-shirt."

He pulled his till from under the counter, set it on his desk, opened it, and then pulled out a plain white business envelope with my name on it, written in cursive with pencil.

"I've been saving money for us to do stuff together this summer."

He opened the envelope and thumbed through eight five-dollar bills. "I have forty dollars. That's got to last all summer. Do you want to spend half of it on this baseball team?"

"Yes."

I could see the disappointment on his face. "Okay, here you go." He handed over four bills.

"Thanks. Thanks a lot."

He forced a smile. "You're welcome."

I had no idea how much twenty dollars was to him.

***

Going out to eat with my father's family was a dreaded event. They'd converse for ten minutes about how to mix and match three meals and three drinks to feed six mouths. After they quizzed the kids on how hungry they were, and before the waitress took the order, Mary would review the plan with my father. "Okay, you're going to get the chicken club with fries and give one wedge of your sandwich to Sherry and another to Rich. And you don't want the fries so Rich and Timmy are going to split your fries. I'm going to get the chicken dinner. I'll give a little chicken and some corn to Cindy, since she eats like a bird anyway. I'll give Rich the drumstick and you and I will split the salad, and you and Sherry can split the mashed potatoes. Sherry will get the kids meal with a hot dog which she'll split with Cindy. We'll get two large milks with three extra glasses for me and the kids, and you just want water to drink."

The waitress would come over, and Mary would order, "He'll have the chicken club, I'll have the chicken dinner, and she'll have the kid's meal. Could we please get two large milks, a glass of water, and three extra glasses, and three extra plates? We're going to share." The waitress would look at the six people at the table and with a confused expression and ask, "Is that all?" After the meal, if there was so much as a tomato wedge left over, Mary would request a to-go box for it. She really respects food and does not want to waste it, which I now appreciate, but I never understood why she just didn't eat the last tomato wedge instead of lugging it around town in a Styrofoam container for the rest of the day.

After watching a few meals shuffled from one plate to another and eating half of what I was accustomed to, I spoke up one morning and asked for my own breakfast plate with all my own food. Mary and my father looked at each other in astonishment like they had never heard of such an idea before. My father said something like, "Are you buying or crying?" Then he went on to explain how the portions were really too big for one person.

Years later, when he was visiting me, I took him out one evening. I had a cheeseburger, fries, and a Coke. He had pie and coffee. The bill came to seven dollars. I pulled a dollar bill out of my wallet and tossed it down onto the table.

"What are you **doing?**" he asked.

"I'm leaving a tip," I said in a what-the-hell-do-you-think-I'm-doing tone.

"A tip? WHATDOYAMEAN? THAT'S A **DOLLARRR**!" he exclaimed, confounded by such generosity.

***

At the skating rink, my father introduced me to his friend's daughter, Gina. We talked a little bit and slow skated to a song called *You're My Shining Star*. We both loved that song. She had the softest hands. I asked for her number and called the next day. We talked for hours and wanted to see more of each other. Because she lived about eight miles away and neither of us had use of a car, I rode my father's bike out to her place and we spent the day together hanging out at the lake and listening to music in her room. She'd sing with along with Genesis

♫ ♫ *There must be some misunderstanding,
There must be some kind of mistake...* ♫ ♫

After that great day together, she started coming to my place, catching rides with her father on his way to work. Gina was the first girlfriend I ever had.

Three days before I was to leave town and go back to Lindale for my junior year, I was competing in the summer track state championships and I wanted Gina to come. I asked my father if we (or I) could go pick her up and bring her to the meet. He complained that gas was too expensive, and that if I had five bucks to put in the tank he would let me go get Gina. He knew I didn't have any money. I contemplated how I could come up with five bucks. I didn't have anything to sell, so all I could do was offer my labor. I went to the back yard, grabbed my father's lawn mower, and pushed it about a half mile to a house that I knew desperately needed their lawn mowed. The so-called grass in their oversized lot was knee high. Mixed in with the grass were pricker bushes; so tall that their fuzzy round purple tops nearly reached my chin. I knocked on the door. Three burly biker dudes with mullets, bandanas, and tattoos, appeared wearing black T-shirts with air-brushed artwork of eagles, American flags, and motorcycles. I stood on their front porch and with a straight face I said, "Hi, my name is Rich, can I mow your yard for five bucks? One of the bikers immediately busted out laughing; the others soon joined him.

One guy held the screen door open and said, "Come on in, man." I reluctantly entered the house and was directed to a chair in their filthy kitchen. There was a beer keg in the sink and dishes piled on it. The counters and the kitchen table at which I was sitting were littered with beer bottles, packs of cigarettes, ashtrays, and a box of dried pizza crust.

Three bikers stood in the kitchen with their arms folded and their butts pressed against the countertops while their buddy started with a series of questions as he pulled a couple beers from the fridge. He tracked down a bottle opener and popped the tops off.

"Say little man, what's your name again?"

"Rich."

"Well Rich, you want a beer?"

I didn't really like beer the few times I had tried it, but having one now seemed like the thing to do. "Sure, thanks."

He brought two beers to the table and sat down. When he pushed one across the table to me, I noticed he had a sequence of tattoos between his knuckles and first finger joints that spelled L-O-V-E. Then he lifted his beer to his mouth with his other hand and I noticed a contrasting tattooed statement of H-A-T-E. "Rich, man, you got any grass?"

"No, man, sorry."

He gestured his head toward the yard. "You're gonna mow that fuckin' jungle for five bucks?"

The interrogation was interrupted when a skinny blonde, who looked like she dyed her roots black, appeared in the doorway. She had cutoff jeans that were hiked up her asscrack and wore a red tubetop over her A-cups. She wore no makeup and her hair was scraggly and oily. She looked like she could be pretty if she tried, but she certainly wasn't trying.

"Tell you what, Rich…you mow our yard and I'll let you fuck my girlfriend." I sat, silent, fidgeting, glancing at him, the girl, the floor, my shoes, the pizza crust on the counter, my beer in front of me, unable to respond. I'd never heard something like that. I studied his stone face for as long as I dared, trying to get a read on whether or not he was joking. What the hell? This can't be real. God, the devil, or maybe Larry Flint himself had just dropped me off in the middle of a *Hustler* Magazine story, or maybe this was a *Penthouse forum* article, except in those stories the girls were always hot and there was never mention of smelly dinner scraps from the night before. I took a nervous gulp of my beer as I contemplated how to respond, or maybe I was trying to buy some time for Blackroots to object. I expected her to respond to his disrespectful comment by picking up a beer bottle and throwing at him. In fact, I was kinda hoping for that so the focus would be taken off me. But she protested only in jest while asking, "Hey don't I get a say in this?"

He looked at me and grinned, showing the rotten, crooked teeth that he had not yet lost, and some gaps where brown teeth used to be. The three bikers and the biker chick were all staring at me waiting for my answer. *'Love will keep us together' is not the right answer to this question.*

She looked me up and down as I sat petrified at the kitchen table chugging my beer as fast as it would come out of the bottle. She smiled at me. Her teeth were better than her boyfriend's mainly in that she still had them all. Then she spoke to me and her boyfriend, "Okay, I'll fuck him, but only if you watch…"

One of my hands started shaking, so I discreetly tried to steady it by grabbing it under the table with the other. Soon they both began to tremble as I spoke. I decided to play it straight. "Nothing against you," I glanced at the lady, then I turned my head to her boyfriend, "but I need the five bucks so I can put gas in my father's car and give my girlfriend a ride to my track meet tomorrow."

I never expected the counter offer. "Okay Rich, tell you what buddy. If you mow the yard, you can have the five bucks **and** you can fuck her. You can't beat that," he said, with another revolting smile as he looked first at me then at her.

I had long imagined how wonderful and fulfilling my first sexual experience would be. During the last week, I even wondered if Gina might be the right person to share it with, and with my departure imminent, I'd been obsessing about whether to raise the issue with her, or possibly just go for it. Never did I envision my first time would involve a biker slut, three Hells Angels wannabes, and hordes of flies buzzing around my asshole. My immediate goal was to get out of that house while maintaining my virginity in all three places. I thought about just making a sudden dash for the open front door. I knew I was faster than these fat guys, but there was still the matter of my father's lawnmower in their front yard. My father would be pissed if I asked him to come here and confront these freaks about getting his lawnmower back. What if they refused to return the mower if I came back for it? Would he come here? Would the bikers tell him he'd have to fuck the slut to get his mower? How would **he** handle the situation? I decided my best option was to try to talk my way out of the house. "Look I don't want to offend anyone here, but I have a girlfriend, and although she is pretty cute (nodding toward the biker girl), I wouldn't feel right doing that, but I would still like to mow your yard for five bucks."

"Aw man, don't get all serious on me. I wuz just fuckin' with ya man…You got a deal man. Five bucks."

I laughed nervously, finished off my beer and shook the biker's slab of a hand. Then I got up, went outside and cranked the old mower.

Progress was slow. I pushed the mower forward two or three feet until it was about to stall, then pushed down on the handle to raise the blade, let the handle down, and pushed forward again. There were tons of rocks hidden in the tall weeds and about once a minute I'd hear the blade smash one against the inside of the mower casing. Many of these rocks were as big as baseballs. The heat wave of 1980 didn't give Idaho a free pass, and even though it wasn't 108 degrees like back in Texas, it was certainly in the 90s, so sweat was pouring down from my head, acting as flypaper for the grass and stickers that landed on my face. It took an hour to do the front yard before I moved to the back which was three times the size. I had just started the back when the semi-bleach blonde whom I had declined to screw, came out with a glass of water. I was so thirsty that I guzzled down the whole glass despite knowing it had come out of that disgusting kitchen. She made small talk for a moment then she joined the guys on their bikes as they headed out.

A few minutes later, I ran out of gas. I pushed the mower into the tall grass so nobody would see it and steal it. I had no money, not even pocket change, so I walked back to my father's house and scrounged forty cents in nickels and pennies out of various car ashtrays that were parked in his yard. I went inside the house and chugged the last twenty ounces of apple juice from a plastic one-gallon container. I rinsed out the empty jug with water and walked to a gas station with it, where I spent ten cents to learn that gasoline eats through plastic. So I rummaged through the garbage and found a 32-ounce glass Gatorade bottle. I still had enough coin to fill it up, which I did and confirmed my assumption; gasoline does not eat through glass. As I approached the biker house with a Gatorade jar full of gas, I could barely see the top of the lawnmower handle protruding from the tops of the weeds. I laughed to myself about what an idiot I was, then filled up the tank and kept on mowing, all the time thinking of my sweet reward, Gina watching me run.

When I finished the job, four hours after starting it, nobody was home. It was getting dark and I was pretty pissed that I hadn't been paid. The track meet started at 9:00 the next morning and these bikers didn't strike me as early risers. I pushed the mower home and came back an hour later, after dark, still no bikers. My father wasn't pleased when he found out that I had used his mower on that lot. "You probably ruined that blade. Do you know how much it costs to get a blade sharpened?"

I explained that I hadn't been paid yet, but I would collect for that job, and asked him to spot me the gas money. He said "no."

I called Gina and told her how stupid I was and how I had failed to come up with a ride. When we hung-up, we were both nearly in tears. I'd be leaving in two days; this was a big event for me and such a trivial matter as my father's unwillingness to help me with a ride for Gina was devastating. For fourteen years he'd done nothing for me. Zero. Not even one day's lunch money. That summer I asked him for only two things: twenty bucks to register for the baseball team (which he provided), and a ride for Gina that day.

I had gone into the summer with an open mind. As much as I tried not to hold the abduction and subsequent abandonment against him, relatively minor incidents caused resentment to surge within me.

When we showed up to the track, my father and I were both surprised to find Gina waiting for me. My father asked her how she got there. "I hitched," she said. He couldn't believe she had done that and, with each follow-up question he asked her, she unintentionally made him feel smaller for being such a tightwad. "Aren't you worried about riding with strangers?"

"Well…it was the only way I had to get here."

After she finished answering his questions, he offered to give her a ride home later, which he did after she watched me win the Mile Run.

The next day was my last full day in Idaho. I'd be getting on a bus back to Texas. My father had made plans to take me fishing. I went out to the garage the night before. He was untangling some fishing line. Mary was in the kitchen making our lunches for the next day. Every wall of the garage lined with bookshelves, floor to ceiling, filled with vinyl 45's, LP's, and 78's. *He will understand. Of course he'll understand. He's a man. I will talk to him man-to-man.*

"Hey, can I ask you something?"

"Sure." He looked up from the rod.

"About tomorrow…would you mind if I spent the day with Gina instead of going fishing?"

He looked at me. The first prolonged eye lock I'd ever had with him.

*Shit. He doesn't understand. Why did I do that? I hurt him. In that way, I **am** like him.*

Grandpa and Grandma

When my mother was six-months-old, her father, before ever laying eyes on his only child, gave his life for his country fighting the forces of evil. Two years later, my grandmother, a World War II widow with a little girl, married the man who'd help her raise my mother, and who'd one day become my Grandpa. Not only did my mother grow up without knowing her real father, but she would ultimately pass that fate to all three of her children—me, Ginger, and her first child, a daughter, whom she put up for adoption.

Our grandparents brought stability into Ginger's and my life. During my teenage years, they'd come to the farm on Sunday afternoons. All day, I could hardly wait for them to show. Grandpa would go out and play football with me for an hour. I'd run pass patterns and he'd throw me the ball as we marched across the pasture. Roger Staubach and Drew Pearson moving downfield against the Redskins. When Grandpa's sixty-year-old arm began to tire, he'd throw the ball underhand—softball style. Grandpa had a pretty good arm; even those underhand throws had some zip on 'em.

When he asked to quit, I usually talked him into throwing some more. "Come on Grandpa, it's a tie game, and we're going into overtime." I savored that encore like a good dessert. My grandfather helped fill the void of an absent father. If Roger Staubach had knocked on my door on Sunday afternoon wanting to play catch, I would have asked him to come another day. Grandpa was my Sunday quarterback.

Sometimes I'd let Grandpa off the hook: instead of forcing him to throw more passes, I'd ask him to watch me vault in my homemade pole vault pit. It was a basic setup. Two vertical ten-foot two-by-fours with a line of nails in them to set the crossbar at the desired height, a hole to plant the pole in, a few crumbled foam mats my school had discarded, and a dirt approach path worn by my own feet. I built the thing as close to the road as possible so when cars drove by, people could stop and watch me. I had my share of fans, one-timers as well as regulars. Most would watch one vault; some would pull over to the side of the road and watch three or four. Once, three cars were pulled off the road at one time as they all watched me clear eight feet with my mahogany pole that Doug had shaped for me. The landing mats were so deteriorated they were practically useless, so I developed a technique to absorb the impact in two separate stages—landing on my feet and then tumbling to the ground. I'd pop up off the ground and look at Grandpa who'd silently shake his head in some combination of pride, amazement, and concern.

After a couple of hours visiting on the farm, our grandparents would take Ginger and I back to their place were we would spend quality family time. It was nice to spend evenings in a clean trailer home with central heat and air, without dogs, ticks, cigarette smoke, and drunks. We'd play board games, eat ice cream, and discuss summer vacation plans. There was a sense of peace at their trailer, and comfort in going to bed knowing I wasn't going to be awakened in the middle of the night by my mother pulling us kids out of bed to take us to a motel, or to a friend's, to get away from Doug, who during his own drunken stupor, had insulted her. At Grandma and Grandpa's, we escaped the chaos for a day. This was my safe place, my sister felt it, too, and I loved my grandparents for making it that.

***

In addition to Sunday evenings, my grandparents took us on several extended summer road trips. The best parts of these vacations were that they'd let me do most of the planning. As a young child, I was fascinated how grown-ups could navigate the streets like a rat running a maze. *How do they always know how to find their way home? It's amazing!* I wanted to know my way around, so I taught myself how to read maps. I was fascinated how each spot on the paper represented a real-life place with its own distinct landscape or cityscape, and its unique people. I became a master planner of ill-advised vacation routes with an unquenchable agenda to turn as many of those black dots into images in my mind.

During the summer before entering high school, I proposed a three-week epic road trip that incorporated almost every place in the country I wanted to see. We left east Texas and hit the following attractions in order: The Painted Dessert, The Grand Canyon, Hoover Dam, Las Vegas, Death Valley, San Francisco, Seattle to visit an uncle, Yellowstone, Mt. Rushmore, Milwaukee to visit Big Grandma, Cincinnati to see Grandpa's sister, The Pro Football Hall of Fame in Canton, Ohio, Graceland in Memphis, and Hot Springs, before finally returning home.

I mapped the whole six-thousand miles and my Grandfather drove most of the route at the posted fifty-five mile an hour limit, sometimes slower. Grandma drove the rest at a blazing sixty.

Each attraction was little more than a place to get out and stretch our legs for a little while. At the Grand Canyon, we looked out over the south rim for about twenty minutes and cruised through Yellowstone, stopping only at Old Faithful. After it erupted, we got back in the car and headed for Devil's Tower Wyoming, the famous sheer cliff from the movie *Close Encounters*, which we marveled at from our car windows as we drove by, concerned that it'd get dark before we made it to Mt. Rushmore. At the Pro Football Hall of Fame, Grandpa and I buzzed through in two hours while Ginger and Grandma grabbed lunchmeat and prepared sandwiches for us in the parking lot.

The most memorable aspect of that trip was our Death Valley crossing. If you draw a straight line on a map between Las Vegas and San Francisco, it crosses Death Valley. So why would a traveler take an interstate onehundred and fifty miles southwest to Barstow, before finally bending north? It made no sense to go south to go north, so I led my elderly grandparents and my ten-year-old sister into the one hundred and fifteen degree desert in July. We drove through a number of dots on the Death Valley map which had intentionally been named to warn people not to visit; places like Devil's Furnace and Stovepipe Wells, stopping long enough to visit a rinky-dink museum that told the story of a particular group of pioneers who crossed Death Valley. Starving and dehydrated, one group survived by eating their mules cooked over a fire they had made from their wagons.

Not only did they not sell gas at those abandoned blips, but I severely misjudged the distance to the first town after leaving the park. Grandpa spoke up while we were still in the park. "How much further to Lone Pine. We're almost outta gas, Rich."

"Oh, we'll make it, we have plenty of gas. *Oh no, Grandpa's right, we're not gonna make it.*

I imagined Grandma waddling down the desolate, boiling highway in her two-inch heels and sweat-drenched dress, while costume jewelry burned her neck and earlobes and the road melted the thin plastic soles of her shoes. She'll lag fifty yards behind the three of us, as we implore her to keep up the pace, "C'mon, Grandma, only fifteen more miles to Lone Pine. You can do it Grandma…"

According to my calculations, which were based on a map with no landmarks, Lone Pine was somewhere between forty and eighty miles away when we reached a fork in the road. There was no sign. There were hardly any signs in Death Valley. *Maybe they melted?* No signs, no people, no cars, no nothing except sand and Joshua trees.

With the gas gauge nearing E, it was clearly my decision. "I think it's this way," I said, choosing the road that had a slightly better surface."

Grandpa obediently followed my advice.

To conserve gas, I advised Grandpa to slow the yellow *Volkswagen Dasher* to forty. Sitting in the navigator's seat, I turned the AC off. Grandma rolled her window down.

I knew that created too much drag. "That's cutting down on our mileage Grandma, we better roll it up."

She complied for about two minutes before beads of perspiration started running down her wrinkled face. Then she rolled the window back down while cursing me, Death Valley,

Rand McNally, and God. A wide swath of black showed between the E and the needle as we rolled into the desert gateway town of Lone Pine. There appeared to be a *Sunoco* station in view when the Dasher began sputtering. It continued to cough and surge for another minute, just long enough to allow us to coast up to the pump. We'd run out of gas at a gas station.

As if I planned it this way, I took credit which I felt was due. "See, I told you we had enough gas."

The price gouging didn't impress Grandpa. "A dollar a gallon! That's ridiculous, Rich."

"Yeah, but just about how many gallons we saved by not taking the interstate through Barstow, Grandpa."

Letters to Me and My Mother

One of the biggest problems that I had with Mom is her insistence on invading my privacy. In the days before e-mail, Facebook, and IM, when a fifteen-minute long distance call could cost an hour of adult wages, teenagers communicated with their out of town friends primarily by exchanging letters in the US mail. I wrote to a few girls, one who had moved from Lindale. I never told her I liked her until I spilled my guts in a letter after she left.

"I wished you were my boyfriend," she wrote back. I would never see her again.

I wrote to another girl, Carla Huskey, whom I'd met at a skating rink in Gatlinburg, Tennessee during one of our annual vacations with Grandma and Grandpa, when I was fifteen. We skated, talked, ate, and played video games until Grandpa came to pick up me and Ginger. When I saw him come in, I had an unprecedented moment of self-confidence. I grabbed the cute girl's hand and led her past the snack bar, past the line of people waiting to play Pac-Man and around the corner to carpeted benches in front of the rental lockers. With her, I shared my first passionate kiss. Our hands swarmed over each other's backs, her tongue softly probed my mouth, my manhood popped to attention. Then Ginger led Grandpa around the corner.

The thrill ended abruptly with his shrilling admonishment, "Rich, what are you doing?"

Jesus, is he talking through a bullhorn? Carla and I turned to look at him standing twenty feet away. For some reason, he didn't come any closer. Ginger was behind him giggling like the prepubescent girl she was. A small crowd gathered to listen to his long distance lecture: "You don't even know that girl....Do you have any idea of the germs she could have?" He continued his inappropriate public objections as if Carla wasn't there, waving his arms like a man flailing at bees. "Get away from her. You don't know where her mouth has been…"

"Write down your address," I told her. "I'll be right back."

I skated past my grandfather to get my shoes. As I did, he whacked me on the back of the head with the heel of his hand. When I looked back at him he was staring at me, smacking his lips, shaking his head in disbelief. Shoes in hand, I skated back to Carla and sat next to her as we changed from skates to shoes. She was laughing so hard I started laughing as well. *What a cool chick.* We kept in touch for five years, then, I saw her one more time. I was twenty and she was eighteen, when I passed through town and took her and her one-year-old son out for dinner. My mom read each letter Carla sent, either by coming into my room and rifling through my collection of open letters or by carefully opening and resealing the envelope.

Then came Gina's letters. After our summer romance, Gina and I vowed to stay together despite being disconnected by distance and her having no phone. Her second letter, about three weeks after my return to Texas, was a mean-spirited surprise. She wrote that she had a new boyfriend. The rest of the letter was comprised of rambling cursing, vague insults, and justifications for why the breakup was my fault. It didn't make any sense. Just a few weeks after our great summer together, the new boyfriend part was hurtful enough, but she failed to explain why she was so angry. Just because she had found someone else didn't mean that she had to be hateful. It couldn't have been something I'd done, because the last time we saw each other was a tearful goodbye. Since then, I'd written to her twice. *What did I say in those letters? They were nice weren't they? Did I say something wrong?* I wanted to call her to see what was going on, but…well…she had no phone. All I could do was write again, asking for an explanation. The letter was never answered, nor was the next one. *Next summer I'll go see her and get an explanation; surely there's some misunderstanding. After we get that cleared up, maybe we can pick up where we left off.*

One night while drinking, my mom probed me as to the reason for my recent somber mood. I had reservations about sharing it with her, but I offered her Gina's letter. Pleased that I was confiding in her, she smiled and exhaled smoke from her nose and mouth. "I've already read it." The admission was bad judgment on her part, and she would not have made it if she were sober. What could have been an opportunity for her to build a bridge and empathize with her son, turned into a heated argument about my privacy.

"Why did you read it? It's not for you."

"Rich, it's my duty as a parent to know what's going on with you. If you don't tell me, I gotta find out somehow, so I can parent."

"So you actually think this is okay, for you to read my private letters?"

"You'll understand when you have your own kids." She finished with the ultimate parental power play. "As long as you live under my roof, I will continue to read whatever I see fit."

We never even discussed Gina.

As the school year progressed, I held solid to my hope of spending the following summer in Idaho, mainly to try and reconcile with the Gina. I'd heard that she didn't have a boyfriend anymore. Then, my mother screened a letter my father wrote to me.

Rich,

Gina was driving home from Seattle this past Sunday. She was on I-90, near Moses Lake. It was late. They don't know if she fell asleep at the wheel, or if she was distracted...

Gina was dead.

Who Shot J.R.?

While I was in Idaho getting acquainted with my father, back in Texas the 1980 heat wave was roasting Mom, Doug and Ginger—forty consecutive days over one hundred degrees. Our chickens fell over dead, grasshoppers swarmed the gardens and fruit trees, eating everything but the peach pits. The farm turned crispy brown. Heat burned away Mom's enthusiasm for gardening. After five years, Doug was still working as a laborer at a trucking terminal. Things weren't going their way. They wanted out of Texas.

Housing prices had skyrocketed in the late 70's. Mom and Doug realized they had cash potential in our house and seventeen acres of farmland. They brainstormed for a way to leverage that money into more money. They decided to sell the farm and buy a motel and restaurant in Bakersville, North Carolina—an economically depressed town of one thousand people in the Appalachian Mountains. In October of my junior year, we left Lindale, Texas to embark on our adventure—running a family business in "Hicksville". I wasn't happy about leaving, but I tried to keep an open mind. *This'll be a fresh start. Maybe I'll be popular.*

***

A week before moving, on Oct. 2, 1980, I played the last football game of my life. Billy Adams came running off the field with an equipment problem. Even though I was the starting quarterback, I seized the opportunity to get some action on defense. On the next play, I ran toward the scrum to get in on the tackle but by the time I arrived the play was pretty much over. To avoid piling on, I tucked both my heels against my butt and did a Kevin Bacon *Footloose* slide on my knees, shins, and cleat tops. Somehow, I sat down hard on the heel of my right foot and snapped my ankle. Sitting on the field, I held my leg up to look at my injury. I couldn't believe I was looking at my own body. No longer fixed directly under my leg, my foot dangled at a severe offset and gross angle. It looked like my foot was structurally disconnected from the rest of my body, attached to the leg only by skin. The surreal, twisted sight. Numbness, Instant nausea.

The trainer came out and put my leg in an inflatable cast. Coach Davis kneeled down and blew air into the device. My teammates found the scene quite amusing, chuckling at the sight of their coach's lips wrapped around the air nipple. The next day, a surgeon secured my broken bones with six pins. He told me I'd be in a cast and on crutches for three months.

***

On my first day at Mitchell High in Spruce Pine, North Carolina, I hobbled through the lunch line on my crutches, pushing my tray in small increments along the tubular track. When I reached the end, a lady took my money. When I didn't move she just stared at me. *Maybe she doesn't understand I can't carry my tray while walking on crutches.* I looked down at my salisbury steak, mashed potatoes, green beans, and dessert, then back at her. *She's not getting it.* "Do you think you could help me get my tray to a table, please?"

"I gotta watch the money, Hun." She suggested no alternative. I was holding up the line. People wanted me outta their way. Clearly, I was on my own. *Look at that dumbass trying to carry his tray while on crutches. He'll never make it. Watch him...*

Some gasped, others watched in stupefied silence as I lost my balance, dropped the tray and one of my crutches, and hopped to the nearest wall on one leg and a single crutch. *Told you he wouldn't make it.*

Four hours and I was already a freak show at this school. So much for the fresh start. So much for being popular.

A lunchroom lady came out from behind the serving line, picked up my crutch, and brought out a new lunch, which she carried straight to the loser table—not losers, as in chess club geeks or artsy drama freaks—losers as in yuckmouth *Deliverance* extras. After lunch, I tagged along with the small group of cousins while listening to them carry on about some guy's custom Trans Am with T-tops, glass-pack headers, overhead cams, *Pioneer* sound system and big-ass woofers that took Molly Hatchet to a new level. As we walked down a hall toward an unannounced destination, I tried to shift the conversation. Using my best east Texas-influenced Appalachian accent I asked, "Ain't there an arcade in this town? Do you guys know the coach who handles the pole vaulters?" They looked at me like I'd just asked them to play dolls.

We stepped outside into a courtyard. I was spellbound at the sight, like a five year old studying an ant farm. *This can't be real.* There were no less than fifty kids smoking.

Each of my new friends lit cigarettes. One was offered to me.

"No thanks; aren't you guys worried about getting busted?"

They laughed. "For smoking?" One kid coughed and spit. "Are you serious?"

I noticed several industrial ashtrays around the courtyard. *A sanctioned smoking area in high school? You gotta be kidding me?*

"Ain't youins got a smokin' area back in Texas?"

Where I came from, students (even seniors of legal age) were suspended for possessing cigarettes on campus. Here, kids were just doing their part to support the local economy.

A couple of men came out and lit up. A girl, about fourteen, approached them. The man whom I later learned was a history teacher pulled out a pack of *Marlboros* from his front shirt pocket, patted out a cigarette, and handed it over to the girl. The volleyball coach reached into his pants pocket, pulled out a lighter and gave her a light. *A ninth grade girl having a smoke with her volleyball coach. Ain't that some shit?*

For the next few weeks, I ate lunch with these car obsessed Appalachian boys, watching them chew with their mouths open, use their shirt sleeves as napkins, and spew small chunks of food from their mouths onto my plate, while listening to them rehash the same meaningless conversations about Nantucket's guitarist or Richard Petty's car. Every sentence in their Appalachian accent tested my interpretive abilities. Later in life, I would be convinced that this was the place where Jeff Foxworthy got his material. *I gotta start sitting somewhere else.* I became a cafeteria nomad, bouncing from table to table, mostly ones that were unoccupied. Not only was I not making it to the *in* crowd, I wasn't making it into *any* crowd.

For the first time in my life I was without friends. Then, one girl who seemed more sophisticated than the others, caught my interest. Teresa Sims, a pretty cheerleader, introduced herself by offering to carry my books to class, which is a pretty big help when you're on crutches. We started talking on the phone as I spent evenings at the front desk of the motel on the off chance someone would check in.

Teresa was obsessed with *Dallas* (the TV show). Caught up in the *JR* hype, my being from Texas fascinated her, so much so that on Nov. 21, 1980, she invited me to her house to watch the much anticipated *Who Shot JR* episode. "I get to watch *Dallas* with a real live Texan," she said.

I met her mother, and I explained how it is I came from Texas to be in her living room. Then Teresa began asking for my thoughts about various characters.

"Actually, I've never watched the show."

"You're kidding? You're from Texas and you don't watch *Dallas*?"

Not wanting to ruin my chances with my only prospect, I fabricated an excuse. "Before I broke my leg, I was always either playing football or hanging out on Friday nights, so I was never home."

She coached me through the episode, telling me who was good and who was evil, and who was kinfolk.

She sat mesmerized, absorbing every detail coming through the snowy screen of her eighteen-inch TV set. During the first commercial I offered no real opinion of the direction of the plot. But I asked a question or two, thinking I was doing a pretty good job of appearing to be interested, until she shushed me when I talked over the return of the show. During the subsequent commercials she called a girlfriend to discuss their hunches on who would pull the trigger at the end of the show.

When JR was shot during the final scene, Teresa screamed at the TV. "Oh my God!"

She looked at me. "Can you believe that?"

This was a test I hadn't studied for. The major TV event I'd just witnessed was less fascinating than watching Mr. Rogers untie his shoes and hang his jacket in the closet. Was it good or bad that Mary Ellen shot him? Who did Teresa want the shooter to be? I stared at her, wanting to say *something*. I didn't even know enough to fake it. Her big brown eyes, full lashes, silky pale skin, the way her hair cradles her neck, she looks like...like Helen Reddy. *No, you idiot, think of something to say. What was the question again? Oh yeah, "can I believe that?"* I went for the humorous angle. "Hey, what's the big deal? He's probably not even dead."

To her, my comment was as insensitive as if I'd been speaking about her comatose mother. She whacked me in the chest with a throw pillow, in somewhat playful objection to my apathy. How could someone from Texas not even care about JR? How could I have lived so close, yet never even have gone to Southfork Ranch?

I didn't realize then, how my reaction may have changed the course of my life. Suppose I had managed to feign some appropriate emotion. There would've been a second date with this pretty cheerleader. We might have fallen in love and had lots of sex. I would have been friends with her friends—popular. This book might have been about an outsider who moves to the Carolina backwoods, settles into a job at the auto parts store in Bakersfield and marries a beautiful cheerleader who has three kids and blows up to the size of a *Macy's Thanksgiving Day Parade* balloon while watching *Dynasty*, *Sex and the City*, and *Desperate Housewives*. But, I failed to step through the portal to popularity. Partly because I didn't connect with Teresa or anyone else at school, my days in this town were numbered in the double digits.

I would be long gone from Teresa, and North Carolina, when I heard a whole *Dallas* season was explained away as a dream, and everything she had watched was twice removed from reality. I wondered for a moment, what her reaction had been as that revelation unfolded on that little TV back in the Appalachian Mountains. Myself? I had no opinion.

***

Besides my leg being in a cast and being deprived of the culture of sports teams, there was another dynamic conspiring to prevent friend making—no leisure time. For a few weeks, my mother had me watch the motel front desk from the time the bus dropped me off after school until I went to bed. It was like being grounded every day. Most evenings, I had no guest interactions. I considered it a busy shift if I gave a bar of soap to Mrs. Stitzlebunk, an old widow who lived at the motel. Eventually, she put a sign up at the counter, which directed hotel guests to go to the adjacent restaurant for service. The motel consisted of twenty units and an innkeeper apartment. My family lived in the two bedroom apartment. My mom asked me if I wanted my own motel room. *No smoke, no bar smell, no pesky little sister? Of course I want my own room!*

For a while, I also served as the overnight motel manager.Before I went to bed, I'd put a sign on the door, which directed potential guests to knock on my motel room door for service. Once, I was awakened in the middle of the night by a wino who wanted to buy a pack of cigarettes, which we didn't sell. I suggested he knock on the innkeeper's apartment and check with my mother. "She's a smoker; maybe you can bum a cigarette from her."

"Can you believe that shit?" my mother asked me the next day. "What kind of asshole knocks on a stranger's door in the middle of the night for a cigarette?"

People woke me up more than once to use the pay phone in the motel office. On only a handful of occasions, did someone actually want to check in.

One late night, a twenty-something Bubba knocked on my door to request a room. As I walked to the office, I saw a girl from my English class in the passenger seat of his car. A week later, the scene was repeated, this time with a different Bubba. Not long after that, Bubba One reappeared at my door for a late night check-in. I noticed the same girl was in the passenger seat of the car and Bubba

Two was sitting in the back seat. *She's making more money than this stupid motel.*

***

After my cast was removed, the doctor told me to remain on crutches for another two weeks. I noticed my skin stretched over the ends of surgically-placed pins like a bed sheet draped over a flagpole. It was odd to see something poking out from the underside of my skin. I began gradually testing my ankle by putting some weight on it. I graduated to walking before doctor's approval.

After lunch, while most students took their cigarette breaks, I'd lay my crutches down and shoot some baskets with a few guys in the gym. I started playing in halfcourt games as soon as the doctor had released me to walk.

There was an intramural basketball tournament coming up before the Christmas break. Only students who were not playing on a school team were allowed to participate. A few guys invited me to join them even though I had just been medically released to walk days before. I'd been attending the varsity basketball games and wasn't impressed at the skill level of the all-white team. *If I were healthy, I'd be a starter on that team.* I was hoping for a chance to rehabilitate and make the squad in midseason. This little tournament was the perfect chance to showcase my skills to the varsity coach, who would be refereeing the games.

The matchups were held during an extended lunch break. Those who weren't out in the courtyard, smoking were in the stands watching jock wannabes play basketball. I started the game with a pump fake and drive for a backdoor layup. It reminded me of my big game back in Lindale a year before. *It's gonna be like that!* We didn't have any coaches so substitutions were done at player's discretion. Five minutes into the game some clown decided to come in for me. I didn't play any more in the first half. During the short halftime I suggested to the group that I start the third quarter, but a dude one inch taller than me objected arguing that we needed his height, so I let him play. Late in the game, I still hadn't played since the first quarter, and I was pretty pissed. *I was a varsity basketball player last year, dammit. I was the leading scorer for my JV team. I could shred that intramural defense with my bad leg tied behind my back and you dipshits aren't even giving me a chance to win this lousy game for you? You don't know what you have in me.*

The game was tied with ten seconds left and our opponent was shooting free throws. *It's time to assert myself. It's time for me to get the ball and shoot my patented high-arcing set shot, and win this game.* I got up and checked myself in for the tall guy who had taken me out of the game prematurely in the first quarter. Cobb was not only his name but also a remark about what seemed to be up his ass when he walked. He was lining up on the lowest block for the opponent's free throw. I motioned for him to sub out as I trotted toward him. But Cobb insisted on staying in the game. His buddy backed him up. "Get outta here man," he said to me in a dismissive tone. "We need him to rebound."

This wasn't an ideal time for a debate, but I knew something these guys didn't: Not only was I the leading scorer on my JV team last year, but at 5'11" I was also the second leading rebounder. Armed with that insight and the knowledge that this stiff had no idea how to box out for a rebound, I countered. "That's why I need in—to rebound!"

Cobb pushed me in the chest toward the bench. I found this very irritating so I gave him a hard karate chop across his extended arm.

"Fuck!" he shouted loudly.

The crowd gasped and hollered in response to the confrontation. Two guys on the same team about to throw down? The varsity coach, whom I hoped to play for in a month, separated us. I jogged back to the bench while Cobb stood on the low block of the free throw lane rubbing his arm. *I don't think I made a good impression on the coach.* The first free throw was good, putting us behind by one point. The rebound after the next shot bounced off Cobb's knee and rolled out of bounds. *Ah-hah, that's what you get.* He immediately resumed rubbing his arm and grimacing, as if I'd injured him so severely he couldn't catch a ball.

The rest of the team backed Cobb. "Fuck, Texas, look what you done did..." The loss was my fault. *No friends to be found on this team.*

After the game I noticed something while taking my socks off. Since the surgery ten weeks before, the swelling had gone down.

With my ankle actually smaller, two pins had penetrated the skin's surface, their stainless steels ends raising a millimeter proud of the skin surface. I recalled the surgeon's post-op remarks. "I cut the pins a little long so we'd have something to grip when we remove them."

It seemed to me, a sixteen-year-old kid who'd skated through Biology with a D, that there wasn't much space between the knobby anklebone and skin. "Won't they poke through the skin?" I asked.

He dismissed my concern with a shrug. So when the pins did poke through, I wasn't concerned.

For several days I didn't mention it to anyone. I continued to shower, sweat, and play basketball without regard for the metal protruding from my ankle like Frankenstein's neck bolts. The area around the pins became tender, then painful and red. When yellow pus formed in the circular crevice between each pin and the rim of the surrounding red skin, I finally brought it to my parent's attention. They scheduled an appointment in Ashville, three days out. But, the next day I started running a fever. My joints ached, not just my ankle, but all my joints. I visited the town clinic where they immediately admitted me to the hospital. The hospital doctor on call, Dr. Kane, wasn't an orthopedist but he was clever enough to figure out I had an infection running down the pin tracts into my bone. The offending pins had to be removed, immediately. No surgery, no anesthesia, just an oral sedative, Dr. Kane, a dainty nurse, and a medical tool that could've passed as *Vise-grips*.

The pills made me delirious, but I was coherent enough to realize the pin removal wasn't going well. Kane grunted and held his breath until I heard the click of his tool losing its grip on the end of a pin. He exhaled in frustration. The process repeated several times. The doctor tried to help the tiny nurse hold my leg down with one of his hands. I'm sure he had no idea how challenging the procedure would be when he agreed to allow Mom and Doug to observe. Kane began sweating; his hands shook as it became apparent his technique wasn't working. "Dammit!" The doctor's tone broke through my delirium. "I need two hands on this tool." Doug took the hint and gripped my leg with both of his big hands to counteract the removal force the doctor exerted on the pin with the medical pliers.

The doctor called for a break; strapped my leg to the table in two places and pulled again, but the bone would not give up the pin.

Kane was in a predicament. A carpenter needing to pull a nail out of a two-by-four would simply use the wood as a fulcrum. But my shin was not a piece of wood. He took another break, toweled off like a tennis player between sets, and returned with a thin book in his hand.

Cancer: A Doctor's Guide to Dealing With the Family

What the hell? Did he see cancer in my ankle? He's gonna give up, put me under, and cut my leg off. Fucking North Carolina. Even the doctors are hicks. Get me the hell out of here!

Kane laid the paperback on my leg and used the surface of the book as a fulcrum for his tool. In his first attempt, he broke the pin free from the bond that had formed around it after nearly three months. "Got it!" he said proudly, holding the three-inch pin in the air like he'd just won a fishing contest. The pin clanged in the metal pan and I exhaled a sigh of relief. With the newly developed Kane pin extraction technique, he got the second pin out with relative ease, and although I didn't have cancer, I did have a bad infection.

I was admitted to the hospital and dosed intravenously with antibiotics. My body's response was measured with a number derived from my blood samples. The number went up each day: 234, 259, 270. Higher numbers mean more severe infection. I was getting worse, instead of better.

"Sometimes it takes a couple of days for the drugs to take effect," the doctor said.

He's lying to me. "What if the antibiotics don't work? Could I lose my leg, Doc?"

"Well...let's not think about that. The drugs usually work."

Usually? It's gone. They're gonna cut it off. I just know it. Who loses their leg because of a broken ankle? This is stupid. I bet these idiots aren't even giving me the right medicine.

After several days, I woke up in the middle of the night in sweat-soaked sheets—my fever had broken. For the first time since I'd been in the hospital, I had an appetite. I didn't need a doctor to tell me I'd just turned the corner in my recovery. After two weeks in a bed, I was discharged on Christmas Eve with both my legs.

Even after I got off crutches things didn't get much better for me socially. Mom and Doug ran the restaurant all day until the lunch crowd was gone, and then they started drinking. I spent most of my time at school, working the front desk, or locked away in my motel room digesting basketball statistics from the newspaper, or perusing the only non-textbook I had, a *Rand McNally Road Atlas*. I memorized the populations of large cities and distances between them. I dreamed of the day I would be free from this town—free from THEM. *Someday I will go to these places in the atlas. Someday, I will go anywhere I want.*

After my ankle setback, there was no chance of playing basketball. In fact, track season was even in jeopardy. I had no car, no social life, and had been asked to the Sadie Hawkins dance by Denise. She was quite heavy. An ill-advised attempt at a homemade perm left her hair a total frizzball. Her teeth were jagged. She had big round glasses that magnified her bug-eyes. She didn't even wear makeup. She was constantly laughing for no reason. Denise was possibly the least attractive girl in the school. I saw her invitation as a sobering indication of my social status.

What made her think I'd want to go to the dance with her?

And with that thought, something hit me: To how many girls have **I** been Denise?

I thought the new kid was supposed to be popular. I wasn't popular. I felt like Denise.

We're Going Home Kids

One night my sleep was disturbed by a banging on my motel room door. I stumbled groggily from my bed and released the door lock expecting to conduct some motel business. But it wasn't a customer; it was my mother. She smelled like a bar.

"Pack your shit," she slurred as she stumbled into my room.

"What do you mean, pack?"

"We're leaving," she said with conviction.

"What are you talking about? Where are we going? I have school in the morning."

"You can go to school when we get to Wisconsin."

"Wisconsin? What about Ginger?"

"She's in the car, waiting."

"Mom, we can't go to Wisconsin. I have an Algebra test in the—"

"YOU, YOU, YOU, it's always about you. This isn't about you and your goddamn school."

Every word was a challenge for her to get out, and she was wobbling like a baby learning to walk. *She's worse than usual.*

"Richard, Doug is drinking. He's being abusive, and I can't take it anymore. We gotta get out of here, now."

Abusive. What does that mean—Abusive?

"Did he hit you?"

No, Richard. He didn't hit me." She extended her hand toward the wall to brace herself. Misjudging the distance, she staggered into it. "He…just…always cuts me down." She started crying.

"Mom, how much money do you have?"

"I don't know. It doesn't matter. We'll have Grandma wire us money if we need to."

Despite my disenfranchised status at *The Appalachian School for Kids of Second Cousins* leaving on a thousand-mile road trip chauffeured by my shit-faced mother driving on slick snow-covered mountain roads at midnight did not seem like a sound escape plan. I didn't like our chances of getting out of the mountains alive and didn't want to go. I could see us pin-balling around inside the car as it tumbled end-over-end down the side of a snowy mountain until the car eventually explodes in a bright orange fireball. In another permutation of my imagination, we're sitting in the parking lot of a gas station in Tennessee, begging strangers for spare change. A stranger offers my mother twenty bucks for a blowjob. She slaps him. He and his buddies rape her and Ginger, then beat the hell out of all three of us.

Even the best case scenario wasn't promising: I'm in a Wisconsin high school three days from now. The teacher announces there's a new student in class and asks me to stand up and tell the class what brings me to Wisconsin. I look at my new classmates, spellbound, unable to legitimize my presence. "My mother and stepfather both got drunk Monday night and they got into a horrible fight. Neither one can remember what the fight was about, but my mom got so pissed that we left, and we didn't take jackshit with us. This explains why you will see me in these same clothes each day for the rest of the school year. So if you're my size and have some clothes that you no longer wear…" Imagine how popular I'd be with the girls in my new school. No, I didn't want to go. If this was her best exit strategy, I'd rather stay put and let Doug continue being a condescending, drunk ass.

My mother continued to sway around my room like an extra in an earthquake B-movie while I brainstormed for a way to avoid embarking on her proposed journey. I considered getting one more drink into her in hopes that she'd pass out. *Hey, maybe I could whack her in the back of the head with a school book and knock her* out. *Then I'll just put her to bed. She's so drunk maybe she won't even remember what happened.* I'd never knocked anyone out before. It seemed so easy in movies. *But what if I accidentally killed her? Do they have the death penalty in North Carolina? Would they try me as an adult?* I dismissed the idea as too risky.

Despite my objection, I had no chance of changing my mother's mind. In her drunken stupor, she was more obstinate than usual. I knew from experience, there was no rationalizing with her when she was in this condition. If I refused to go, then my sister would probably be dead within an hour. Soon, we were in the car heading for Milwaukee, about 737 miles away.

On each curve of the windy mountain road, my mother straddled either the white line on the right or the yellow lines on the left, and then overcompensated like an eight year old driving a go-cart for the first time. With no guardrail to stop us, three feet of crushed rock was the only thing between us and an end-over-end movie-style tumble. She weaved, drifted, and zig-zagged the big El Dorado on the same route she and Doug routinely traveled to the nearest liquor store. Ginger implored her to let me drive.

"Your brother has no experience driving in snow. And he doesn't know these roads like I do."

I noticed the gas gauge was on E. This, above algebra tests and our safety, was our last hope to end this madness. "Mom, there's no gas stations between here and Johnson City and we don't have enough gas to make it there. We're gonna run out of gas and freeze tonight. Do you want all three of us to die?"

Unresponsive, she drove the Cadillac closer to nothing.

Realizing we were doomed if we didn't get the car turned around, Ginger asserted herself despite her tears. "Mom, don't go any further. We don't have enough gas. If you care about us, you'll go back."

I don't know if it was my sister's plea, fatigue, or the booze wearing off, but finally, Mom relented. She pulled over and started sobbing.

"It's okay, Mom." Ginger rubbed her back and consoled her from the back seat. "Will you take us back home, Mom?"

My mother nodded and continued to cry.

I just stared out the car window into the black and waited for the pathetic moment to pass. I want my childhood over. *I want out of this house, out of this family. AWAY.*

Mom didn't want to go back to the innkeeper's apartment where Doug was. I had two beds in my motel room, so she lay in the bed next to mine. In the darkness, she told me why she wanted to divorce her third husband. "He is so cruel, especially when he drinks." *Maybe you should both quit drinking?*

After a moment of silence, I asked. "Why did we move here, Mom?" I waited for a response. *Is she ignoring me?* Her snore answered my question.

I went to school the next day and made a D minus on my algebra test. I was content that things had returned to normal, at least for now. *I need a better plan than that to get outta this town.*

Brother Sal Ahmey

    Jim Ahmey was one of my best friends back in Lindale. Just before our move to North Carolina, in October of my junior year, his parents had extended an open-ended invitation for me to stay with them until I graduated high school. Mom resented the Ahmeys for that offer and viewed them as a disruptive force against her utopian vision of a successful family-owned business. But after five months of cooking food and preparing rooms for people that never showed, and with tensions between us at an all-time high, my mother gave her okay for me to leave. I didn't know what to expect from this setup, but I had one prevailing thought on the Greyhound bus ride from North Carolina to Texas: *Whatever I'm headed to, can't be any worse than what I'm leaving.*
    Sal Ahmey. That was Jim's father's name. Sal Ahmey? What kind of parents name their son after sandwich meat? It didn't take long for me to learn that Mr. Ahmey was more explosive than my mother, and he didn't need a drop of booze to set him off, either. Jean, Jim's step-mother, told me her husband had inherited his ill-temper from his father (also named Sal). The elder Sal, Jim's grandfather, was a foreman for the railroad, and was such a legendary prick that Johnny Cash recorded a song about his tyranny over his crew.
    Jim had some odd habits. He played center on the junior varsity football team, and was constantly racking himself when he snapped the ball, which was usually to me. Jim complained that I

wasn't receiving his snaps properly; my hands weren't in the right place. Fearing repetitive testicular trauma would eventually render him sterile, he hedged against possible future low sperm count by collecting his procreation material in film canisters, then storing them in the freezer. He'd preserved a dozen samples before Jean found his stash and confronted him. Jim simply pinned the rap on me. It'd be years before he'd ever reveal to me the story how he ratted me out to save face. As far as I know, his folks still think I'm a deranged curator of cum, which is one of the reasons I'm writing this book, to set the record straight.

Jim got a kick out of feeding boogers to their little mutt lapdog. When Trixie saw Jim picking his nose, she'd come scampering across the room, cute, red ribbon bow in her hair, anticipating her tasty morsel. One day, the four of us were watching TV. With her treat already collected between his thumb and forefinger, Jim called Trixie's name affectionately from across the room. "Trixie. Trixie…" But this time Jean saw the whole thing. She cried out in disgust as Jim fed the dog. Jim's father didn't know what was going on. His wife had a horrified look on her face and was shaking her head while chastising Jim for some mysterious behavior. Mr. Ahmey demanded an explanation. "What is it, Jean?"

She couldn't speak; didn't know how to put into words what she'd just witnessed.

Mr. Ahmey was out of patience. "Spit it out Jean; what is it."

His beloved little girlie dog being fed boogers was more than enough to light Mr. Ahmey's fuse. He jumped out of his recliner, grabbed Jim by the neck, placed his leg beside his son's and, using some hand-to-hand combat maneuver he must've learned in his military training, pushed him backwards onto the ground. Mr. Ahmey scrambled to a superior position on top of Jim, forcing all three hundred of his pounds onto his son's stomach and chest.

"Dad—

I can't—

Breathe."

His father's face was pink-red with anger. Jim's was the same color due to oxygen deprivation. "Breathe? You don't deserve to breathe!"

He poked his finger in Jim's face and hollered the most confusing verbal threat I've ever heard, "SON, I'M GONNA PURRRRGE YOU!" I don't know exactly what Mr. Ahmey meant by that threat, but I'm pretty certain he wasn't offering to stick his finger down Jim's throat, to assist him in throwing up for the purpose of him eating more dessert. Perhaps he thought his son was possessed by demons, needed cleansing.

That was typical of how fast Mr. Ahmey could snap. You might be having a pleasant conversation about any topic, but the moment you espoused an opinion he didn't agree with, he'd be all over your case. One morning at the breakfast table, he went on an unprovoked rant. "HORSESHIT! That there's a crock of HORSESHIT." His face boiled. Rage burned in his bulging eyes, which were already magnified by his large wire-frame glasses. "How can you be so stupid? Someone needs to kill you, you nigger sonofabitch. That's what; somebody oughta put you out of your miserable ignorance!" As usual, Jean tried to settle her husband down. "Oh Sal, don't let the newspaper get you all upset, dear."

I learned not to express an opinion on anything more controversial than the weather.

***

Sal Ahmey knew his son had used pot before, and correctly suspected he was still occasionally using. This was a source of great consternation to Mr. Ahmey. He thought everything Jim did had some connection to the drug culture. Mr. Ahmey thought all blacks were on dope, and Jim should avoid socializing with them. According to Mr. Ahmey, Jim's music, clothes, haircut, friends, and negative attitude were all causing him to be, and be seen as, a *dopehead*. I believed Jim's parents considered me a good influence. I figured they liked the fact that for the first time in years, Jim's best friends, me and Robbie, weren't stoners.

Jim's father lectured him about a propaganda chain letter that southern Baptists were widely circulating, regarding the evils of rock music. The letter claimed many popular bands were possessed by Satan. Groups like Led Zeppelin, AC/DC, and The Eagles were spreading the devil's message subliminally in their lyrics through a technique called backwards masking. Play a record backwards and besides damaging the needle and the record you hear weird noises. With an imagination you can hear something like "The devils out in the tool shed making us suffer." After attending a meeting in which concerned parents played records backwards, discussed album art, and heard references to a beast in *Hotel California,* Sal Ahmey, along with many other concerned parents tried to censor their kid's music.

Mr. Ahmey routinely degraded his son in the presence of others. One afternoon, at the Ahmey's home, Jim and I came home from school to see a visitor's car parked in his driveway. Oblivious to our arrival, Mr. Ahmey was ranting in the living room. "I can't get him to listen to anything..." We both knew he was talking about Jim, but we didn't know to whom. We walked into the room. It was Dr. Burger, the pastor at our church. Obviously, Mr. Ahmey was seeking spiritual counseling on how to deal with his son. His father pointed at Jim and commented. "Dr. Burger, look at Jim's belt-buckle."

Mr. Ahmey continued talking, now speaking to Jim. "Now that's more like it, son."

Jim and I were confused. I rarely heard his father compliment Jim about anything. Usually he humiliated Jim in front of company. A compliment? *What could Jim have possibly done to earn a compliment?*

Speaking to all of three of us, Mr. Ahmey praised his son. "*Yes*—that's such a positive word—*yes*. The message is strong. It's good. It says YES. *Yes* I can do this! *Yes*, with the right attitude, anything is possible!"

Jim's Father sought the preacher's affirmation. "That's the kind of message Jim should be sending to people, Dr. Burger."

"Yes, Brother Sal, what a powerful statement it is." Dr. Burger agreed on queue.

Jim's belt buckle was the psychedelic emblem for a rock band named *Yes*. Ironically, *Yes* was one of those bands called out in church chain letter propaganda as being messengers for Satan.

Jim and I could barely contain our laughter. He'd earned praise from his father while trying to defy him. No matter how hard

Jim tried he couldn't do anything right. In this case he couldn't even succeed when he tried to rebel.

One of the requirements of residing in the Ahmey's house was that we go to church each Sunday. Jim, Robbie, and I would share the back seat with one of the blue-haired old ladies whom Jean volunteered to drive. The interchangeable faces, wearing funny hats, that rode with us would invariably go on-and-on about what fine young men we were. *Yes, we are. Yes, we can do anything.*

Had they known Jim was the mysterious vandal who'd frequently done donuts with his Ford Pinto on the 13th green of the Hide-A-Way Lake golf course, on which they lived, they might not have thought he was so fine. But, we were well-dressed, on our way to church, smiled when addressed, and used "yes ma'am," and "no ma'am" in our responses to questions.

One Sunday morning, Dr. Burger followed his routine of asking one of the men in the congregation to close the service with a prayer. Twenty-five years later, the words still ring in my head. "Brother Sal Ahmey, will you lead us in the closing prayer?"

Mr. Ahmey had a hard time stringing two coherent sentences together without showing his disdain for something. Since he tended to mumble and grunt unintelligibly, and the last half of his so-called sentences often trailed off when he realized he'd lost his train of thought, I was thinking Dr. Burger could've made a better choice. Even his seventeen-year-old daughter's twenty-seven-year-old boyfriend would be have been a better pick

Standing next to Mr. Ahmey, I noticed his arms and legs begin to shake. *This is not good. This is an impossible task. There's no telling what's gonna come out of his mouth.*

My mind flashes back a few weeks to January 10, 1982. We were watching a football game in the Ahmey's den. The Cowboys were up by six points against the 49ers in the NFC championship game. The 49ers had driven to the Cowboy six-yard line. Less than a minute to go in the game and San Francisco needs a touchdown to win. Dallas needs to hold for a chance to go to the Super Bowl.

Jim and I are standing behind the couch watching over his father's shoulder as Joe Montana brings the 49er offense to the line of scrimmage.

Sal Ahmey is one of those fans who love to hate his favorite team. Watching any football game with him is an uncomfortable experience. He emulates his pessimistic approach to life in the way he cheers for his Dallas Cowboys, cursing someone on nearly every play.

"They're going to lose this goddamn game, and there is no reason for it; no reason at all. They had them sonofabitches, and now they're going to lose on this play, right here, on this play…"

Jim interrupts his father. "No, Dad, Too Tall is gonna sack Montana, or Everson Walls is gonna get an interception."

Mr. Ahmey shakes his head and snorts in disgust that Jim would even suggest such a preposterous scenario. "Everson Walls? Everson Walls? Bullshit, Jim. That stupid nigger ain't gonna do shit. That's why they're gonna lose, because of that goddamn stupid nigger!"

"Oh Daaaad, you'll see," Jim says in his special whiny voice he reserves exclusively for timid rebuttals of his father. "Everson leads the league in interceptions. Everson is awesome."

Jim had no idea how wrong he was about to be, and how angry his prediction would make his father.

Montana rolls right. He's chased backward and toward the sideline by D.D. Lewis and Too Tall Jones. Montana's running out of room. It looks like Jim might be right, Too Tall is gonna get him. Then, an off-balance Montana heaves the ball in apparent desperation toward the back of the end zone. Everson's in position. For one moment in time, it looked like Jim was a prophet. Too Tall almost got the sack, and now Everson Walls is about the make the play that will put the Cowboys in the Super Bowl. Out of nowhere, 49er receiver Dwight Clark runs behind Walls and leaps high into the air. Everson flails with one arm in a futile attempt to influence the play. Clark continues his ascent and at his apex, snatches the ball, and a spot in the Super Bowl. Candlestick Park goes crazy. The TV announcers are beside themselves in disbelief, telling us what I already knew—that we have just witnessed a legendary event. Years later, polls and lists would list it as the single most memorable play in the history of the team sports.

I've never seen a man more angry than Sal Ahmey at that moment. He screamed with all his might, "NOOOOO!

NOOOOOO! You stuuuupid nigger!" Then he got up from the couch and got in Jim's face, challenging him to defend Everson Walls. "I told you Jim. I told you! That goddamn nigger. He can't cover shit." Sal Ahmey's face was beet red. Snot rolled out of his nose. Slobber pelted Jim's face. There was contempt in his eyes—contempt for Jim, contempt for Everson Walls, contempt for the world and everything in it that didn't go the way he wanted.

His father poked his finger hard into Jim's chest. "SEEEEEE, I TOLD YOU, YOU DON'T KNOW SHIT, JIM." Mr. Ahmey was reacting as if Jim himself had blown the coverage on Dwight Clark and cost the Dallas Cowboys and their biggest fan, Brother Sal Ahmey, a Super Bowl berth. Perhaps Brother Sal was a superstitious man and he believed Jim's prediction actually cursed his beloved Cowboys.

Jean Ahmey emerged from the kitchen to see what all the yelling was about. She spoke passively, trying to not further agitate Mr. Ahmey. "Sal, Hon, why don't you calm down?"

In his best Archie Bunker imitation, enunciating every whiney word of his demand very slowly, Mr. Ahmey responded. "Jean, why dooooon't youuuuu shut the hell up? You don't know a goddamn thing about it."

I'm sure Joe Montana has no idea of the emotional crisis he created in the Ahmey household that day. As the 49ers celebrated their victory, Jean retreated to the study for a good cry, Jim vowed that he would kill his father, and I learned to never make a statement around Mr. Ahmey that could be perceived as contentious. I restricted my dialog with Mr. Ahmey to complimenting him on his ugly ties, discussing the weather, and lying to him about how well his son is doing in school and how widely respected he was.

***

And now, Brother Sal Ahmey was about to close the Sunday morning service with a prayer in his own words. Like Sal Ahmey watching the Cowboys, I expected the worst: *God, our Lord in heaven, please watch over our son's and daughter's so they don't lay with niggers.*

I say my own little prayer for Sal Ahmey's prayer. *Please don't let him say something bad. Please let him get through this okay.*

Much to the astonishment of everyone, he gave an eloquent, heartfelt closing prayer. Brother Sal spoke of love, fellowship, and the greatness of God. He spoke of his reverence for God's gift of salvation and personally thanked the Lord for the chance to be born again. Thanked him for the freedom to worship in this church, for all the blessings in his life. The Lord was working inside Mr. Ahmey. The three of us fine young men were amazed at his eloquence in espousing such feelings. Perhaps it didn't surprise the blue hairs, because they were always going on and on about what a fine Christian man Brother Sal was to bring us fine young men into the house of God.

In the church foyer, we basked in the afterglow of the miracle prayer until every hand was shaken and Brother Sal Ahmey had received the last of his well-deserved back pats. Then, our group rode his coattails into the church parking lot. Jean was glowing with pride and walked closer to her husband than usual, clutching his huge right arm with both her hands. For the first time since living with the Ahmeys, I felt a sense of family.

When we got to the car, Brother Sal's good mood snapped like a twig. The euphoria was pierced in an instant. "GODDAMNIT, JIM!" he screamed in his booming voice, for everyone in the church parking lot to hear. The suddenness and volume of the outburst shocked me. I looked immediately at Jim, expecting to catch him engaged in some offensive behavior, like having his finger buried in his nose up to his knuckle, or perhaps scratching his privates with a hand buried inside his pants. Despite Jean's attempt to get her husband to lower his voice, Mr. Ahmey turned up his volume even higher as we arrived at the car.

You'd think he'd just discovered Everson Walls trying to hot-wire his green Ford LTD. "I told you, Jim, to lock the goddamn doors! You told me they were locked. These doors aren't locked! What the hell is wrong with you, son? Are you stupid, or what?" Deacons, Sunday School teachers and little old ladies of the congregation watched Brother Sal Ahmey's tirade in disbelief.

On the drive home, Robbie and I smirked at each other, united in the witness to the juxtaposition of Mr. Ahmey's prayer and his parking lot cursing fit. Jim swore to himself he'd kill his old man and Mrs. Ahmey cried into an overused wad of Kleenex.

***

Most football fans remember the play that would become known simply as *The Catch* as one of the defining moments in NFL history. I witnessed a lot more than a throw and a catch that day. To me, The Catch has always reminded me of two very disturbing things: the blind hate and racism in the hearts of men, and the foolish things that can drive a wedge between a Father and son.

Twenty-five years later, I learned Everson Walls saved a former teammate's life by donating a kidney to him. As a kid, I never juked imaginary defenders in a vacant lot pretending to be Everson Walls. While I have pictures of myself wearing an OJ Simpson jersey, I never had an Everson Walls shirt or hung his poster in my room. Even though some football fans remember him for a play that didn't go his way, Everson Walls will always be my favorite football player. Mr. Ahmey, often abrasive, overbearing, and bitter, will always be the man who opened his home to me, fed me, praised me, and treated me like his own son. Well, what I mean is, better than his own son.

As odd as it sounds, I believe Everson Walls and Mr. Ahmey are alike more than you may think. Whatever in Everson Wall's heart that compelled him to give a man his kidney, stems from the same human goodness in Mr. Ahmey's heart that led him to open his home to me.

March 30, 1981

     The locker room. Today, when I walk in, I hear reserved voices that don't fit here. This is a place where seventeen-year-old boys are normally seen popping one another with towels and heard fabricating stories of sexual conquests that never actually happened. Today, my teammates are partitioned into several huddles. Serious discussions are going on. Single words, not sentences, reach my ears: *shot, chest, President.*

     President Reagan had been shot. Everything else I hear is supposition.

     I think about the Kennedy assassination, about the film of it that we watched in our History class just last week. I was one month old when it happened. *Has my life seen its second presidential assassination?*

     Coach Robinson comes out into the dressing area and breaks the mood. "Let's go you pansies; the President wants you girls to run today." Pleased with his creative wit, he smiles and retreats to his office while we slowly begin getting dressed for our workout. Robinson is like that; the only time he smiles or laughs is when he amuses himself, and I have no idea he's about to do that in a depraved way that I will never forget.

     Wendell Robinson was the head football coach and athletic director at Lindale High School. An unsightly man, he was widely known as *Block* not only because his head was shaped like a cinderblock, but also because his acne-pitted face resembled the texture of one. He was gargantuan—6'2" and 300 pounds of relentless, ruthless ass.

Every kid who came out made the team; that was school policy. To circumvent that rule, Block tried to get kids to quit football on their own. When he wanted a kid gone, he employed a host of public humiliation tactics to persuade him to quit. If the other marginal athletes didn't jump on the bandwagon and join him in ridiculing those he wanted off the team, they risked becoming targets themselves. A lot of team members picked on the weaker guys as a survival tactic. If Robinson saw you were tough enough to be a bully yourself, you were spared his bullying. Many young men of higher principles simply left the athletic program rather than deal with his intimidation.

When two guys got into a disagreement, Block often insisted the boys put boxing gloves on and fight it out in front of their teammates. His idea of building boys into men was to let them beat the hell out of each other to toughen them up. The fights wouldn't end until he declared it over, or until the weaker boy was physically unable to continue. To play, you had to be tough. To prove you were tough, you had to fight. Declining to fight would be the ultimate act of cowardice in the testosterone-filled environment, and a sure way to find oneself on the end of the bench, and as the object of ridicule. Accepting and getting the hell beaten out of you was the only way to salvage self respect, and to stay involved in the high school sports. The threat of mandatory boxing matches magnified each boy's personality. The aggressive bully who relished the chance to beat someone up could simply choose any meek kid he pleased, instigate conflict, and be rewarded with a chance to pulverize the poor kid in one of Robinson's sanctioned fights. The kids low on the ass-kicking totem pole would do all they could to avoid interaction with bullies.

Robinson never had the starting quarterback squaring off against the star running back. His prized athletes only had to fight opponents who had zero chance to land a punch. He was an unscrupulous fight promoter and fixer all at the same time. Many matches had a clear agenda—to get the weaker competitor to quit his athletic program. In the process he fed his insatiable fetish of masterminding the public humiliation of boys. I got the hell beaten out of me by a succession of upper class mini-Robinsons as the bloodthirsty crowds cheered like Romans watching a lion dismember a Christian. More than one boy's athletic career ended when his mother confronted Robinson about her boy's story, as best he could remember, about how he came to suffer a concussion.

I'm wearing only underwear, midway through my transition from student to athlete, wondering if the President is dead or not, when the subdued locker room atmosphere is again interrupted by the shrill of Coach Robinson's voice. He comes from the coach's office into the dressing area, screaming my name as he scans the room. His voice, deep, loud, and thick. "Schnabl! Schnabl! Where's Schnabl?"

He's gonna do something to me.

As an attention getting technique in the classroom, Robinson routinely whipped tennis balls at students. He once drilled a meek, effeminate ninth-grader, Dusty, with a fastball right between the eyes, sending his glasses bouncing off his desktop and onto the floor, causing him to cry in pain and shame. "Dry it up, Sissy (he had long before taken to addressing Dusty as "Sissy"), before I give you something to cry about." Coach Robinson taunted Dusty unmercifully in the classroom, creating open season on him, just as he had done with me, except he could be more innovative with his cruelty toward me because the coach/player relationship was not restricted to the classroom. Like a fish in a larger tank, the boundaries of his abuse expanded in locker room and on the practice field. He turned my complex and sometimes self-effacing humor, which most adults seemed to enjoy, against me. I didn't realize my good nature is what made him his primary target. A day rarely passed that he didn't seize an opportunity to disgrace me, often in front of the team, but sometimes in small groups or in private. Because of my last name, *Schnabl*, he'd always greet me in the same disturbing manner. He might walk into a field house full of athletes, eyeball me from across the room, and in his booming voice, bellow "Heil Hitler" while extending his arm in an emphatic Nazi salute. For three years he referred to me as either "stupid Kraut" or "Nazi." Ironically, I'm not even German. During my junior year, when he learned my birth last name was Ochoa, not Schnabl, he began calling me "Nazi-Taco." For four years he made sophomoric remarks about Hitler, bratwursts, beer, Volkswagens, German Deutschemarks, even the Holocaust.

Robinson chose his targets carefully. Most of these boys had the same set of traits. Good hearts, broken homes, weak or no father figure, and their worse quality: they didn't possess the tear-off-their-heads-and-shit-down-their-fucking-windpipes attitude he wanted in his program. He worked hard to align the other guys against his chosen whipping boys. The collective mind of his Neanderthal-thinking mob was putty in his hands.

Yes, he's gonna do something to me, and it's not gonna be good.

His scan ends when he locks onto me like the *terminator*—the bad *terminator*, not the good one. Our eyes meet across the locker room. His eyes tell me he's gonna hurt me. My eyes speak to him. "I have heard your eyes, and I am scared." An enraged psychopath closes in on me for some sort of attack. *What the hell have I done now?* I've never seen a human being this big, this angry. He's ten feet from me, getting closer as he yells as loud as humanly possible. "HOW MANY TIMES MUST I TELL YOU? THIS IS IT FOR YOU! I'M GONNA KILL YOU, SCHNABL!"

***

I knew Block was a violent man. I'd seen him break Tony Scott, one of the toughest kid in school, down to tears when he put every ounce of his might behind three brutal licks to the boy's ass (which was covered only by paper-thin track shorts) for leaving his sweat top hanging on a chain link fence after a workout.

Coach Robinson had an arrangement with the sports-crazed superintendent. All football players took Health class with Coach Robinson, and it was scheduled right before football practice. Turns out, we never had class, instead practiced football right through that time slot. "Health? What could be more healthier than running?" he'd say. It was almost time for report cards, and one student, Stan Denman, objected to Robinson's announcement that everyone would be getting the same grade—B. As everyone else cheered their B, Stan's voice was heard above the others, "Nooo!" To Stan, who was competing for valedictorian, accepting a random grade would be akin to two coaches agreeing before a game, "Let's just play for fun and not keep score."

Robinson came up behind Stan, put one hand on his shoulder, with his free hand, clutched one of Stans' wrists and pressed it into the small of his back. "Is a B good enough for you, Denman?" At first it seemed like a playful act, and that's exactly what Robinson was trying to sell.

My friend could not be coerced that easily. "Nooo."

The bully coach hiked his student's arm higher and asked again. "Is a B good enough for you, Denman?"

Stan's face contorted with intensity. His principles were still stronger than his innate sense of self preservation. "No!"

With each negative response, the perpetrator hiked his victim's arm a little higher behind his back, toward his neck. Tears puddled in Stan's eyes. My friend was often the lead in school plays (he'd one day be the Dean of the drama department at a major university) but this was clearly no act; it was torture. "You're hurting me!" He made sick noises in his throat. The tears were kinetic now, streaking down his checks. He begged for mercy. Individual reactions of the witnesses would make a good psychological case study. Some boys watched in horror. Those inclined to help, like me, were not man enough, mature enough, to stop the abuse. Others cheered Robinson's plan to remove the only obstacle between them and the highest grade they'd ever make. They didn't want to take a test on CPR, or how to save someone from choking.

And that's how Robinson got Stan to quit the team.

***

Block is only an arm's length away. But he's concealing something behind his back. *It must be his "board". He's gonna whip me.* I hear someone with a better vantage point scream. "Oh Shit!" The monster shouts one more threat, but I've stopped processing words as I determine the object previously obscured is a pistol.

I retreat into a corner of the room, working to preserve every second of my life. He follows my path. He has me cornered. It's geometrically impossible to put space between myself and this madman, without getting closer to him first. I consider running straight into him and to try knocking him down. *Fight or flee?* I take a step toward the nearest door, but I'm running in waist deep water. My legs and mind become disjointed.

I fall to the brown, musty, locker room carpet, face first, my underweared ass sticking up in the air. I get back up quickly and try to run but my normally dependable legs have turned to jelly. I try to hurdle a bench but my foot catches the underside and I topple over it.

Lying on the ground, I turn my head and look up at Robinson—a Goliath, veins bulging from his forehead as his contorted face boils red with sadistic pleasure. He stands over my trembling body, pointing a pistol at me. At that moment, I join an exclusive club—a fraternity composed mostly of war veterans and victims of crime—those who've stared down the barrel of a gun, with no doubt it was about to be fired. That sensation, that image, would come to dominate over other life experiences, brandishing a greater veracity than births, weddings, funerals, the first kiss with my true love, so indelible, it may be the very last thing erased, years after Alzheimer's sets in. Distracted by the fact that I have one or two seconds to live, I don't think of anyone in particular, I only think *I'm dead. I don't wanna die.* Death is an absolute certainty. I close my eyes, and girl-cry the most horrific scream imaginable. "NOOOO!" I turn my head away and cover it with my arms, expecting the next face I see to be that of Jesus. The first shot rings in my ears but I feel no bullet enter my body. *Did he miss? How could he miss? Maybe I'm hit and I just don't know it. Maybe I'm already dead.*

I open my eyes and see smoke coming from the gun and a maniacal look on Robinson's face. *If I'm dead, I sure ain't in heaven because this is not the face of Jesus.* I try to get up but my legs are still useless; they fail beneath me again. As I fall for the third time, I catch a glimpse of Jim Parker's expression. Gripped in shock, he stares at me with utter pity. Not yet man enough to try stopping his coach from killing me, yet understanding that he is witnessing the last moments of his friend's life. I can think, but not speak. *Help me Parker. Help me!* There is no other noise or competing commotion, a room of young men stand frozen, not breathing. I am Kennedy, he is Oswald, and the last seconds of my life are a slow motion Zupruder film. In the next frame my assassin will blow my brains all over the locker room at Eagle Stadium. *I bet this sonofabitch will get away with it. He gets away with everything. I bet every last coward in the locker room will testify that it was self defense, just so they can keep their places on the team.*

I look up from my position on the ground and extend my arm toward him as if I expect to stop the next bullet with my bare hand. Robinson has a deranged smile as he discharges another round at my palm. I'm not breathing, my diaphragm paralyzed like I've been punched in the gut. I turn my head away and feel a prickly sensation in my side. *I've been hit. But I'm not dead.* I gasp for a single breath. Robinson fires one more time, this time at the back of my head. I feel the air leave my lungs, hear more ringing in my ears, but no pain.

An eternity passes. There's nothing but silence and the smell of gunpowder. Trembling uncontrollably, I turn around and look up at him and his brutal grin. He's no longer extending the pistol in my direction, but holds the smoking gun at his side like a victorious gunfighter. *He's out of bullets.* I look down at my own side. There's nothing but a small abrasion. How could he miss three shots from such close range? *Did I dodge the bullets?*

Robinson smirks, looks at the gun, studies it nonchalantly, looks around the locker room as if he's confused as to why everybody has stopped what they're doing to witness a possible murder, announces loudly, not really to me, but to every stunned student athlete in the field house, "Calm down, Schnabl, it's just a starter's pistol." He smiles. He laughs. He is very amused. He contemplates what he has just done—how well he sold the gag. *Yeah, that was a good one.*

After a moment of silent recognition of what just happened, almost everyone joins Robinson in laughter—perhaps in nervous relief, perhaps because they are amused. I do not laugh. *I will kill this man. One day, maybe five or ten years from now, I will devise a plan to kill him. I will do the world this service. This will be my purpose in life.*

I'd go on to have nightmares about the assault for years. As I write today, Coach Robinson's pistol attack stands as the single most frightening moment of my life—the most bizarre behavior I've ever witnessed in another human being. In the days that followed, I argued the pros and cons of killing him—now, not five years from now. *If I get caught, I might be treated with leniency because I'm seventeen, because of all the witnesses that will attest to what he did to me, because I'm estranged from my parents. People might feel sorry for me. I might even be seen for what I am—a victim who fought back. But, I will be a suspect. If I kill him now, I will be caught. This is almost certain. I don't think I'm very good at killing people. I have no experience. I can't pay for a good lawyer. I will wait. In five years, I will not be a suspect. In five years, I will be bigger, stronger, smarter. In five years, I might be able to get away with it.*

In 2002, twenty-two years after the pistol assault, the Texas State Coaches Association voted Coach Wendell Robinson into the *Texas High School Football Hall of Fame.* His esteemed colleagues and some of his old players got up and told stories about what a hoot Coach Robinson is. "He molded us into men," one of his old star players said.

Myself? Had I known about it, I would've shown up and told those good ole boys a few stories about a man who had dedicated his life attempting to emasculate young men and successfully influenced many to turn the wrong corner. Maybe I would've brought a starter's pistol. *Yeah... that would've been funny.*

The Last Supper

    I'd lived with the Ahmeys for four months. Fearful of becoming the object of Mr. Ahmey's wrath, I exhibited model behavior, demonstrating my appreciation by helping around the house. I got along well with Jim, his father, and step-mother. Problem was, none of them got along with each other. As the school year drew to an end, the Ahmeys were due for a break from their confrontations being acted out in front of a live audience. Jean and my mother had a talk and agreed I'd go back to North Carolina "just for the summer."

    On the morning of the last day of school, I packed all my clothes in a trash bag and put them in the back of Jim's car. After class, he drove me to the bus station in Tyler. As far as Jim and I knew, the master plan for me to live with them until graduation had not changed. I figured Jean's kind heart and my friendship with Jim would prevail over any other family dynamic, and I fully expected to be back for my senior year. I shook Jim's hand at the bus station. "Thanks Jim, for everything." His normalness and smile reassured me. "Alright Bro, have a good summer."

    By now, I had come to hate the slow pace of Greyhound. The bus stops at every little town, sometimes to pick up one or two packages, sometimes only because the schedule says so. This gave me plenty of time to think about what I was heading toward. *What's it gonna be like when I get back? Maybe she's changed. Maybe, this is gonna be a fresh start.* After a twenty-four-hour ride, it was late in the evening when I arrived at the bus station in Johnson City, Tennessee—two hours later than Mom and Doug had expected.

There were no hugs. My mother celebrated my arrival by cursing me, Greyhound, the Ahmeys, and anyone else who may have had a hand in her not understanding the arrival time. It was not a cheerful reunion. They had been drinking, which meant my mother wanted to confront me about everything that had been bothering her. Before we even got to the car, she began criticizing the Ahmeys for inviting me to live with them. "Those two nosey bastards... And what a piece of work he [Mr. Ahmey] is. It wasn't that great, was it, Richard?"

This is not gonna be a fresh start.

The three of us loaded into their violet Cadillac, which they bought before moving to North Carolina to give the locals the impression that they were successful Texas business people—Doug in the driver's seat, Mom riding shot-gun, and me sitting in the back. Mom opened the lid of a small cooler on the passenger front floorboard and grabbed a handful of ice. She added the fresh ice to the small, rounded shards that remained in each of the two glasses sitting in the drink holders between them in the front seat. The familiar sound of ice ringing against glass was followed by the gurgle of Jim Beam as it caressed the cubes until they crackled. Almost as an afterthought, she added two-fingers of Coke to each plastic tumbler. She handed one of the cups to Doug who took a sip and then licked his lips before pulling out of the parking lot.

My mother had a lot more she wanted to talk about. "What do you plan on doing this summer?"

This was not small talk; it was a test. Asking seemingly innocuous questions was her method of baiting me into confrontation. She was looking for a chance to exert control. I knew there was only one answer that would keep peace, but I wasn't about to say, "I plan to cheerfully wash every single dirty dish in your restaurant all summer long, and if anybody happens to check into the motel, I will clean their rooms even if they piss the bed." Instead, I told her what I'd been thinking on the bus ride. "I wanna get a job, or maybe mow yards and save up for college." I knew my mother was against college, and I immediately regretted giving her the opportunity to rebut my controversial idea while in her adversarial mood. She knew few people who had gone to college, and one of them was Doug. He had only negative things to say about his college experience not landing him a high paying executive position.

"Where do you plan on getting a lawnmower? Besides, you already have a job at our restaurant and college costs a helluva lot more than you can make this summer, Sonny Boy." She was contentious, her demeanor reflecting four months of bridled anger. In the captivity of the car, there was no chance of escape. My safe place was gone. After four months of being a voyeur of parental oppression, I had returned to my role as a target. *I sure hadn't missed this.*

I knew from experience her "jobs" were lacking a critical component of other jobs—paychecks. "Food and shelter is your pay," she'd always say.

"I was hoping to get a *real* job this summer, so I can save money." If my mention of college was my first mistake, vocalizing a grievance regarding pay, without a union backing me, was the point of no return.

"Let me tell you something. We've been working our asses off here while you've been on your little vacation. Your sister never asks to be paid..." The car lighter clicked. Doug gripped it between his thumb and forefinger and brought it toward the cigarette dangling his mouth. He lit the Marlboro with the hot coil that looked like an orange *Lifesaver*. His freshly lit cigarette popped to attention as he took a no-handed deep drag while his right hand jabbed the lighter back into its hole. He exhaled, exchanged a knowing look with my mother and shook his head at the audacity of my expectations. I could read his mind. *Do not let up on that kid, Judy. Lay the hammer down. He deserves it.*

The smoke cloud was unbearable as they both puffed away. My eyes were burning. After stringing a dozen sneezes together, I asked for mercy. "Can we roll down the windows, please? I can't breathe."

"There's not a goddamn thing wrong with the air in here," she said. She turned her body sideways in her seat, rotated her head to face me, and then spewed a burst of smoke toward me. "Let me tell you something. You'll work in the restaurant from morning to night every goddamn day this summer. Do you understand? EVERY DAY."

Every day? There'd be no days off? Not one? Jean Ahmey, take me away...

Instead of letting the situation diffuse until the next day, I made the mistake of engaging her, asking to take two hours off one morning to do the *Rhodenderan Festival* 10K Run. She was in no mood to concede any liberty to me. "You don't get what I just said, do you?" She shifted again in her seat to face me. Kneeling, her weight pressing against the backrest of the front seat, she leaned toward me to emphasize her next words. I withdrew my head to the furthest corner of the back seat and turned it to the side as she began screaming. "YOU WILL BE WORKING, YOU GODDAMN SELFISH BRAT!"

Having established her policy prohibiting leisure time, next on her agenda was to confront me about girls. I had taken an eighth-grader, Cindy, to my Junior Prom. I picked blackberries, collected cans, and sold roses to save the fifty dollars needed for the event, and accessories like pictures and corsage. I'd been missing out on so much of the typical high school experience, and was determined the prom would not be another item on the lost-forever list. I figured I'd be a little bit less of a loser going with a cute eighth-grader, than if I'd gone by myself. I knew Cindy mostly from hanging out at the community pool. On our Prom date, I wasn't able to sustain a conversation with her and spent most of the evening in silence or listening to her giggling. Thankfully, the loud music cranked up and gave us an excuse to not talk to each other. We rarely spoke again until a month later, when she asked for half of my prom pictures. We never had a second date. We never had a kiss. Proms are overrated.

Now that I was in my mother's car, she decided to scold me about something she knew nothing about. "That girl is too young. She's gonna end up pregnant. You're not ready to raise a child. What the hell are you doing? You'll ruin your life if you haven't already..."

"Mom, you don't even know what you're talking about; it's not like that."

"I don't know what I'm talking about? Bullshit, you little shit. Don't tell me I don't know what I'm talking about. I got pregnant when I was seventeen. I know what I'm talking about!"

She forbade that I date Cindy. I hadn't yet developed the skill of humoring her to avoid conflict. If I had, I would have said, "Good advice Mom, I agree with you; I don't want to date her again." Instead, appalled at her presumptions, I made ugly faces and argued for the right to see who I wanted even though in the case of Cindy there wasn't much chance there'd be a second date. I argued for principle. I had to draw a line somewhere—establish some boundary. I had to fight for the right to be me.

Arriving "home" provided a sense of relief. At least we weren't in a confined space together. Sometime during my four-month absence, the family had moved out of the innkeeper's apartment and into a nearby rent house. I had come home to a place I've never been before. I found my way to my room. There was a bed, a nightstand and three boxes containing my personal belongings; things like trophies, track medals, a small radio, baseball cards—stuff I hadn't taken with me to the Ahmeys. I spent an hour trying to make the room my space. I thumbtacked my Cheryl Tiegs poster on the wall. In my opinion, Cheryl Tiegs was hotter than Farrah, who, at her best never matched the Cheryl Tiegg's *Sports Illustrated* one-piece fishnet swimsuit pictorial—the one Mr. Brown, my junior high principal confiscated, I believe to this day, for his own personal use. Across from Cheryl, I pinned a poster of Earl Campbell. The juxtaposition of the posters had them eyeballing each other. Cheryl, wearing her skimpy pink bikini, trying to seduce the big, bruising Houston Oiler into choosing a romantic interlude instead of trampling her like an overmatched defensive back. I arranged my trophies on a shelf and pinned my track medals and ribbons to a bulletin board. Then, I was called for dinner. My mother, Doug, Ginger, and I sat down to what would be our last supper.

A collection of events conspired to condemn this dinner before it ever started. The antagonizing lectures from my mother on the way home had set the tone. Mom and Doug had gotten even more liquored up since we arrived home. Further irritating me was the fact that I was tired and hungry from my bus ride from Texas. And to top things off we were having chili, full of kidney beans. My mother knew I hated kidney beans.

I've always detested the combination of the smooth glossy exterior encapsulating the powdery, pumice-like filling of this disgusting red bean. I do not like them in the south. I do not like them in my mouth. I will not eat them at the prom. I will not eat them served by Mom. I do not like them, Mom I say.

We started eating the chili, which on this evening, to commemorate my homecoming, contained a double batch of kidney beans comprising about sixty percent of the chili mass.

A haze of cigarette smoke hung over the table, settled into my nose, throat and lungs. Cats rubbed against my legs, dogs panted under my elbows. Another ten sneezes—snot on my lips, chin, and in my hand. I left the table, went to the bathroom. I had been breathing clean air for four months, and it spoiled me. I just want to breathe!

Back at the table, I began picking out the beans and setting them aside, just as I'd always done. My mother was intent on drawing lines and establishing boundaries herself. "You're going to eat every last one of those godamned beans or I will shove them down your throat. Don't think I won't."

Before putting the next spoonful of chili in my mouth, I added a few beans that I had piled on the side of my plate, but I did not add a vocal response, nor did I acknowledge her command by making eye contact.

"Did you hear me?" she said, demanding I verbalize my submission.

"You see I'm complying, don't you?" My use of educated English always annoyed my mother. She was particularly linguistically-challenged when she was drunk. She'd often slur my offensive vocabulary word back at me in a mocking way. It was like arguing with a fourth grader.

But this time she had a nonverbal response of her own—a Deacon Jones style head slap.

I absorbed the blow and responded by scooping up spoonfuls of kidney beans from my wastepile in a demonstrative manner, trying to prove a point to her, but mostly to myself, that even if I did exactly what she said, she would still antagonize me. I shoveled beans into my mouth until I nearly gagged. Red chunks dribbled down my chin.

Ginger began to nervously spin a damp wash cloth which she had been using as a napkin. Water droplets pelted my face. I thought this was inappropriate dinner behavior, so in an annoyed voice I said to Ginger, "Can you stop that?"

My mother came to her defense, reprimanding me. "Go to your room!"

"But I haven't finished my kidney beans," I protested in a sarcastically polite tone.

She lurched from her chair and moved toward me. I thought I was about to get slapped again, or maybe punched, but this time I was pelted with small chunks of food flying from her mouth as she put her face right in front of mine and screamed at me like an out of control baseball manager confronting an umpire. "Who do you think you are? Don't you say shit to her! She's my daughter, and you don't get to talk to her like that!" Her yelling pierced my ears. Her chili, rum, cigarette breath permeated my nose. Her beans, her slap, her face, her screaming, her breathe. Taste, touch, sight, hearing, smell—she was attacking all five of my senses.

I finally reached my breaking point. I couldn't maintain my relatively submissive attitude. Passive-aggressive was not working. This conflict, which up to this moment had followed the same script as a hundred previous confrontations—her boisterous belligerence against my subdued, witty rebuttals was about to take an unchartered path—my defending myself with the same fervor with which she attacked.

I raised my voice to a tone I'd never used before with her, "She's slinging water all over the place while we're eating, and you're in *my* face?" I didn't know what to say next but didn't want to lose my new found courage to counter attack. I used her favorite technique—I repeated her statement back to her "Who do YOU think YOU are?" My mind was spinning. Adrenaline surged. *I'm doing it. I'm talking back. I'm standing up for myself.*

Infuriated by my overt disrespect, she started coming toward me again but Doug restrained her. "Go to your room," he yelled.

His demand was fine with me. I just wanted the night to end—no point arguing with an unreasonable, bitter drunk. I retreated to my room. She staggered in behind me and started tearing things off the wall and throwing them at me, struggling to maintain her balance as she screamed the same obscenities over and over, sometimes changing the order just to mix it up. "Get the FUCK out of my house, you GODDAMN BASTARD, you. Get the FUCK out of my house. You BASTARD! You SONOFABITCH."

My mother did something NFL linebackers only wished they could; she brought down Earl Campbell with one arm. She tore everything off the walls. The room was raining so many red, white, and blue track ribbons, it looked like a ticker tape parade.

"Mom! Stop. Please stop!"

She grabbed a handful of wire coathangers and threw them, first across the room, then at me. Then she began swinging them at me, swearing. "GODDAMN SONOFABITCH. Don't FUCK with me. Don't you dare FUCK with ME!"

I had seen *Mommy Dearest* and I no interest in playing a role in the sequel. I dodged her wild swipes. She threw herself off balance with her errant roundhouse swings and wobbled like a punch-drunk fighter while I scurried to a strategic position—the floor space on the opposite side of the bed. Her knees buckled and she tried to brace herself against a wall that wasn't there. She clawed at the bedspread before disappearing momentarily beneath the bed's horizon with a thud. Howard Cosell's voice played in my head. *Down goes Frazier! Down goes Frazier!* Then she peered over the rim of the bed, her head appeared to me as a possessed puppet controlled by an unseen devil, his hand inside of her, controlling her actions. She stared at me with utter contempt. I clasped my hands together as if in prayer, looked into her eyes and begged. "Mom, please just stop."

"Stop?" And then in her best Linda Blair voice, "FUCK YOU!" She crawled across the bed; her fistful of coathangers snagged my letterjacket before she resumed swinging them at me. But she was a drunk Mummy and I was Muhammad Ali doing a rope-a-dope. She couldn't touch me.

Her tirade ended only when she was physically exhausted. She looked at me panting, pissed about my speed, agility, and elusiveness. "Pack your shit, because you're going to your father's tomorrow." Then she staggered out the door and slammed it behind her.

I sat on my bed, regarded the disaster that was my room. My radio was smashed, a circuit board hanging out of it, clothes and coat hangers covered the floor. My Cheryl Tiegs poster ripped into two pieces, perfectly bisecting her boobs. Several of my treasured sports awards were damaged. I found the gold plastic bat from my baseball trophy inside one of my shoes.

Alone in my room, I contemplated both my immediate future, and my long-term outlook. Even as I wondered where I'd be tomorrow night, I self-affirmed myself into believing that somehow I would manage this situation, and come out okay on the other side. *She's sick. Her behavior is not a reflection of my worth as a person. Somehow, going through this will make me stronger.* In my heart, I believed all these things.

In the morning, there was no remorse or apology. She enforced her threat. Just a couple days after arriving at the Greyhound station in Johnson City, I was back there again to ride another bus, this one to LA, where my father and his family were visiting his wife's parents. The plan was for me to join them in California for the last few days of their vacation before we would all head back to Idaho where I'd spend a second consecutive summer. *I hope I'm welcomed back at the Ahmeys when my senior year starts.* As I got on the bus, I thought about one of Coach Davis' clichés: Today is the first day of the rest of your life. I'd be spending that day with a very interesting new friend.

Kill or Be Killed

The bus in Johnson City was crowded. In an effort to ward off strangers, most people sitting next to vacant seats filled them with a barricade of purses, bags, and suitcases. To further discourage boarding passengers from sitting next to them, they avoided eye contact. I'd walked almost all the way to the back in a futile search for a spot next to a friendly face, or at least a spot that didn't require me to ask someone to reorganize all their worldly possessions. A hardened white man in his thirties shot me a knowing smile while gesturing toward the seat next to him with an extended arm and open hand like a *Price is Right* model presenting the second showcase. I sat down and thanked him for his politeness. His pinkish-red face was pitted with acne scars, and covered in two days of stubble. Even though he was seated, I could tell he was a little guy, several inches shorter, and thirty pounds lighter than me. Clumps of brown-red curls protruded from under the rim of his black watchcap, covering the back of his neck. I guessed he was thirtyish. *It's the first of June and 80 degrees outside. Why is this guy wearing a winter hat?* Wearing a denim-colored, buttonup shirt and generic dark blue *Dickies*, we weren't ten minutes into the ride before Mike confirmed what I was thinking. "It was for assault." He paused to study my reaction. I smelled lingering cigarette smoke on him, maybe even menthol, like my mother's. *These seats are too close.* "But don't be scared man." Mike's most remarkable feature—his creepy smile—was like the scene of a car accident. No matter how hard I tried to avoid looking, my eyes kept shifting involuntarily toward it to steal glimpses of his pale, thin lips framing his patchwork collection of yellow nubby teeth. "I's just defending a woman, know what I mean?"

"So, where ya headed, Rich?"

"I'm going to LA to see my father."

"No shit? I'm going to LA, too! That's great, man. Isn't that funny?"

No, actually, it isn't very funny at all.

He told me what it was like in the *joint*; including stories about the first time he got head from a man, and how he killed a *nigger* inside the pen.

"Hey man, it was one of those kill-or-be-killed situations, man. Know what I mean? I ain't saying all niggers is bad, ya know, man, but this motherfucker—I'm glad he's dead. We's all better off with that sumbitch dead. Don't get me wrong, I don't hate all niggers, man…ya know? I had this nigger friend in the pen. He's a good man. He looked out for me, man. Know what I mean? He's big and strong, ya know? Sumpen like six-five, two-fifty; but he was so gentle, man, ya know—a gentle giant. He told me sometimes he cried himself to sleep 'cause he was a nigger. He hated being a nigger, and he told me I done right by killing that other nigger, so I don't feel bad 'bout it, ya know?"

I wanted to sound tough, just in case at some point he wanted to start some shit with me—like I could empathize with his kill-or-be-killed predicament. "Yeah Mike, that's some fucked up shit, man. I know where you're coming from."

"You been in a situation like that, Rich?"

"Well—" My mind scrambled to reciprocate a tough guy story. I thought about telling him about the time when I was in second grade and I beat the shit out of two sixth-graders who kicked my friend's marbles, or how I beat up a snotty nose tattletale for telling the teacher I'd peed my pants. I decided my stories didn't quite measure up.

I managed a generic reply. "Sometimes you gotta fight to protect yourself, man. That's all I'm saying."

Mike's eye's lit up like my remark was the most profound thing he'd ever heard. "Now that's a fact, Jack." He celebrated my condoning his murderous ways by insisting we share a special prison handshake.

Voices of self preservation in my head tried to settle me, each in their own way:

That was good, Rich.

Yeah, maybe a little too good. He thinks you're a kindred spirit. Don't act too tough. But don't be too weak either. Middle of the road.

Yeah, middle of the road, Rich...

"Let me tell you something about this handshake, Brother. Don't let the wrong people see you do it. Know what I mean? You could get your ass killed if you ain't careful. I ain't trying to scare you or nothin', I'm just saying...be careful."

"Right on, Mike. Right on." *You can get killed for shaking hands wrong? Who knew?*

Our conversations over the next two-plus days consisted mostly of him talking, and my short but polite acknowledgements: Really? Wow. Oh yeah? Ah-huh. Mike was either unable or unwilling to interpret body language or verbal clues that people (in this case me) send when they don't want to converse. At first, I maintained our dialog out of politeness, then out of fear.

By now, I was a bus riding veteran, this being my fourth long distance Greyhound solo trek. On each of the previous rides, I formed brief cordial alliances with people sitting next to me. Mike was the first to demonstrate how sharp his switchblade was by shaving all the hair off one of his forearms—a service which, when Mike offered to perform for me, I politely declined. At night I tried not to sleep, scared he might stab me with that switchblade, just like he did to that unfortunate black man in the bighouse.

It was the long meal stops I came to dread the most. My forty chaperones scattered to various local eateries—Sambos, Big Boy, Dairy Queen—leaving me alone with Mike for an hour or more. *Mike and his knife.*

At our first meal break, in some little town outside of Nashville, Mike didn't eat. Polly's Pie Pantry was famous for its homemade pies, yet he just sat across the table from me, drinking water and digging dirt from under his finger nails with his switchblade. I realized he didn't have any money, or at least none that he was spending. I didn't have much myself, but at least I had enough to eat. I started to budget my meals so I could feed both of us. I also bought a one-pound package of off brand, crème-filled cookies for seventy-nine cents which we shared while riding.

I was trapped in the ambience of Mike: His stories, his beady little eyes, his pink nose, flaking skin, his aroma, and his whiskey flask that through some magic was never empty. At each stop, people would get off and sometimes there would be plenty of open seats, but I figured he would take my moving a little personal. My strategy was simple: Listen to his stories and not disclose too much personal information. I wanted to avoid giving him the perception that we were really bonding. On the other hand, I couldn't risk pissing him off by being rude, or even assert my desire for privacy. *I really need my own space, Mike. It's not you, it's me. I think we should see other busriders. Can we just go back to before we met and act like we don't know each other?* No, that wouldn't work. I needed to straddle the line between friend and foe.

Somewhere in New Mexico, the US Border Patrol stopped our bus. Two agents boarded and walked down the aisle looking at people, their heads turning back and forth like tennis spectators. As they neared the back, where Mike and I were sitting, the first agent paused in front of me. "May I see your ID, young man?"

The agent's request didn't surprise me. People often spoke Spanish to me, to which I always replied, "no comprende." Years before, when we lived in California, we had taken a family car trip to Tijuana and points south in Baja. On the return crossing, the agent asked the standard questions of my mother and Doug and then directed some questions to me. He waved us through after I spoke English with a Wisconsin accent.

Although I didn't have ID with me on the bus, I expected this situation would play out much like my Tijuana border crossing. I figured in the worse case I'd offer to recite the first thirty-five US presidents in order. But, before I could even open my mouth, Mike took it upon himself to speak for me. "Officer, this here boy ain't done nothin'. He's just sitting here riding the bus to go see his old man…"

The officer retained his professionalism, "Sir, what is your relationship with this boy?"

I wasn't too comfortable with Mike acting as my spokesperson, so I spoke before Mike could answer. "I just met him on the bus, sir"

The agent was perturbed. Still using a professional tone, he spoke firmly to both of us. "Look, when I ask a question of one of you, I expect THAT person to answer the question. Understood?"

"Yessir," I said respectfully, while Mike acknowledged his understanding with defiant silence.

"Now, I need to see both your IDs, please."

Mike produced his ID and I produced an explanation. "Sir, I don't have ID. I had a temporary driver's license from Texas, but I left it in my pants pocket and it got all crumbled up in the washer."

The walkie-talkie on the officer's vest crackled. He moved his hand across his chest, turned his torso away from us, clicked it and said his piece about some business unrelated to us. Mike took advantage of the short break in the interrogation to whisper in my ear. "Don't call that motherfucker *sir*."

The other officer ran Mike's license. Meanwhile, I answered questions like name, birth date, and address. *Maybe this is a blessing. A guy like Mike—something's gonna come up on his record and he'll be pulled off the bus and arrested. Then I can relax and not worry about his switchblade. Maybe they'll even handcuff him, charge him for murder and read him his rights as he sits next to me on the bus. That would be awesome.*

After the check on Mike, the agent returned his license. "Have a good day gentlemen." Before leaving the bus, he turned and then thanked us all for our patience and apologized for the delay. *Thank God.* I'd been to Mexico, and didn't want to get shipped there today.

The Border Patrol experience reinforced Mike's disdain for law enforcement. And he wasn't shy about expressing his opinion loud enough for all around us to hear. To add credibility to his position, he cited examples of prison guard brutality he'd seen or been subjected to. One disheveled man about Mike's age heard his ramblings and began commiserating with him across the narrow aisle. The scraggly-haired guy was traveling with an equally unkempt woman whose dirty blonde, rat's nest, Gary Busey hairstyle matched his. But, her most notable feature was the nastiest looking shiner I'd ever seen. Her eye was swollen shut. The colors of trauma—red, black, purple, yellow, blue—extended from above her eyebrow to half way down her check. Scraggly claimed a gang of *niggers* had beaten the hell out of him and his girlfriend and then raped her. Shiner neither confirmed nor denied the story; in fact she never spoke at all. *That's odd; if they beat the hell out of him, where's his black eye?* I looked at her a little closer; trying to visualize her with combed hair, minus the shiner. *Either this guy's a liar, or those guys must've been pretty desperate.*

Mike and Scraggly's conversation evolved into an ad hoc KKK meeting in which they shared their stories of how they had come to hate niggers, nigger-fuckers, nigger-lovers, sand-niggers (Arabs), uppity niggers, and niggers with badges, until the beaten-up couple got off the bus in Las Vegas. *Great place for those two. I hope they turn their lives around in Vegas.* I was relieved at least for the whole state of Arizona, Mike had found someone else to talk to—his real kindred spirit. But, after Scraggly and Shiner went off to beat Cesar's Palace, Mike's attention was back on me.

We were four hours short of LA. That's how close I was to getting Mike out of my life forever. It was around three a.m. and almost every passenger was sleeping. The bus was mostly empty. I had a whole row, both sides of the aisle, to myself. In the row directly behind me, Mike looked like an exhausted sentry in the dark, upright, but slumped sideways, his watchcap-covered head pressed against the window.

I created a sleeping palate by bridging most of the span of the aisle with a suitcase on top of which I added enough loose clothes to bring the arrangement up to seat level. Lying face down, I spread my body across the walkway, situating my crotch facing over the narrow un-bridged gap.

I was awakened by a hand moving across the front of my jeans. I stirred slightly, as if adjusting my sleeping position. The hand was gone. *I'd been so cautious the last two days. How could I let my guard down like this? What do I do now?* His hand ran across my pants a second time, this time pressing harder to feel what I was made of. I knew I had to do something—but what? *Mike and his knife.*

Maybe I should jump up in his face, threaten him, waking up the other passengers in the process. Or, I could tell him politely, "Excuse me Mr. Hardened Criminal, but I'm not that kind of boy," and then change seats. Perhaps I should tell the busdriver; maybe he would protect me.

I rotated ninety degrees, so my manhood faced forward. I hoped the combination of my stirring, and my privates being a little less accessible would deter him. But, moments later he curled his arm around from underneath and touched me again. I feared confronting the murderer with a switchblade. I thought a non-confrontational approach gave me the best chance of not getting knifed in my privates. I grunted and popped upright, acting incoherent, like I was waking from a nightmare. I turned around; there was Mike sitting in the dark like the boogeyman. There was enough transient light for me to tell he was looking at me—studying me. I asked him a contrived, stupid question. "Where are we?"

He laughed and spoke softly, like he was telling me a secret. His words and they way he spoke them conveyed a sense of hopelessness. "We're in the desert, man, the goddamn desert."

I knew he touched me, but I didn't want him to know that I knew. "Man, I had a weird dream. I was in a cage with a bunch of monkeys..."

I didn't sleep anymore that morning; instead I sat rigid and alert, counting the dark miles between me and LA until the sun rose and bathed me in the safety of its light. My father wasn't waiting for me at the bus station. Mike insisted on waiting with me, therefore, I got some "bonus time" with him at the bus station. With LA's reputation as a haven for runaways, I don't think he was convinced I had a Father coming to pick me up. "Are you sure you got someone here?" He started talking about how a friend of his was gonna get him into the porn business, and how a young good-looking guy like myself could make a lot of money. "If you don't got nowhere to go, you best come with me to my buddy's house, so I can look after ya."

When my father finally showed up, I introduced Mike to him not as a ball-grabbing pervert on his way to porn stardom who offered me a co-starring role in his movies, but as a "good guy who'd been looking out for me." Mike said we should keep in touch. We exchanged that weird prison handshake. I gave him a bogus phone number and prayed I'd never see him again.

***

I met a lot of my father's family while in LA. I discovered one had to climb pretty high on my father's family tree to find someone who had actually died. This was good news, I thought, until we spent a day visiting a collection of ninetyish Great Grandparents, and Great Aunts who'd not seen me since I was a baby, back when they were 83.

"My God, I can't believe how he's grown. Would you look at him? He's almost as big as you, Richard.

What's your name again?

What's that, dear? Talk louder please.

Richard? Oh, that's right; just like your father.

How tall are you?"

I couldn't wait for us to leave for Idaho, where I had some friends.

The Stolen Lawn Chair

Every place in Sandpoint reminded me of Gina and the time we'd spent together the previous summer. Just walking past a snowcone stand or an arcade might bring a sudden sense of loss. One night, I went to the skating rink with my father's family—the place where I'd met Gina the year before. I saw familiar faces from last summer, the same couples. Little had changed about that skating rink. The same video games, the same grumpy old man at the snack bar, even some of the same songs. How could Gina be dead, yet everything else be unchanged? The same DJ's voice boomed the same words over the intercom that, one year prior, had given me the excuse to approach her. "Alright, couples skate, couples skate only. So grab that special someone…" I half expected her to show up, embrace me, explain the terrible misunderstanding, grab my hand and lead me out to the floor to skate together. The music started, the DJ chatter replaced by the voice of Phil Collins.

There must be some misunderstanding—

That song! I remembered Her singing that song along with the radio last summer, as we lay on my bed in the basement, kissing.

There must be some kind of mistake

"You know…I'm a virgin," she said.

"Okay…"

Was that an invitation? A warning? A complaint?

My blue balls screamed at me to touch her downstairs, to finally get on the scoreboard, but I was too afraid of rejection. *Maybe next year.*

***

My father was particular about his stuff. The focal point of his living room was not a fireplace nor a TV, but an eight piece drum set. "I use this to make a living and no one else is allowed to touch it. This is not a toy." I was also told to not play with his audio recording equipment, which he used to make eight-track tapes for his music store customers. Inspired by routines of Cheech & Chong, Red Foxx, and George Carlin, my friends and I of course ignored his rules and used his high-tech equipment to choreograph sophomoric skits and x-rated parodies of *Bette Davis Eyes* and *Looking For Love In All the Wrong Places*.

The most outrageous bits captured on tape were my prank phone calls. Bringing strangers into the mix was especially challenging because it created unpredictable dialog. I called the Zorns at two a.m.

A sleepy voice answered. "Hello?"

"Yes sir, I was just looking at the white pages and noticed you were the last name in the whole damn phone book, and I'm calling to ask you how you feel about that."

"Do what? What time is it?"

"Time for you to get a clock."

I asked an insurance company if I could insure my burning house. I called a furniture shop to complain that the bed I bought there had just snapped in half during a rough sexual encounter. As if using my father's precious recording equipment was not defiant enough, much of our production included one of us mindlessly banging on his drums. I was sure that tape was classic comedy, even better than the professional stuff I'd grown listening to. Most of the bits were laced with profanity, some blasphemous.

My father's wife, Mary, was not the target demographic for our work. Her finding the tape I'd carelessly left in the recorder was truly unfortunate. Her Catholic religious convictions were absolute. Hanging around the shower head of the house's only bathroom was a laminated picture of the Virgin Mary, apparently in the midst of some kind of open heart surgery. Just below the big red heart on Mary's chest, written in bold, black *Magic Marker* was a note-to-self. *Pray to stop the killing of unborn children.* A handwritten note on the inside face of the food pantry door asked God to "bless the food in this house." It's unlikely there were any reminders in the house to check on show times for the latest *Cheech and Chong* movie. Not only was Mary not amused by my creativity, but she was deeply offended by my jokes about nuns, priests, and popes. When she played the tape for my father, he was outraged that I'd used the most revered item in his home—his stereo system—for child's play. He called my mother and told her I must be on drugs. I'd now been falsely accused of being on drugs by both parents.

Even before she found my tape, I sensed my presence was annoying Mary. Because summer days in Idaho were so long and only two channels weren't snowy, TV was a rare indulgence for me at my father's house. One morning, *This Week in Baseball* was almost over when Sandy, my seven-year-old half-sister, came in. "My mommy said I could watch *H.R.Pufnstuf.*

"Sandy, I'm watching something right now; it'll be over in ten minutes."

She started crying, and then quickly disappeared. Mary came into the room, beside herself that I had denied her daughter TV access. She must've been applying makeup because one eyelid was coated in blue eye shadow from eyelid to eyebrow. The other had not yet benefited from this handiwork. "No sir, she always watches her program on Saturday morning. This is **her** time," she said, shaking her head in disbelief at my audacity as she rotated the tuner.

***Her** time? Exactly when was **my** time, Mary?*

***

That summer, after keeping my nose clean for twelve years, I had my first brush with the law since the chocolate milk incident. On the Fourth of July, while walking to the park to meet friends and watch fireworks, I saw a lawn chair on a porch. I thought I'd be the envy of all my friends if I showed up with my own chair. I looked around and saw no human activity other than a car coming down the street far in the distance. So I ran up onto the porch and snagged the chair. When I got back to the sidewalk, I noticed the approaching car seemed to have something on the roof. *Oh shit! Maybe it's a police car.* Already regretting my poor judgment, I took a step or two back toward the porch with the intention of returning the chair. *No, that would look suspicious.* Frozen by indecision, I finally turned around and continued walking with it. *Lots of people are walking around carrying lawn chairs tonight.* When I saw that the oncoming car was indeed a police car, I panicked. Instead of just walking down the sidewalk with a lawn chair, I dashed a few steps toward a parked car. I stashed the chair against the car and tried to walk down the sidewalk like nothing had happened. The cop pulled up and rolled down his window. "What was that I saw you hide behind the car?"

"Oh that? Ahhh...well...I ah...found this lawn chair on the sidewalk and...um, I didn't want someone to trip on it...you know, so I...um moved it out of the way..."

"Let's have a look," he said, getting out of his squad car.

"I saw you running with this chair from that porch," he said, challenging my story.

I knew I'd been caught red-handed now, so I fessed up and told the cop my intentions, "I was gonna sit on the chair while watching the fireworks, then on my way home pass this house again and return it...I swear to God, officer...if you could just let me go I promise I'll never take another lawn chair again..."

He wasn't sympathetic and took me to the city jail where I spent about an hour before my father came to pick me up.

"I should have let you sit in jail," my father told me on the ride home. He was still upset about the comedy tape. "From now on, you're not to hang around those friends," referring to the buddies who'd made the comedy tape with me; the same ones I was on my way to meet that night. The conversation on the short drive home from the jail ended with a question from my father.

"What the hell is wrong with you? Are you on drugs?"

"No."

I'm not on drugs. What about you? What the hell's wrong with you? What kind of Father have you been? You're the one who should be arrested.

One Way Ticket to Anywhere

Several times during the summer, both Mary and my father referred to my time there as a *visit*. Clearly the expectation was for my visit to end when summer did. As long as I had a place to crash back in Texas, that was okay. I hadn't talked to any of the Ahmeys since I left at end of May. With the school year fast approaching, a phone call to Jean Ahmey was overdue. I needed to assess my chances of bunking at their place for another nine months. Although I wasn't certain I'd receive an encore invitation, I was hopeful the kindness in Jean's heart would prevail over the intra-family hostilities.

Jean spent ten minutes catching me up on what had been happening over the summer. "Sal and Jim aren't speaking, Rich. Sal's got a bad back and he might lose his job."

It sounded like she was laying the foundation for a rejection. She shifted topics to trivia she'd read from *The Lindale News*. Jean always combed through every word of the town's weekly rag, and the longer she regurgitated meaningless copy print, the more evident it became she was averting the subject of me. *Yeah Jean, that's great. Carl Worley won a golf tournament. What about me, Jean? What about our arrangement? Remember when you said I could finish school living at your place? Is that offer gone?* I heard the newspaper crinkling on her side. "Uhm…Mike Morman attended a debate camp at Baylor." *Why aren't you asking me when*

I plan on arriving, so you can arrange a ride? This conversation is going nowhere. I couldn't take it anymore. I had to be direct.

"Jean, it's not going too well up here. What are the chances of me coming back?" I assured her this arrangement had a definite end in my mind. "I promise I'll be gone from the house the day after graduation."

She sucked air from the microphone; then blew it back in. *She's gonna say "no."* Struggling to find the right words, she spoke of the stress in her marriage, between Jim and his father, between her and Jim. "…and, Rich, Sal went to the doctor and he's going to need surgery." *Yeah, yeah, I know—it's not you it's me. You still want to be friends.*

"You know how much you mean to us, Rich. You're like a son to us, but this just isn't a good time." *I know. I get it. You **love** me, but you're just not **in love** with me.* Her voice broke into a hybrid of words and sobs. Sniffles, then, "I'm sorry, Rich." If there was a trace of anger or resentment in me, it melted into disappointment, even understanding. Then I found myself in a role reversal—me consoling her. "Oh, don't worry, Jean; I have lots of options. You've already done so much for me." She cried more. The nicer I was, the more she cried. "Thank you, Jean. Thank you for everything." The conversation was over and the door to the Ahmey house was closed.

I considered my options. Back in the Appalachian Mountains, Mom and Doug were coming to realize not enough of the nine hundred people who lived in the shacks and trailers around Bakersville, North Carolina had palates for Thursday night Tex Mex, or reason to stay in motel rooms. The chaos of alcoholism, depression, and a failing business was driving them toward bankruptcy and ultimately divorce.

Three months earlier, my mother had kicked me out of the house after the Great Kidney Bean War. I hadn't spoken to her since. An outcast in the family, and a misfit in school, I decided I'd be better off staying in Idaho than going back to a school, town, and family in which I already knew I didn't fit.

My father was making tapes in the living room when I approached him. "What do you think about the possibility of me staying here for to finish school?"

"I thought you were going to stay with that friend of yours in Texas?"

"Well, his dad lost his job, so things aren't working out there."

A surprised look came to his face. "Oh—" He broke eye contact and started fidgeting with a stack of records. "Ahh— what do you plan on doing after you graduate?"

"I wanna to go to college somewhere." I saw fear in his eyes—fear of responsibility for me.

"Oh." He seemed uncomfortable being put on the spot. He evaded the question. "Let me talk to Mary about it."

Later that day, Mary approached me while I was in the basement doing laundry. "Our house is so small, kiddo, you know that. We really don't have much space here. And I don't think this is where you want to be anyway. Is it? What do you really want to do?"

"I'd like to go back to Texas and graduate with my friends, but the people I was staying with aren't able to invite me back."

"Have you asked any other friends? You can go anywhere you want—back to Texas, to your mother's, or wherever you think is best. We'll get you a one way bus ticket to anywhere you want to go."

It sounded more like a vacation offer than a living solution.

I could be free. Only one problem—I didn't have work, money, a high school diploma, or a place to stay. The bus ticket to anywhere had its appeal, but what would I do when I got to *anywhere*? I knew I'd be starting my senior year in two weeks; I just didn't know where. Clearly, it wasn't going to be in Idaho. Not that I was especially excited about that proposition, anyway.

As Mary spoke, I didn't show my resentment, but it surged through my veins as surely as did blood. Because of the abduction, his fourteen-year disappearance, and his failure to subsequently pay any child support that had been court ordered sixteen years ago, I had no respect for my father to begin with. Now, after less than three months of parental duties, he was having his wife talk me into leaving. I understood they were already having a hard enough time feeding three kids on his custom eight track tape business, but I didn't require any money. I just need a place to sleep. *I'll get a job and take care of my own food. Just a place to sleep.*

"I think you belong back with your friends in Texas. I'm sure one of your other friends will let you stay with them," she said, with a *Stepford Wife*-like finishing smile and head nod, her tone and body language purveying a sense of finality. To her, the issue was solved just by making a declaration. "You'll be fine, kiddo."

I thought about running upstairs and confronting my father.

Why am I the odd one out? Why don't you send one of your other kids away to live at their Grandma's for a year? That would open some space around here for me.

Just give me the twenty-thousand in child support you owe, and I'll be on my way. Don't worry about interest or cost of living adjustments.

Why don't you get a real job so you can finally live up to your obligation to me? Maybe you could afford to feed me while I finish high school, if you'd get off your lazy ass and punch a clock somewhere for a year, instead of trying to raise a family by selling old records to your friends.

What do you mean, you can't feed me? Just tell the foodstamp people that you have another kid now, and they'll give you more coupons. Tell one of your other goddamn kids you can't feed them. I was here first.

I need nine months—nine months here to finish high school. You've done nothing for me your whole life, and you won't even give me a bed for nine months?

All these things ran through my brain, but I said none of them. There is a balance between obedience and speaking one's mind, and my mother's heavy hand had conditioned me to error on the side of obedience.

I asked Mary, the lady who had more regard for unborn children than she had for me, her husband's son, if I could make some long distance calls to Lindale. I wasn't able to reach my best friend, Robbie—*the number you've dialed has been disconnected or is no longer in service.* I was down to B-list friends. I talked to two who dutifully said they'd check with their parents. Each called me back within an hour to tell me, "sorry."

The only thing between me and homelessness was my mother. I hadn't talked to her all summer. I reluctantly called and humbly asked if I could come back and live with the family at the motel.

"Richard, I think it would be better if you just quit school and joined the Army." She went into recruiter mode, listing the benefits: Food, shelter, training, travel, discipline, and a paycheck. *Seventeen years old, and I'm begging my mother for the chance to stay in school? What the hell is wrong with her!*

Don't get me wrong, I liked food and shelter as much as the next guy, and I knew I needed to learn discipline from someone who wasn't an alcoholic or deadbeat, but when I told her the idea of dropping out of high school, under any circumstances, was not something I'd consider, she was insulted. "Why is it so goddamned important that you finish high school? If you want, you can always get your GED later and no one will ever know the difference."

"A GED? Are you kidding me? Good Enough for Dopeheads, Mom. That's what GED stands for."

"Let me tell you something Richard, the real world doesn't give a shit about whether you finish high school. Look at Doug. He has a college degree and it hasn't helped him." As a high school dropout herself, she didn't understand why I was so adamant about finishing high school.

"Mom, even if I wanted to join the Army, I'm not old enough. The Army doesn't take seventeen year olds, and I won't be 18 for a long time. My only plan is to finish high school." *I'm not joining the fucking Army. I will not be a high school dropout. I will not be like her.*

All I wanted was a place to sleep and some food to eat for the next nine months. Having moved forward from the dropout discussion, she started with terms of my return; which were exactly as I anticipated: I'd take auto mechanics class at school, I'd not be allowed to play any sports. I'd cheerfully work in the restaurant every day in exchange for room and board. I wouldn't be allowed to drive either of the cars, not even for a date. I'd never have any money for a date anyway.

I offered compromises. "How 'bout if I give up football and just play basketball and run track?"

"Richard. You're not playing sports. You've wasted enough time with sports. You're not gonna make professional…"

I conceded to the no-sports requirement, with a backup plan in my mind. In February, when track season comes, I'll be eighteen.

At that point, if she still doesn't allow me to compete, I'll seek some other living arrangements, perhaps a friend, a dirt-cheap apartment, homeless shelter, whatever. She can't stop me from running track, not if I was eighteen. I could plan my escape later.

I was hoping to win some concession.

"Could I use the car one night a week?"

"No, you're not responsible enough to drive a car. And, even if you were, we can't afford insurance."

"Could I get a twenty-dollar-a-week allowance for my work?"

"No, your allowance is food."

I began to discuss her next requirement—the one I considered most oppressive, the one that would surround me with exactly the kind of people I wanted to avoid—that I take automechanics class. I tried to explain that by taking high level academic courses like Chemistry and Physics, instead of automechanics, which consumed three class periods, I'd be better prepared for college. She argued college was a waste of money, which we didn't have anyway, and that it held no promise for a better job. "Look at what you did to the station wagon, Richard," referring to the time I lost the gas, radiator, and oil caps, all within two weeks. "Automechanics is more important than college."

"Mom, if I go to college, I could get a well-paying job and afford a good mechanic."

"Where are you gonna get a job? What do you even want to study in college?"

"I don't know for sure…"

"You don't know?" she said, insinuating I'd just proved her right.

"Maybe I'll be a coach."

"A coach! Great, just what the world needs, another one of those goddamn egomaniacs. Maybe you can be like Coach Robinson."

It was time for me to assert myself again. "One thing I do know is I'm not going to be a mechanic, so I'm not taking automechanics."

"Then you better stay at your father's, because you're not coming back here. I raised you for seventeen years. Let your father take a turn for a year."

I wasn't going to tell her that I wasn't welcome in my father's home either, because I figured it would give her credibility—proof it was my fault nobody wanted me. Reality set in. I had no place to go, and neither of my parents cared. Tears snuck up uninvited, but my voice was still held up. I was determined to keep it from reflecting my despair. I didn't want to let my mother know she had broken me. We weren't going to reach any kind of agreement, so I said goodbye and hung up without knowing where I'd be living the following week when school started, but certain it wasn't going to be with either of my parents.

I was about to be a homeless teenager. Fifteen years ago, my father wanted me so much he stole me from my mother. My twenty-one-year old mother was distraught; unable to function I'm told. The day I was returned to her was the happiest day of her life. Now, they'd both come full circle, Each telling me I wasn't welcome in their homes, both of them believing the other should assume responsibility during my last year of high school. It was an unspoken game of *chicken* and neither of them flinched. The toddler who was the gamepiece in an epic tug-of-war battle was now a teenage hot potato. Even if I had to live under a bridge in Bumfuck, Egypt, I was going to finish high school. Nothing else mattered.

A one way ticket to anywhere? I looked at a road atlas and circled places I thought would be fun to live. Then, I went to the library and researched them. In the end, the thought of going someplace where I didn't know anyone was too intimidating.

Over the next couple of days, Mary frequently asked how my arrangements were going. Her quizzes not only compounded my anxiety, but also made me realize how unwelcome I was. So I lied. I told her I'd arranged to live with a friend back in Lindale, and my one way ticket to anywhere would be to Texas.

I'm gonna be on my own. The burden of food and shelter will depend on my own resourcefulness. Maybe my father will be overcome with a sense of obligation and, before I get on the bus he'll hand me two-thousand dollars in cash and show some remorse. "This will help. I owe you so much more than this, but this will keep you warm and fed."

Don't be silly; this is a man who drives across town to save a dime on a cup of coffee.

I didn't know how I would possibly manage, but if I had to face homelessness I wanted to do it in my hometown, where I knew people who might help. Surrounded by friends, I'd have a chance to get food. I had some ideas of some secluded sleeping places around Lindale. Behind the high school, just beyond the baseball diamond, there was a wooded area which would be my initial squatting place. Hardly anybody ever went back there. I would build my own little shelter and sleep there at night. I went to the library and read about how to build such a shelter. I'll surely find a job. Between school, work, sports, and showers in the locker room, all I'd really need was a blanket, a place to sleep, some toilet paper to wipe my ass, and maybe a place to wash my clothes once in a while. I'll have two months of manageable weather to make some money before it gets cold. I just have to find a job and everything else will work itself out.

***

Mary and my father drove me to the bus station. I went inside by myself. As I slipped four twenty dollar bills across the counter to the clerk, something occurred to me: The most money my father had ever spent on me was this $75, for the purpose of getting rid of me.

If he felt any guilt about sending his seventeen-year-old son into an unknown future, it didn't show. On this, the last day of my childhood, we hadn't spoken to each other. We waited for the bus in the parking lot. Mary, standing next to me, played the role of a priest administering last rites to a death row inmate. She held my hand and prayed. "Our Father who art in Heaven..."

She filled my mind with happy thoughts. "Your friends are going to be so happy to see you..."

My father, still upset over my mischievous escapades such as stealing the lawn chair, the prank phone calls, abusing his lawnmower, and allowing my friends to bang on his drums, stood by himself, twenty feet away. Stoic as an executioner, and defiant in his right to ignore me, I wondered if he knew the switch he was about the flip would take him and me past the point of no return.

The *Dad I never had* will, after today, never have the chance to be anything else.

"Here's a little something, Kiddo," Mary said, as my bus approached. She handed me a twenty-dollar bill and fifty dollars of food stamps. The silver, ribbed panels of the Greyhound reminded me of a spacecraft I had drawn as part of my second-grade book report. A spacecraft coming to take me to a whole new world, one without parents—the *real world*. The vastness of her blue eye shadow, exacerbated by her squinting against the setting sun, made her eyes appear as Easter eggs. "You know, he really cares about you. You need to say goodbye to him."

Say bye to him? What I really should do is demand some money. Twenty bucks doesn't go too far.

I walked over to my father. "Well…" I paused, electing not to extend my hand in invitation of a shake for fear it might be ignored. "Take it easy…"

For several seconds he was unresponsive, avoiding eye contact, staring into the distance, as if he were looking around me, at something else, for someone else. I'd seen that look before, in the man at the bus station last summer—the man who, for a moment, I mistakenly believed was my father. The emphatic apathy of my father echoed in my head. I'll never forget it.

I don't need you. Never have. I was angry with myself for not having the courage to say it aloud.

After I turned toward the bus, he mumbled something behind me, something like "take care." I didn't know if it was directed to me or if he was just talking to himself. As I boarded, I was convinced I'd never see him again and, to be honest, I didn't care. I had concerns about how I was going to eat and where I was going to live. My relationship with my father, who'd never done anything for me anyway, was near the bottom of my list of concerns. He had just flipped the switch inside of me.

Most boys make a gradual transition into manhood, incrementally weaned from the nurture of their parents in a series of stages: small decision making, transportation, shelter, and ultimately financial support. Even when a kid goes off to college, it's understood they'll call to ask for money, come home for occasional weekends, holidays, and summers and continue some semblance of family interaction. For me, the moment I stepped onto that bus, I knew my childhood ended. While my friends were getting their curfews extended to midnight, I was jumping into adulthood with both feet, and hoping I'd never see either of my parents again. As I walked down the aisle, searching for a seat, more than ever before, I knew I was alone, abandoned in a purgatory somewhere between the kid's table and manhood. Through all my mother's rage and father's apathy, every other time I'd gotten on one of these buses waiting for me at the other side was a solid arrangement for food and shelter. This time, there was nothing. I had twenty dollars cash, fifty dollars in food stamps, a trash bag full of clothes, and a plan to build a fort. My imagination casts me into the future. I land in a void. Finally, something tangible: I'm in an empty hallway at Lindale High School. A few familiar faces appear, politely smile, and pass. This is all I have. Nothing more.

With a full year of high school still unfinished, and estranged from both my parents, my work experience consisted of selling roses, picking blackberries, and washing dishes. It was a sobering thought, and I would spend most of the trip contemplating its significance. I likened myself to the ten-year-old Bobby Brady in the *Brady Bunch* episode in which he planned on running away from home. When his step-mother, Carol, asked him what skills he had that he could use to support himself. He replied, "I can fingerpaint." I had nothing on Bobby Brady. Outside of friends, there was no safety net in Lindale for people like me—no shelters, soup kitchens, or charities waiting to help me out. I thought back to that afternoon when I was four, when I marched my little friend away from our playground outside our apartments, several miles into town. We were on our own all afternoon. It would be kinda like that, except this time, it was forever. It wasn't self pity, but Spock-like logical thinking that steered me toward my conclusion. *I have no one; but I'll manage. I must manage. Everybody does it. I'm just doing it a little sooner.*

The Lady on the Bus

Choosing a seat on those bus trips was unnerving. To bus people, two days was worth the hundred bucks they saved by not opting for a three-hour plane ride. After the Mike experience three months before, I didn't want to take any chances; I decided to choose a seat based on safety. I found a spot next to a frumpy lady in her fifties. Our worlds could not have been further apart, but at least she wouldn't try to grab my crotch. She was the type of person I normally wouldn't pay much attention to. More neatly dressed than most busriders, she was about two-thirds of the way into her Seattle to Missoula trip. After exchanging introductions, I dismissed her name from memory, wedged a jacket between my face and the window and tried to sleep. She recognized my inability to do so and saw it as an opportunity to babble about her young grandchildren she had just visited in Seattle, and her son (about my age) back home in Missoula.

When you're in the midst of a life-altering personal crisis that you'd rather not talk about, even the most generic conversations can be uncomfortable. After talking about her kids and grandkids for a while, the nice lady, reduced to a voice and featureless silhouette in the dark, caught me off guard with polite smalltalk. "So, are you heading home?"

"Well, not exactly. I'm going to the town where I used to live to finish high school."

"Oh, that's nice. Are your parents already there?"

"No, I'm on my own."

She was confused. "You're in high school?"

To avoid her pity, I told her I had an offer to stay with my friend, and that I already had a job lined up. I lied to put her at ease. She was caring and authentic, not phony-voiced, like most ladies her age. We talked (mostly I talked and she listened) for three hours. Perhaps she sensed apprehension in my voice, because she was so reassuring, saying some of the same things that Mary had. Odd, how those things had a completely different meaning coming from her. "You're gonna be just fine, Rich." When Mary said it, it sounded contrived. When this lady said it, I believed it.

We were almost to Missoula before she presumed to offer advice. "It sounds like you have some good friends. The more friends you have, the better your chances will be. Lean on your friends now, ask for their help and accept it whenever it is offered. Express your appreciation to them. Years later, seek them out and let them know you have not forgotten what they did for you. The feeling you give them when you let them know you remember will make them feel better about themselves. You may not believe it, but, by doing this, you will be giving them even more than they gave you. You just have to be patient to return the favor." I could tell this lady highly regarded my well-being, and to see that a stranger cared about me moved me in a way I hadn't known before.

A little after midnight, we emerged from the black night and pulled into the well lit bus terminal in Missoula, Montana. For the first time since I took my seat next to her, I took note of what this lady looked like. This woman—who over the last three hours had been only a voice and a shadow—had a certain sadness in her eyes. I knew that sadness was for me. She gathered her things around her seat as she prepared to depart. Before she got up, she extended her hand, which held a twenty-dollar bill.

"Take this, Rich."

I tried politely to refuse, but she quickly settled the issue.

"I'm not *giving* you this money. I am *loaning* it to you. Money is a tool. Right now you have more use for it than I do. I might use this to buy flowers for my garden, but you can use it to buy food for a week. How could I enjoy my flowers knowing that? Don't be silly; please take the money."

She put the folded bill in my hand, wrapped both her hands around my fist and squeezed as if she were trying to press the ink permanently into my palm, like she wanted me to have it forever. My pupils had been in night vision mode for a while, so the light pouring in from the city made it seem almost like daylight inside the bus. "This, what is happening to you now, will make you stronger, and before you know it, you will become successful. Believe me when I tell you that, because I can see it in you." Her voice began to fracture. "When that day comes, twenty dollars won't mean anything to you, and you'll come across someone who needs it more than you, somebody who's trying their best in life but just can't seem to get a break, somebody facing a challenge just like you're facing now. Give it to them, and your debt to me will be repaid. In this way I get to help not only you, but someone else I will never know."

With tears now streaming down her cheeks, she released the trembling grip that her two hands had on my one and stood up. All the other Missoula-bound riders had gotten off. Fresh busriders were beginning to embark. From her standing position she looked down at me and said, "You're going to be just fine." Then she turned away and lumbered up the aisle in a side-to-side sway typical of a lady much older than she appeared to be—like my grandmother.

"How profound," I thought. That phrase, *I get to help*, would stick with me forever. Here was a lady who sought opportunities to help people because it enriched her life as much as the person she helped. I will be like *that* someday, I promised myself. In the mean time, I may make fun of other kids, throw eggs on passing cars from overpasses, and act like the obnoxious imbecile I am, but eventually, when I grow up, I will be like that lady.

From my seat, I watched through the window as she greeted her son with a warm hug. They stood outside, talking and smiling as they glanced up at me. They were so close, if not for the bus window; we could've had a conversation. But I was glad for the barrier; glad the conversation was over. Glad because nothing more needed to be said. When the bus pulled away, they waved to me, as if I were a family member—as if I were her son. They waved to me like my father had not. As we moved a little further, I saw her son consoling her. *I wish I were that kid. Wouldn't it be great to have a mother like that?*

Suddenly, I was struck by an impulse. My brain shouted, but my mouth did not. *STOP THE BUS. STOP THE GODDAMNED BUS.* And when the bus driver stopped, I'd grab my trash bag full of clothes from the overhead, run off the bus and join my adopted family in a three-way hug. I bet that lady would take me in. I bet she'd do anything to ensure her kids were taken care of. I'd finish high school living at her house in Missoula, and become best friends with my new brother. Maybe we'd get bunk beds. We would hike in the mountains together and raft the rivers. I can reinvent myself, be born again in the arms of a Montana girl who knew nothing about my favorite song, who would watch in awe as I won the Montana state championship in the mile, and pole vault. I'd get a track scholarship to Big Sky University, or whatever college they have up here. This would be my life.

Would I do it? Would my one way ticket end in Missoula? Would I behave as I always had, following my impulse? Would I have the guts to do it? Would I have the guts not to? Which choice took more guts? Who cares about guts, what's the best thing to do? It was fifty-fifty.

Yes, I will.

No, you won't. What if she says "no"?

She won't say "no." She wants to take care of me.

No, she doesn't, if she did, she would've offered.

She didn't offer because she thought I had a place to stay. She didn't offer because she thought I had a job.

Had you just told the truth, you'd already be on your way to your new home. Forget about her.

I think she did offer. All that talk about friends, she meant *she* was my friend. *That* was her offer. Yes, I will scream right now for the bus to stop.

Stop it, you big pussy! Be a man. It's not her responsibility to take care of you. It's too late now anyway.

No, it's not too late; it's only a quarter-mile, I could run that in one minute. Okay, carrying a trash bag full of clothes, maybe seventy seconds. And they will see me running before I get there. I can make it back before they leave.

What if they're gone, you'll be stuck in Missoula for the night, and will Greyhound even let you finish the trip after you get off the bus? There's bound to be some rule about that. Besides, it's more like a half a mile. It's too late.

You're right; it's probably a half a mile. Fuck it.

There was no more decision, no more choice, no possible action for me to take except to sit on that slow-moving bus making its way through the black darkness of the Montana Rockies and toward the woods behind Lindale High School. There would be no Montana girl. There would be no brother with bunk beds. There would be no adopted Mother.

The darkness was oppressive; I couldn't see where we were going. There were maybe twenty other people on the bus, but I was alone, a four year old lying in my bed, afraid of the dark, afraid the boogey man may come out of my closet, or maybe come out of the shitter in the back of the bus. Maybe the boogeyman was back there. I faded in and out of light sleep, jerked awake repeatedly like I had stuck a bobby pin in a light socket.

At first I didn't know where they came from or why they were there, but new thoughts pounded inside my head. Something, and someone, I'd never thought about much at all—my mother's real father—my grandfather—the man who gave his life for his country nineteen years before I was born.

Did he know he was going to die? What was he thinking as his transport boat drew closer and closer to that beach? As bombs burst around him in the water, his platform kept moving closer to the enemy. How scared was he? Did he have any idea that his courage would be revered by patriotic Americans for generations, perhaps centuries, maybe longer—that what he was doing was the most glorious thing we—the United States of America—had ever done and will ever do? Did he know this? That his sacrifice—not the moment he would come home to meet his newborn daughter for the first time—would be *his* finest hour?

Was he proud? Did he have a sense? Did he need the historic perspective I took for granted to absorb the magnitude of what he was doing? Did he know what he was about to die for? Or did he think, "I'm a goddamned pawn of the US government and crooked politicians fighting somebody else's war."

Did he wonder about me? "Will my baby girl ever have an enlightened son who sees me as a hero?"

I thought of my grandmother, the day the Chaplain came, and the nights and days that followed—a pain like no other in the world. And, a few years ago, maybe I was about twelve, when Grandpa, Grandma, Ginger, and I sat up in their king-sized bed with our backs against the headboard during one of our Sunday night sleepovers watching that movie on TV, *The Summer of '42*. How Grandma cried when the Chaplain came and how Grandpa appeared oblivious. Did he really not notice or did he feel her same pain? Four years after watching that movie, I finally cried for her—with her.

I thought of my sister, poor Ginger, still in that house with my mother. Why hadn't I protected her? Why had I made her life even harder than my own? Is she okay right now? Is she now the target of my mother's rage?

And I wondered. Where is this all coming from? Since when do I think about deep-meaning heavy shit like this? At first I wondered, then convinced myself it must be so. That lady on the bus had given me a helluva lot more than twenty dollars. When she held my hands in hers and squeezed, it was as if she had transferred her compassion, her depth, her kindness to me. Was she an angel? Was God using that lady to reach me? It could've been nothing else. I didn't get on my knees and accept Jesus as my savior, but goddamnit, in some bizarre way I was born again. I was spiritual, and I would never be the same person—and that was a good thing. I was the enlightened grandson of a war hero and just like that, starting on this day, genesised from a random encounter with a stranger, whose name I failed to note, I had captured empathy and compassion.

Finally, the stars in the big sky of Montana faded into the blue glow of dawn. We were in Wyoming. I was relieved, relieved that I could see the world and see the other people on the bus. I was not alone, and now I felt better. I thought about what I almost did the night before. I convinced myself that I had indeed made a decision—the right decision. Proud of myself for not running like a toddler to cry on the bosom of a stranger, and assured by a frumpy middle-aged lady, that I was gonna be just fine. I believed it, but still wondered how.

The Clothes on My Back and a Broken Sack

Late at night, on the last Friday of August 1981, I arrived at the Greyhound terminal in Tyler, Texas, after a fifty-hour bus trip. My plan was to somehow get to Robbie's apartment in Lindale, and have him sneak me into his room where I might be able sleep on the floor. In the morning, I'd set out to find a job and build my fort in the woods. With only three days until the start of our senior year there was no time to waste. I knew Robbie would help any way he could. I had to make it to his house, but Lindale was fifteen miles away and I hadn't been able to arrange a ride from the bus station.

Robbie's phone was still disconnected. Not that he had a car, but maybe he'd have more phone numbers, perhaps of a friend who might give me a ride. If nothing else, I wanted to let him know I was coming.

I called the Ahmeys, hoping Jim might be able to pick me up. Mr. Ahmey told me Jim was grounded from the phone. I didn't ask why, but I assumed it was for something like driving his blue Pinto over someone's yard ornaments. He told me Jean wanted to say "hello." The conversation with her was short and awkward. Having been through that emotional conversation a few days earlier, I didn't even tell her I was in town even though I knew she'd soon find out. I forced a polite end to conversation before she had a chance to start reading from the newspaper. I knew for certain Jean would come to the bus station and drive me to Robbie's. But asking her would be selfish. It'd be like I was pinning my predicament on her. *I'm back Jean, and I need a ride to Lindale so I can build a fort in the woods and sleep on the ground because you're kicking me out too, just like my mom, just like my dad. By the way, "do you know how to build a shelter?"*

No, Jean didn't deserve that, and neither did I, really. Walking fifteen miles would be easier than that.

After dropping a few more dimes, I was out of people to call. I'd come almost two thousand miles, but the last fifteen—the path between Tyler and Lindale that I'd traveled hundreds of times in a car, but never on foot—was going to be the most difficult part of my trip. I was tired. I just wanted to crash, but I hadn't traveled across the country to sleep in a bus station in Tyler. I hoisted my trash bag full of clothes onto my back and started my march toward the closest thing I had to home—a town named Lindale.

I tried hitchhiking for a bit, but cars raced by without slowing. After a few miles, realizing just how much hitching was slowing me down, I gave up on that idea. *Who's gonna pick up a stranger carrying a trash bag late at night?*

I occupied my mind by trivializing my hike, comparing it to hardships faced by notable adventurers on their epic journeys. I wondered how Shackleton's Antarctic team might view a fifteen-mile walk on a hot Texas night. I thought about Terry Fox, a nineteen-year-old boy, with terminal cancer, who ran (not walked) half way across Canada on one leg and a bleeding stump to raise money for cancer research, before losing his battle. I'd often use this coping technique to help me manage tough situations. I imagine how much harder it *could* be, or how much worse it is (or was) for other people. *Lewis and Clark. They...*

I passed a sign on Highway 69:
Lindale 10
Mineola 22

My trip is easy. I have both my legs, the wind chill is ninety above zero, not ninety below, there are no Grizzly Bears trying to eat me, and at least I'm not going to Mineola.

I was smelly, broke, tired, hungry, and thirsty, but I was only ten miles from Lindale. *I've done ten-mile training runs before.* I was just a long run away from lying down for the first time in three days. I picked out a sign on highway 69, and with my bag bouncing on my back, jogged for a couple of minutes, until I reached that sign. *I'm two percent closer than I was when I started that run.* I picked out a reflector post ahead and treated myself to walking until I reached it. Then, I jogged to the next reflector. My plan was to alternate walking and running all the way to Robbie's. I'd just started my third cycle of running when my trash bag burst. All the clothes I owned were scattered on the shoulder of the road.

Using the moonlight and headlight beams of passing cars, I took two long-sleeve shirts and laid them flat on the pavement. Then, I took my underwear, socks, and T-shirts, rolled them into compressed units and placed them on the shirts. I amused myself slightly by sticking an orphaned sock in a shirt pocket—*almost like a fancy handkerchief.*

I tied all my clothes, except my one pair of jeans, into two small bundles, using the long sleeves and the bottom corners of the shirts to form loose knots. I laid the jean legs over my shoulders and looped a bulky denim crossover knot on my chest. I suppose it looked a bit like a sailor getup with a giant neckerchief and a flap over my shoulder blades. Walking was not a problem, but when I tried to run, one of the bundles loosened causing socks and underwear to spill out. I'd stop for a minute, sometimes walk backwards to retrieve a liberated sock and then rework my knots.

I had just passed Tyler Pipe, about five miles short of Robbie's place when an old Camaro pulled over onto the shoulder in front of me. I jogged up toward the car and heard a voice inside yelling something—maybe my name. What a relief to see my good friend, Steve Freeman, behind the wheel.

"Hey man, what are you doing out here, Rich?" He laughed with amazement.

Well...my mom sent me on a bus to come back here and live with the Ahmeys, then the Ahmeys sent me on a bus to live with my mother, then my mother sent me on a bus to live with my father, then my father—

"Long story, man, long story…"

***

Robbie's family situation was similar to mine. He'd been estranged from his father since early childhood. While my mother was often antagonistic, his was emotionally detached. Whenever I was at his apartment, she was either in her bedroom or sitting in a zombie-like trance at her kitchen table, smoking cigarettes, starring out the patio window at a gray, wood fence four feet beyond. When she did speak, her voice was deep and depressing, like she'd just awakened. Devoid of expression and action, she was a cereal-for-dinner mom. She was not Jean Ahmey.

Within ten minutes of being picked up by Steve, I was sitting at the small kitchen table in Robbie's apartment, eating bologna sandwiches and planning with him in hushed voices—as to not awake his mother and sister—about what to do next.

My first priority was to find work. The next morning, I caught a ride to the Hide-A-Way Lake Country Club. I'd washed dishes there for a short time a year before and left on good terms. My experience and willingness to work weeknights, and to close down the kitchen after midnight, got me hired me on the spot. I was elated to land the minimum wage job and the free meal that would come with every shift. The club was seven miles from town, and I had no means to get back and forth to work, but that was a problem I would deal with later.

I returned to Robbie's place ready to start the business of building my fort in the woods.

"Rich, we're not going to the woods."

"Why not?"

"Because I talked to my mom. She said you can stay a few weeks, until you save some money."

I'd landed a job, with free meals, and now had a roof over my head. I'd traveled such an emotional distance since I'd arrived in town just a few hours ago with a seemingly insurmountable list of problems that, when I opened my mouth to speak I couldn't even utter the words *thank you*. I'm sure he wondered why I wasn't talking, why I looked like I might cry. Days before, I came to terms with the fact that my parents didn't care what happened to me. Now, I knew my friend did.

At the risk of Robbie thinking I was queer, I gave my best friend a hug. I didn't sob or bawl like a baby, stroke my hand through his bushy brown 70's hair or anything like that. It was a short hug, maybe two seconds. I knew at that moment, I had a lifelong friend—not just a buddy who'd laugh at my smart-ass remarks or the crazy shit I did, but the kind of friend who would one day be the Best Man at my wedding. What I didn't recognize was the recent cycles of rejections and acceptances were dovetailing into a chrysalis. Forever lagging behind my classmates in emotional maturity, these profound human interactions with parents, strangers, and friends were turbo-charging me past many of them with a newfound empathy, gratitude, perspective and life experiences they lacked.

***

On the first day of school, I went to the office and requested an application for free lunches. I wasn't able to answer a lot of the questions, so I gave tongue-in-cheek responses to make my point that if anyone needed free lunches, it was me.

Name: Richard Ochoa [this was later contested by the principal because my school records showed Richard Schnabl]

Address: Same as Robbie Hudson [I had no idea what his address was]

Father's Occupation: food stamp collector

Mother's Occupation: estranged

Monthly household income: There is no household, I don't even know where I will be living next week, but my income is $3.15 an hour.

The principal reviewed my application and issued me a *free* lunch ticket, which looked no different than the *reduced* lunch ticket I'd used in years past. I hated classmates seeing me present that white *business card* to Mrs. Hicks, who sat behind the till at end of the lunch line. I'd sometimes jockey for a place in line to avoid having a cute girl behind me. The shame of *that card*, so overwhelming, sometimes I would pay rose-selling cash from my own pocket to avoid presenting *that card* in front of some uppity Hide-A-Way cheerleader. When I did present it, I cringed at the clicking of Mrs. Hick's holepuncher calling attention to my indigence like a scarlet letter. But, things were different this year;

when I got *that card*, I saw it not as a source of embarrassment, but a critical component to my survival. Humility had taken hold; hunger was a greater concern than pride.

I had a job, which meant in a week I'd have some money. I had a floor to sleep on, free lunches and dinners on weekdays, and nine months between me and a high school diploma. *I might just pull this off.*

A Friend With a Bed

Robbie's floor was never intended to be more than a temporary solution. His family's apartment unit was sized for two, and I made four. After I got my first paycheck, I visited an apartment complex with a big sign out front: *$99 move-ins*. "I'm sorry," said a lady with big Texas hair and costume jewelry. "I can't rent to minors."

Other than a sack full of clothes, I had nothing to put in an apartment anyway. What I really needed was to rent a room in someone's house, but I couldn't find anything like that. Then, another friend came through. Glen Ballard, a prototype geek with aspirations of being class valedictorian, caught up with me during lunch. Glen was conceited and condescending, often trading a chance to be friends with his classmates for the opportunity to exhibit intellectual superiority over them. A classic know-it-all, with an answer for everything. Ask him who was buried in the *Tomb of the Unknown Soldier* and he would likely claim to know. This made Glen one of the most widely disliked kids in school. In our small circle of friends we called him *Gland* because he had a tendency to be an arrogant prick. He enjoyed the nickname, often using it to refer to himself.

"Rich, my parents want to have you over for dinner tonight."

"Thanks Glen, I appreciate that, but I have to work." Since I was all for a free meal, I asked if I could come on the weekend instead.

"This is important, if we eat early, can you go into work a little late? I'll give you a ride."

I didn't understand how eating at Glen's place could be more important than the three bucks I'd make for an hour's work, so, not wanting to be greeted with stacks of dishtubs upon my arrival at the club, I again declined politely.

Glen revealed the mystery. "I'm not supposed to tell you this, but my parents want to meet you. If they get a good feeling about you, they'll offer to let you stay at our place for a little while. It'll get you off Robbie's floor and into a bed." I thanked Glen without hugging him.

***

Before dinner, Glen's Father took me down the hall to his daughter's room. "Dede, this is our guest, Richard Ochoa." The twelve year old squared up, made eye contact with me and smiled. Mr. Ballard continued the introduction. "Richard, this is my daughter, Dede."

She extended her hand. "It's nice to meet you, Richard."

Poor kid; I bet they sent her to finishing school.

In the wake of the formality of the moment, an awkward silence permeated the room as the three of us glanced at one another. Mr. Ballard broke the ice. "Dede, show our guest your Rubik's cube, please." Her little hands twisted that block faster than I could follow. Every so often she'd pause for a moment, study the pattern and then rotate the sides in some sequence that made sense only to her. In three minutes the cube was solved. Mr. Ballard had only begun to show off his seed. "Would you play the flute for Richard?" She played without reading music. "Dede's first chair," Mr. Ballard said, after she finished. I resisted my impulse to ask him if Dede could fetch. He didn't strike me as a man who enjoyed a good joke at his child's expense. There was too much at risk for me to be myself.

Dede was about to read to me in Spanish when Glen's Mother, Marsha, addressing me and her husband as *gentlemen,* requested us for dinner, bringing *The Dede Talent Show* to a merciful end. *Well, at least I know why Glen is so pompous.*

I found Marsha Ballard to be kind, down-to-earth and personable. It was obvious that she was driving this idea to meet me. A polio survivor with an iron lung in her study, she had limited use of one of her arms which dangled limp and twisted at her side, palm facing out, fingers curled up. Marsha seemed well read without the pretentiousness of her husband. If Glen's father carried the arrogant genes, clearly his mother, although physically frail, was the one passing on the genius ones.

Initially Mr. Ballard dominated the dinner conversation. "Well…uh…Glen had a 720 Math. No, wait." He squinted his eyes, pursed his lips, then rested his chin in the valley between his thumb and forefinger. After a moment of intense thought, he resumed. "Glen had a 760. It was Robin who had the 720." He dabbed a napkin at the corners of his mouth then returned it to his lap. "Dede isn't going to take the SAT until we know she can ace the math, right, Dede?" *Geez, does this guy have a knack for great conversation, or what?* I wished we could change the subject. *How 'bout them Cowboys? Are they gonna do shit this year? What do you think of Everson Walls? No, that wouldn't be a good topic; these people don't even have a TV.*

Marsha waited patiently for her husband to finish his synopsis of their children's academic performances, and then asked me a few questions about my situation. She inquired about my grades, and asked what my plans were for after high school. "I'm hoping to get a track scholarship," I told her.

"You need to turn your grades around, Rich. If I may be forward, it might be too late for a scholarship."

"I think I'm gonna make good grades this year. I'm done with math and science, so I have some pretty easy classes." She and her husband raised their eyebrows in shock at the notion of taking it easy. *Yeah…well…I ain't no Ballard. Don't wanna be a scientist. You don't have to be a Ballard prodigy to play sports and be a coach.*

Over dessert, Marsha asked me if I'd like to stay with them a few days. Her husband gave me a single, deliberate nod to affirm he agreed with his wife's offer. Glen took me to work, dropped me off, picked me up at midnight, drove me to Robbie's to get my bag of clothes and then back to his house.

One night, a few days after the interview dinner, I found an envelope with my name on it taped to a ladder rung of the bunk beds I shared with Glen. Inside the envelope was a short letter.

Rich,

Wesley and I have discussed your situation. We each admire your strength in dealing with it. I'm certain, one day your parents will be so proud of you for finishing high school. We cannot agree with you more about the importance of this. We would like to do something to help you achieve your goal of getting your diploma. You are welcome to stay with us until you and Glen graduate. We have discussed this with Glen and he is in agreement. If you choose to stay, you will be treated like one of the family. You are welcome in our home, your home.

Marsha Ballard

I had a place to call *home*—an interlude within the chaos that had become my life. Marsha Ballard got a hug, and there was nothing weird about it.

The letter from Mrs. Ballard didn't address our transportation problems. Although Marsha and I frequently had substantial conversations, I'd no more than exchange polite greetings with Mr. Ballard after that first night. So, when Glen went on a two-day band trip, and Mr. Ballard had to drive me to school, we rode in clumsy silence. How do you start a conversation with a man who doesn't watch sports, or for that matter even TV? *School, that's it, I'll ask him something about school.* "Did Glen tell you he aced his physics test?"

"Yes, he did. That's not surprising, though. We got his teacher to give us a syllabus and textbook last spring. He studied the material over the summer, so I'd be disappointed in anything less."

"What a great idea. I should've tried that."

"You should try studying—period." He was not smiling or ribbing me, just stating facts as he saw them, and doing it in the same condescending way that his son alienated classmates.

"Yeah, well, I'm gonna turn my study habits around when I get to college. I'm looking forward to a fresh start. I'm gonna make good grades in college."

"Okaaaay." He drew out his one-word response as if to say, "Why are you telling me? I don't give a rats ass what you do."

"Hey, wouldn't it be great if Glen and I went to college together?"

He took his eyes off the road for a moment, and looked at me. He shifted his head and shoulders away from me in an exaggerated, contrived manner like a stage actor might use. Wes Ballard was literally taken aback as if I'd said the most insulting thing he'd ever heard. He couldn't have been more offended than a grand dragon being asked for his daughter's hand in marriage by a black man. The idea of his son and I attending the same college was absurd.

"Ahhh…well, Glen is expecting a nomination to West Point. Failing that, he should be accepted to MIT. As a backup, he's already been accepted into engineering school at UT. I don't think you'll be going to any of those schools, Rich. You have to understand, Glen has been preparing his whole life for college. It's not something one starts to think about their senior year."

"Where's MIT? Do they have a football team?"

Wes Ballard rolled his eyes, shook his head and laughed from deep within his throat. I joined him. He may have thought I was joking. But, I knew he was laughing *at* me, not *with* me.

I should have just kept quiet. I think the silence was better.

Even though I found Mr. Ballard's pretentiousness annoying, I wished my parents were capable of exhibiting parental pride like he did. In fact, given the choice of an apathetic father or one who incessantly boasts of my achievements, I'd choose the latter.

After a few weeks of midnight rides, and other taxi duties, Glen's enthusiasm for having a roommate started to wear down. He'd pick me up at the lodge, after I closed the kitchen.

"Thanks for the ride Glen."

"Your welcome, but this sucks."

That was so *Glen*. He'd give you the shirt off his back and then complain that he's cold.

It was important for him to be well rested in school. He was making a push for valedictorian, the elusive perfect math SAT, sashes and colored cords to wear at our commencement exercise, and a nomination to a military academy. He couldn't afford the time it took to be my taxi service. Every day he reminded me of the unwanted things I'd introduced to his life: snoring, sneezing, foot odor, fingerprints on his records, pubic hairs on his toilet seat. My relationship with Glen was suffering from overexposure. It was all Glen, all the time. Glen's heart was huge but he had tendency toward obsessive compulsiveness and was annoyed by almost everything I did. He'd yell my name in the middle of the night to shut up my snoring, then in the morning ask politely if I slept well. Clearly, Glen was conflicted between being a good guy and wanting his privacy back. It was obvious the Rich-and-Glen roommate thing was not a long-term solution.

My Own Place

There was never a risk Glen or his parents would ask me to leave, but he and I agreed if a better situation came up, I should consider it. Glen was more proactive in the idea, and approached a substitute teacher, Bob Staton, to pick his brain for alternatives.

Bob Staton, entrepreneur, local real estate man, part-time mail carrier, dabbler in the oil and hunting businesses, and long-time substitute teacher, was by far, the most well known man in town. For several decades, each kid who attended Lindale schools had the pleasure of Bob completely disregarding a daily lesson plan in favor of his back-when-I was-a-youngster stories. A crafty student like me could easily divert him from collecting assignments, administering tests, or assigning homework the real teacher had ordered. More than once, I walked into Mr. Praytor's Algebra class without my assignment, prepared for a zero, a humiliating verbal assault, and the possibility of a board across my ass from the militant math teacher. Instead, I was treated to Bob's story about how he made a hundred grand in a business deal on his way to becoming the richest son-of-a-gun in town and the most prolific substitute teacher Lindale had ever seen.

Bob modeled himself as a teacher of life. That meant he focused on real-world lessons like demonstrating to us on the chalkboard how to write checks. A classmate once asked him for assistance with a word problem about a plane flying from New York to Chicago into a headwind. "New York, that's a helluva a city. How many of you have been to New York?" Before long, we were getting a lesson about how New York was laid out in five boroughs and how residents of the city didn't have cars because they could walk everywhere they wanted to go.

The personification of a "good ole boy," Bob spoke at an uneven pace and exaggerated southern drawl, enunciating every syllable as a separate word, which annoyed some people but mesmerized me. In my science class, he once read a short story about the moral dilemma of a hunter who'd accidentally shot and killed another hunter in the woods. Two black girls were talking so loud their voices competed with his. He paused to address them. "Look, if you young lay-dees won't mind resuming your con-ver-sa-tion in 'bout for-ty-five minutes after the bell rings, I'd sure 'preciate that." They ignored his plea. "Ex-cuse me again lay-dees, I'm won-dren, do you peo-ple not understand En-glish?" With defiance in their eyes, the girls stared back. He continued reading. In an obvious attempt to antagonize him, they talked louder. A white girl turned and shushed them. Bob addressed the girl's attempt to apply peer pressure with a not-so-subliminal message intended for the loud-talking black girls. "That's o-kay. [long pause] Let 'em talk. If they don't wanna lis-ten, that's fine. [long pause] It's too late for those two any-way; they'll just be a bur-den to the rest of us, when they're each on well-fare." Today, Bob's remarks might be picked up by local media outlets, broadcasted on the evening news, and tweeted. But in 1981, comments like these helped him portray an image of a wise and worldly man who had an answer for most everything. Bob Staton, a no-nonsense problem solver who tells it like it is, had taken on the task of solving my problem.

Bob called the Ballards and got their input. Then, Bob Staton—*The Wizard of Lindale*—came to the school one day to see me. He called me out of class and brought me to the teacher's lounge for a cup of coffee. We sat in the corner of the hallowed room sipping from our mugs like we were having some kind of business meeting while I skipped World Geography.

"Rich, do you know Gary Camp, Lindale class of '76?"

Bob and his new business partner, Gary, had just purchased a three-bedroom house two blocks south of *the* fourway stop. Gary was moving his new CPA business into one of the rooms in that house. The rest of the house, except one bedroom, would be rented to Howell Realty. "If you want that spare bedroom, me and Gary'll put a bed and dresser in there, and you can have it for a hundred sixty a month." A furnished bedroom in the middle of town—this was exactly what I had been looking for.

Coach Robinson came into the Teacher's Lounge and eyeballed us from the other side of the room. Had I been with anybody else, Block would have come over, whacked me upside the head, and told me to get the hell out of his lounge. But, I was with the only man who out-Lindaled Coach Robinson. *Yeah, that's right, asshole; I'm with him, Bob Fucking Staton, talking business. So piss off.*

I ran the numbers. The first fifty-five hours I worked each month would go toward rent. Since I'd been averaging almost forty hours per week, I figured I'd have plenty left for other necessities like food, Pac-man, and Asteroids. I could unburden the Ballards, mainly Glen, and have my own place. The school, gym, track, stores, pool hall, Robbie's place, everything (except work) was so close I could walk, just like New Yorkers did. I accepted Bob's offer with a handshake, and impressed him by pulling out eight twenties on the spot, becoming the only seventeen year old in town with his own place. *My own place. How far I've come in such a short time.*

***

Gary Camp was a preppy cowboy. He wore cowboy boots, Wrangler jeans, and Izod shirts—sometimes pink or yellow. He graduated near the top of his Lindale class in 1976 and married his high school sweetheart, Susan, who was Miss LHS. Gary was an ambitious young accountant who usually arrived at the house before I awoke. Eventually, I depended on him as an alarm clock on school mornings. He'd come into my room, turn my radio on full blast, and do a God-awful dance beside my bed. One morning he might do a herky-jerky rendition to *Dancing Queen*, first tumbling his hands around each other, then extending his arm upward, holding the pose a long time before finally adding the classic pointed finger to complete his interpretation of Travolta's "Saturday Night Fever" pose. The routine was predictable but always funny. I'd wake up to the sight and sound of Gary shaking his booty like a Solid Gold Dancer to *Angel in a Centerfold*. When the Macarena came out fifteen years later, I'm pretty sure it was inspired by a collection of Gary Camp morning dances.

As far as accountants go, Gary was pretty funny. More importantly, Gary was a righteous man. When it came time to pay my second month's rent I walked into his office with bills in my hand.

"About your rent, I'm getting a good return here with my office and my share of rent from Howell. So just pay Bob $80 a month from now on, and you'll be set." *All these people coming to my assistance, this is great.* I was able to go to K-mart and buy a *Sound Design* stereo for my room. *Sound Design* made stereos for people like me—people who didn't know anything about audio equipment but wanted big-ass, light-as-paper speakers and a vast array of red and green lights flickering across the front panel. The stereo weighed about the same as an empty cardboard box, but you couldn't convince me all those lights didn't translate into a good system.

I was settling in. My life, once characterized by conflict and contest was now circumscribed by independence and determination. Every problem had been solved, except transportation. But, that solution would soon prove worse than the problem.

"I Thought You Was Roadkill"

There was a seven mile stretch of east Texas piney woods between my room in town and the country club where I worked. I knew several guys who lived in the ritzy community and my Monday-through-Friday solution for getting to work was to bum an after school ride from one of them. None of them were particularly excited about giving me a lift, so each day, during last period I'd obsess about finding a ride like it was a prom date: *I don't want to ask Brian because people have told me he's ridiculed me for being a beggar. Maybe I'll ask Brad. Except Brad gave me a ride yesterday and I don't want to wear out my welcome. I sure the hell won't ask Bart again. Him and his stupid rule against people sitting in the back seat of his Firebird. Besides, when he's in a bad mood Bart says "no" without even giving me the dignity of an excuse. He's so arrogant. Yeah, Bart is Glen Ballard without the compassion.*

As a last resort, I'd hang out in the parking lot after school and stalk a "Hide-A-Way boy" as he walked toward his car. I always managed to find someone willing to help, even if not enthusiastically. I never failed to heed the advice from the lady on the bus: I always let my driver know how grateful I was for these favors that made my life manageable. "Thanks insert-name-here, because of you, I'll have a chance to eat dinner before I start work." But these weren't mature adults whose hearts warmed at the chance to help someone; they were sixteen-year-old, image-conscious

Hide-A-Way kids with Z-28s and new pickup trucks; and to most of them, I was an accessory that didn't go well with their mag wheels. After a couple of paydays, I remembered another lesson the lady on the bus taught me. "Money is a tool." I started giving two dollars for each lift. Soon, guys were approaching me in school. "Hey Rich, you need a ride today?"

Brad had helped me out a handful of times before I rolled out my pay-for-ride program. When he dropped me off after a ride one day, in a generous mood, I gave him five bucks for not being such a smug ass back in my begging days. A few days later, a Johnny-come-lately to the ride game muscled in on the action. "Let me take you today, Rich." After we arrived at the club, I gave him two dollars and thanked him. He appeared offended. "Two bucks? That's it? I heard you was givin' five."

Paying for a ride not only helped me get one, but just like in the school lunch line in years past, I could again afford the price of dignity. My long hours and reduced rent meant suddenly I was the guy with money. Spoiled kids who lived in big lake houses and drove expensive cars begged me for my business. Within the dynamic of these transactions I was somehow equal. *Money is a tool.*

Getting home from work was not as easy. Finding someone to take a few dollars to let me ride with them to someplace they were headed anyway was one thing, but there was no parking lot full of kids at the country club heading toward downtown Lindale at midnight. I was lucky to have a friend, Kenneth, who worked as a waiter at the club. On the two or three nights a week Kenneth worked, he'd always offer to drive me home. As a waiter, Kenneth was done with his shift more than an hour before I completed the closing duties of a suds buster. But he'd wait on me anyway, knowing how much that ride meant to me. Sometimes he'd sit in the empty dining room studying. Other nights, he'd even help me mop floors and take out trash, even though he was off the clock. Sometime around midnight, my work was done.

On nights Kenneth didn't work, I ran home. I considered it not only transportation but also training, and I could do the seven miles wearing smelly, food-soaked jeans in under an hour. I hoped the roadwork would pay off when track season arrived. But the runs were unnerving, spooky. The chirp of insects screamed into my head and bounced around inside it. Wind whistled through the pines and oaks and swayed their branches, giving them breath and mobility to morph into slow-moving monsters whose nighttime charter was to obscure the howling creatures among them. *Probably just dogs. Do dogs howl like that?* Every so often, a car passed. The tire hum and engine purr brought a camaraderie between me and the driver— a moment of comfort. *I am not alone. Aren't wolves afraid of cars?* I tried to block the eeriness out, visualizing myself running in the district meet, sitting on Edward Anderson's heels and then kicking past one of the state's top distance runner on the home stretch. As I ran the dark country roads, the dream of beating the three-time district champ, a track scholarship, and the prospect of being eaten by a pack of wolves, kept my mind occupied and my body moving swiftly.

At one a.m., I approached Joe Pool Park, my symbolic gateway to town. Turning off the Farm-to-Market road onto a residential street, with less than a half a mile to go, this was where I usually lengthened my stride and picked up the pace. I loved that last stretch. Rows of houses marked my return to civilization and light from their porches alleviated my concerns about unseen potholes or snakes. *Almost home. Tonight will not be the night I have to fight off a pack of wolves.* I moved like fluid through the night. I was six miles into the run, which didn't begin until after sixteen consecutive hours of school and work, yet I felt strong and fresh. I had the endurance of youth. *I am fast tonight. Real fast. I can feel it.*

I heard a car approach from behind, but it wouldn't pass, the driver choosing to birddog me instead. *Sure, I'm running fast, but not faster than a car should be moving.* I glanced over my shoulder. It was a cop car. I hadn't done anything wrong, the lights weren't on, so I turned my head forward and kept running. The siren wailed as the police car pulled past me, then stopped. The door opened. The car was enveloped inside a blinding white light. The light spoke to me through a bullhorn.

"Freeze!" *The voice of utter authority.*

I stopped in my tracks. Exhausted, I bent forward and put my hands on my knees.

"Get your hands above your head, where I can see them."

"Okay," I shouted, throwing my trembling arms obediently toward the moon.

A light within a light moved toward me. The cop was holding a flashlight with one hand, his other ready to draw his pistol—a gunfighter at *OK Corral*. He approached cautiously.

"Don't move."

I'm not.

"I SAID DON'T MOVE!"

"I'm not moving, sir."

A spotlight shined from his car. His flashlight shined in my face. *Lights, lights, what's with all the lights?*

"Where are you going?"

Instinctively, I brought my hands down to speak.

The chubby, baby-face cop freaked out, screaming like a drill sergeant. "I SAID GET THOSE HANDS ABOVE YOUR HEAD, OR I'LL TAKE YOU DOWN!" His voice cracked. *Jesus, what's with this guy? Is he afraid of me?*

He patted me down.

"Where you going?" I sensed his tension recede slightly after he found me unarmed.

"I'm going home, sir."

"You can bring your hands down now. You got any ID?"

"No, sir."

"What's your name?"

A simple question for most, but not for me.

When I was born, I was given my father's first and last name, Richard Ochoa. My mother didn't like the last name of the man who abducted me, so when she enrolled me in kindergarten, she tagged me with the last name of her husband, Schnabl. With a few signatures on school registration forms, she had wiped out my real name. There were no adoption papers or other documentation that connected me to the child attending school as *Richard Schnabl*.

Once school records established me as Richard Schnabl, she used those as my identification for everything else. Wherever I went, new schools, doctors, libraries, the fabricated last name followed me without legal basis. Although she never hid from me that Carl Schnabl was not my real father, I never questioned why I carried his name, until one day in driver's ed. "Alright, a couple people still owe me birth certificates," Coach Johnson said. Without laying eyes on what was inside, I walked up and presented a large brown document envelope that my mother had given me.

Coach Johnson pinched the silver clasps on the envelope together, folded the flap back and pulled out a document and examined it for a moment. He chuckled and shook his head. "Schnabl...What's this?"

I gave him a stupid look. He thought I was up to my usual pranks. I thought he was up to his usual good-natured ribbing of me.

"You're already late turning this in; you need to take this seriously." He showed the document to the other instructor. "Do you have a birth certificate, Schnabl?"

Well, if they're not looking at my birth certificate, what are they looking at? What's my mother done now?

"What's wrong?" I asked.

They showed me a certificate of birth for *Richard Ochoa.* "Who is Richard Oca?"

"I don't know." That's all I could say. I know *who* he was. I just didn't know *why* he still was.

The class thought this funny, cracking up in appreciation of what they thought was my latest stunt. The instructors didn't know what to do with me. *Who am I?*

That night, I approached my mother as she and Doug sat on the swing on the wooden back porch, sipping on their drinks. *I hope I'm early enough.* "Mom, do you have any adoption papers on me?

"What are you talking about, Richard?" *Damn, she's drunk as ten Indians. And defensive.*

"To get my learner's permit, I need proof of my last name."

"You tell them twelve years of school records should be good enough."

Mad at me, mad at the school, mad at the man, just mad. "Mom, what's my legal last name?"

"What do you want it to be?"

I am bothering her with life. Have another drink, Mom; I'll just handle this on my own.

I used *Ochoa* for my license and social security card, while continuing to go by *Schnabl* at school. I was two people.

When we moved to North Carolina during my junior year, I saw an ideal opportunity to use my birth name. But Mom had other plans. We were buying a family business in a small town. According to her, we could avoid explanations and gossip if we mismatched kids, Ginger and I, each converted to her current husband's last name. Instead of three different last names, all four of us were *Hansons*.

Somehow, she convinced another school district to enroll us with a contrived name. My North Carolina name became *Rich Hanson*. Not accustomed to responding to *Hanson*. Teachers and classmates probably thought I was retarded or deaf as they tried to get my attention. "Hanson? Hanson? Rich?"

"Huh? What? Oh…I'm sorry. I'm not used to…nevermind."

When I returned to Lindale for my senior year, I spent fifteen minutes in the principal's office explaining my name changes and convincing him the transcript showing Richard Hanson's school records in North Carolina was actually mine. I didn't want to go on being three people. Tired of being subjected to my mother's whims for last names for me to use, I asked to be registered for my senior year under my given, legal, birth name.

"You're a minor, Rich. You'll have to get one of your parents sign to change your name," the principal said.

"That's my point. I don't want to change my name, Mr. Caldwell; I just wanna start using the right one."

"Well, then one of them will have to come up here and sign papers."

He had no idea how preposterous that suggestion was.

"Can I do it when I turn eighteen?"

"Yes."

Thanks for your help, you idiot. When my birthday comes, I'll prove I'm eighteen by presenting my birth certificate, which says I'm Richard Ochoa, so I can change my name to Richard Ochoa.

So, I re-enrolled in school as *Schnabl*, which I changed to *Ochoa* on my eighteenth birthday. For you baseball fans keeping score at home, it sounds like the official scoring of a baserunner caught in a rundown: That's Ochoa to Schanbl to Hanson to Schnabl to Ochoa.

The town and school papers referred to me as Richard Ochoa-Schnabl. My classmates never stopped calling me *Schnabl* so; if you ever find yourself in a social setting with someone from Lindale, ask them about Rich Schnabl, not Rich Ochoa.

With Barney Fife contemplating whether or not he should shoot me for not having ID, I tried to figure out the right answer to his question, "What is your name?"

First I gave my legal name. Then I considered that no one in town knew me by *Ochoa*. So I mentioned my "Lindale name." Lindale was a small town and I thought my unusual name, *Schnabl*, might gain the officer's recognition. It did not.

"What's your address, young man?"

"Uhm…actually, I don't know what my address is, but I live in that house between T-Macs and Dr. Kinsey's house."

"Ain't that Howell Real Estate?"

"Yes, but—"

"How old are you?"

Finally, a question I could answer. "Seventeen."

"I'm gonna take you home and speak to your parents."

Yeah, well we got a helluva drive ahead of us, mister.

"Sir, my parents don't live here."

"What do you mean, they don't live here?" The cop acted like he doubted me. I knew I wasn't coming off as credible. *This kid has no ID, changed his mind about what his name is, claims he's a seventeen-year-old high-school student with no family in town, and he's running from work to a real estate office, at one a.m.?* He had me sit in the back of his patrol car while he sat in the front, talking police lingo over his radio to his boss or somebody who might tell him what to do with a kid who didn't know his name.

The parallels between my legal predicament and the state of my life struck me as profound. I had no ID, no proof to the world who I was—even *that* I was. My credentials—a learner's permit issued by the state of Texas—had long ago been reduced to a collection of meaningless paper crumbs after a cycle in the washing machine. I am a ghost, dropped into a little town of families, trying to fit in, trying to achieve status as a viable human.

The Lindale cop asked a question I didn't want to answer. "What's your parent's phone number?"

Which parent? My mother and father are divorced. No, don't explain that mess.

I didn't want a cop calling my mother in North Carolina or my father in Idaho in the middle of the night to tell them their son was being arrested for running. "I don't know their number, sir." I followed that with the bold move of asking the cop a question, but I did so in the most respectful way I knew. "Sir, would you mind telling me what I've done wrong?" This was not a wise approach.

"You talk back to me one more time and I'll have CPS down here so fast your head'll spin. You hearing me son? I'm investigating you for curfew violation and vagrancy. You could be fined up to one thousand dollars and spend six months in jail. And that's just for starters. Do you understand what I'm telling you?"

Let's see, one-thousand dollars is three hundred hours of washing dishes...

"Yes sir." I didn't know who CPS was, but they sounded like some bad-ass sonofabitches I didn't want any part of. Six months in jail? I was scared. *What if this guy locks me up and throws away the key?* I thought about the bus pervert, Mike, how hardened he was. Was that my destiny? What if this cop puts me in a cell with somebody who'll kill me if I don't give him head? Was I gonna have to *kill or be killed*?

"Before I can release you son, I haveta verify you are who you say you are, and you ain't *wanted*."

Wanted? I'd seen those posters at the Lindale post office:
Wanted
For running in the middle of the night
Richard Ochoa-Schnabl
Do not approach him. Police say he is as fast as Edward Anderson and considered extremely dangerous.
Beware: he smells like spoiled meat.

"Is there any adult in town who can vouch for your identity?"

I imagined Brother Sal Ahmey after being awakened in the middle of the night by a phone call from the Lindale Police. He might go downstairs, pull Jim out of bed and beat the hell out of him for having such a dumbass friend. I might be better off risking an ass kicking from these mysterious CPS operatives than face Brother Sal Ahmey.

"Sir, I live in a room that Bob Staton and Gary Camp rent to me, but I really hope you don't have to call them at this hour."

"Bob Staton? Bob Staton can vouch for you?" The officer seemed impressed, maybe even awed. *Bob Staton.* It appeared I'd said the magic word.

"Yessir, Bob kinda takes care of me."

The officer got back on the radio.

"Our runner here says he rents a room at Howell Reality from Bob Staton."

The voice on the other side crackled through. "Yeah? Bob told me he rents that room out to a high school kid; does the kid have a key to the place?" *A key, yes I have a key, they hold up just fine in washers and dryers.*

The cop drove me to my room. I opened the door with the one thing that was always in my pocket—my key. I was free. I wouldn't have to give anyone head tonight.

Exhausted, I fell asleep with my smelly clothes on. I woke up in the morning smelling like a dishpit. In the absence of hot water, which was not an amenity at my place, I wiped down my entire body with a cold, damp towel, and then went to my closet to find something to wear.

I had no clean pants, underwear, or socks. I found one shirt that I'd handwashed in my usual method; in the bathroom sink with cold water and a bar of soap. It had large grease stains on the bottom front. It was my "last-resort" shirt because I had to wear it tucked it inside my pants to hide the stains, a style which I did not particularly like, nor was fashionable in 1981. Most of my shirts had smaller food stains, grease spots, rips, or some kind of mar. Since I worked in the same clothes I wore to school, I just accepted this as an occupational hazard. My clothes might stop me from getting a girlfriend, but they weren't going to keep me from graduating.

I rifled though the cardboard box in which I kept my dirty clothes. I found a pair of underwear without skid marks and took a whiff. They smelled like ass. *I'll be going commando today.* I sniffed a succession of dirty socks. They reeked. I decided to go sockless as well. *It's time to do some laundry.* A pair of dirty jeans in the box were slightly cleaner and far less stinky than the ones I'd slept in. I slipped them on and grabbed the stained, but smell-free (at least to me) shirt.

I put the jeans on, zipped carefully, pulled the shirt over my head, and laced up my New Balance running shoes, which were closer to gray than their original white. I was ready for school.

***

It was so dark on those runs home that sometimes I could barely see the road surface. One night, half way between work and home, I stepped into a pothole with my surgically repaired ankle. Falling into the darkness of the night, I was unable to brace myself for the fall.

The next thing I processed was a man's voice with an extreme Texan accent.

"Awlright, he's movin. I told you he's alive. Hey, man, what happened ta you? Kin you hear me? What was you doin' in the road man?"

My mind slowly focused, and I realized the faint questions I just heard were directed toward me.

I sat up in the grass and squinted toward two figures standing above me in the darkness. I put my hand to my head. I felt a bump, like half a golf ball under my skin. *Oh, fuck, my brains are coming out.* Awareness was slow in arriving. *Why am I lying in the grass on the side of the road?*

"Shit, I thought I done run you over with my rig. You was laying right in the middle of the goddamn road. I thought you was roadkill. I thought for sure I hit your ass."

Finally, I managed to ask the trucker to clarify. After nearly running me over with his eighteen-wheeler, he stopped his rig and pulled me off the road onto the grass. He was with a woman, but she didn't speak, apparently content in allowing him to act as historian.

The trucker offered to take me to the hospital, but I insisted I was okay. "Do you think you guys could give me a ride into Lindale?"

The three of us got into the truck. *That's one way to get a ride.* I listened to the driver babble about how he ain't never seen this kind of shit before.

"Man...I'm telling you, I damned near ran you over with my truck. It's a goddamn miracle that you's alive."

A *GODDAMN MIRACLE*? I laughed at his choice of words and wondered if he was smart enough to use blasphemous irony on purpose or if he just lucked into saying the funniest thing I'd heard all day.

Mister, I live this shit every day.

The trucker was impressed I had my own place. I asked him to pull his rig into the T-Macs gas station parking lot, which was right next to my room. We shared the obligatory unifying handshake of the times; not the nice-to-meet-you business handshake, but the you-and-me-are-in-this-shit-together handshake, which begins with your fingers pointed skyward and your thumb pointed back toward your own face, and progresses to the mutual wrapping of your partner's thumb in your own palm and fore-finger—a bond which is maintained through a few tugs.

I got out of his rig and hobbled toward my room on my sore ankle. *He may be an uneducated truck driver, but that man may have just saved my life.*

I wondered what he and his mute girlfriend were thinking as they watched me limp away. *That poor sonofabitch, he don't got no sense and no parents, but at least he's alive.*

My Wheels are Coming Off

Clearly, I needed more efficient transportation than my two legs, something that could get me to work and back for the next eight months. One of the kids I often paid for rides, Brett, told me he'd give me a good deal on his '69 Ford Pickup, which still ran. The truck had a jury-rigged three-speed-on-the-floor shift kit that wouldn't engage in either first or reverse. On my test drive, Brett showed me how to use creative clutch pumping to circumvent the need for first gear.

I gave Brett two hundred dollars; in return, I got only the truck. No title, registration, or bill of sale, just the truck, which in terms of public safety, was not fit enough to drive to the junkyard. It had an expired inspection sticker and registration, mushy brakes, dead battery, and prickly little wires sticking out from bald tires. The vehicle's condition, combined with its driver, an inexperienced, uninsured, unlicensed seventeen year old with no repair money, made me the proud owner of the most effective deathtrap in town.

After a week of parking downgrade with no obstructions in front of the truck, which enabled me to push, coast, and pop the clutch, I could finally afford a battery. The brakes would begin responding only after several pumps to the floorboard. Even then, they managed only gradual stops. Brett loved tweaking the carburetor, which probably explained why the truck smelled like a gas pump. I considered these factors and compared them to the alternatives of running home from work, being mistaken for road kill, eaten by wolves, and harassed by the police. I was determined to drive this truck until the wheels fell off.

I couldn't afford a mechanic, but I heard the high school autoshop class was looking for vehicles to work on, and their labor was free. I drove the heap to the school's garage. Mr. Seaver, the automechanics teacher, told me he'd check out the brakes.

Later, I went by the shop to talk with him. "You got no brake pads left. You need new rotors and a master cylinder, too. You got metal on metal and not 'nuff pressure to stop."

No brake pads left? *Were they stolen?*

Metal on metal? *Is that bad?*

"How much will that cost?"

Mr. Seaver spit tobacco juice into a Folgers coffee can. "'Bout three-fifty."

I was hoping it'd be less than the fifty bucks I had. "Can I get away with replacing just one of the parts?"

"Nope."

"So...if we just replace the brake pads and add some brake fluid, that won't help?"

Mr. Seaver spit more tobacco juice in the can. "Nope."

I wasn't about to spend more on brakes than I'd spent on the truck, so I drove it to work even more gingerly than before. On my late night drive home, nearing the place where I'd been almost dismissed as roadkill two weeks before, I felt a sudden and extreme oscillation in the steering. I took my foot off the gas hoping to gain stability. The more I slowed, the more the steering wheel wobbled. I watched in bewilderment as a runaway tire did an impression of an impatient motorist, passing my truck as it rolled down the centerline. *Wow, where did that thing come from? Did I hit that tire?*

The wheel veered left and disappeared into the glare of oncoming headlights. Next, my windshield shattered in sync with a crash. My truck shook. Shards of glass landed on my lap, the rearview mirror glanced off my right thigh. It felt like an accident, but I was still coasting forward. *Did some punk throw a rock at me?* I pumped the brake pedal, downshifted to second to assist my brakes, and pulled onto the grassy shoulder of the back road. My truck came to a stop and dipped forward slightly. After gently recoiling, it kept going, tilting back and to the left, made a thud, and shifted me into the driver's side door.

I got out and inspected the bizarre scene. My whole wheel was gone—as in missing. Not there. The truck rested on its left rear hub, the five lug bolts reduced to sheared and mangled fingers. Admittedly, I didn't know a lot about cars, but I didn't need an automechanics class to deduce that the tire making an illegal pass across a double yellow line was the one missing from my truck. *Where the hell did that tire go?* When I last saw it, it was passing me, heading toward an oncoming car. I started looking for my wheel and pondering my shattered windshield.

My hypothesis was confirmed when I found my tire in a ditch a long way behind my truck. Rubbing my hands around the bald circumference, I felt small glass pebbles. My liberated tire had rebounded off the front of the oncoming car and landed on my windshield. Most people go their whole driving lives without ever breaking their own windshield. I had shattered two before my eighteenth birthday.

What do I do now? The brakes were going to get someone killed. The truck would have to be towed to someone who could fix the broken lugs and windshield before even addressing all the other problems. Seaver's boys up at the school weren't part of the solution. They were the ones who hadn't tightened the lug nuts. *This vehicle isn't worth the money it'd take to tow it.* I had literally driven this truck until the wheels fell off. *It's time to cut your losses.* I left the key in the ignition, the door unlocked, and started running home, abandoning Brett Garland's truck on the side of the road.

One of Us Needs a Car

When an opening came up, I gave Robbie the inside track on a busboy job at the Lodge. He didn't have a car either, so now we both had transportation problems. Gary had a friend in the used-car business in Tyler, so he sent Robbie and me to see him. By now, I was back up to three hundred dollars in savings and had turned eighteen. I had everything I needed to make my first deal. The salesman, Steve, had only a few cars that appealed to me. I was intrigued by a gigantic, eight-year-old Oldsmobile Delta 88. It had sparkling silver paint, burgundy crushed velvet interior, and spoked rims. The rear fenders seemed to stretch forever. The seats were immense and their velour texture so comfortable, that one could easily sleep on them, which, given my situation, was always a possibility. Steve was asking two grand, but since we were friends of Gary and all, he'd take my three hundred down and let me make monthly payments over two years. Robbie promised he'd pay for the gas we needed if I would loan him the car occasionally. My first legally binding contract obligated me to pay thirty-six hundred dollars over two years for a car with a sales price of two thousand dollars. I drove the car off the lot thinking I had pulled one over on Gary's buddy. *Such a big car for only three hundred dollars and a promise; I hope Gary won't be mad at me for screwing his buddy over like that.*

I drove back to Lindale while Robbie followed behind in Gary's borrowed car. *Two months ago, I was a human clothesline, walking this same highway toward nothing but a town and some friends. Now, I'm driving my car to my own place.* I was proud of myself. *I bet Gary's gonna be proud of me, too.*

Robbie and I couldn't wait to show him the car. When we brought the pimpmobile back to my room (his office), he couldn't stop laughing. "Boys, this is a real pimp-mobile." Convinced Robbie and I were playing a well-orchestrated gag, he kept asking who the car belonged to. He rattled off a list of every black friend I had, confident that eventually he would guess the identity of the true owner. He circled the car several times kicking the tires. "You guys crack me up; this is a good one." *I knew it. I knew he'd be impressed. He can't believe it either. I got me a nice Oldsmobile, just like you, Gary.*

I opened the driver's door and invited him to sit behind the wheel. He sat in the driver's seat, caressing the soft, velvety seats and shaking his head. *Yeah, nice seats, huh, Gary?* The three of us were all laughing. For me and Robbie, it was a we-hit-the-lottery laugh. To Gary, it was a these-clowns-are-a-couple-of-screwballs laugh.

"You guys are telling me Steve sold you this car?"

"Yes, it's my car," I said proudly.

"Show me the contract."

I opened the glove box and presented the papers to him.

He examined the contract. The moment he realized we weren't putting him on, his demeanor changed. His reaction surprised me. "I can't believe you did this! Two thousand for this monstrosity? Twenty-seven percent interest? He charged you twenty-seven percent interest? Why did you buy a car at twenty-seven percent interest?"

My euphoria was fading. "You're saying that's bad? You said he'd give us a good deal."

Gary's opinion meant a lot to me. Though he was only seven years older and I'd known him only a short time, he was my surrogate father.

"You can't pay for this, Rich."

"Why not?"

"Because I'm an accountant and I said so. I thought you guys said Robbie was gonna buy the car. He doesn't have to pay rent. He might could afford a payment."

"Well, he didn't like any of those cars."

"Really?" He turned toward Robbie. "Didn't you try to talk him out of this?" Translation: "We both know Rich is a dumbass, but I thought you knew better."

Robbie could barely get the words out between his laughs. "I told him, Gary…I told him."

Gary persuaded us to let him try and fix the deal. We went into his office and called Steve on the speakerphone. Gary chewed him out for putting me in such a ridiculous vehicle at a high price and an absurd interest rate. In typical used-car salesman fashion, Steve defended the deal. "Hey Gary, them boys picked that car out on their own. And on the interest rate, this is an eighteen year old making minimum wage with no credit."

"You can do better than twenty-seven percent, Steve."

"You wanna co-sign, Gary?"

Gary looked at us. "Can y'all step outside for a minute?" We went outside and sat in my new-used car—my car that I was about to lose.

Gary called us back into his office. "Steve agreed to tear up the contract if one of you buys a more practical car from him. He'll drop the interest rate to eighteen percent. He said there was a little red Pontiac Robbie liked."

Robbie ended up buying a Pontiac Astre. Gary approved of both the car and the contract. Even though I missed that giant Olds, I was thankful I had Gary looking out for me. He was filling the void in my life that Coach Davis left. Robbie's new car and his willingness to work almost every night meant my days of running home in the dark were over just in time to avoid the cold weather.

Okay, the car was big, the interest rate was a little high, but surely Gary liked the car itself. He probably just didn't think it was the right car for me for that price and that interest rate. He probably was just saying the car was too big. I looked up *monstrosity* in the dictionary at the school library.

Monstrosity – An object that is very unpleasant or frightening to look at, often because it is large and strangely shaped.

I guess Gary didn't like the car.

Squeal Like a Pig

I was halfway through my senior year, feeding myself, paying rent, going to school every day. Then, one night at the restaurant I decided to play a little gag on Kenneth. The waiters had small, wooden cubby holes above a drink counter in which they stored incidental items: pens, name tags, keys, etc. After finishing my closing chores, I noticed a pad of blank guest checks in Kenneth's slot. I grabbed the pad, flipped a few sheets over the top-binding and doodled a cartoon likeness of him engaged in a sexual act with a pig. For good measure I added dialog boxes filled with clever remarks.

I expected after using the top guest checks, Kenneth would approach a customer's table, pull out his tablet, look down, see my artwork and giggle. It didn't work out that way.

Just after I clocked in the following Monday, my manager, Suzane, appeared in the kitchen with a scowl on her face, making a come-here movement with her forefinger. Parents, teachers, neighbors, coaches, bosses, police—I spent my life in trouble with authority, so as I followed her across the dining room, down the spiral staircase to an office adjacent to the empty banquet hall, I sensed she wasn't going through all this trouble to tell me she'd noticed how clean my dishes were. I formed a mental list of things I could be in trouble for. *I bet someone saw me throwing the rubber kitchen floormats off the back door balcony into the country club swimming pool.* This was a little shortcut I'd invented to clean the mats without spraying and scrubbing them. *Maybe one of the waitresses saw me nursing from the nozzle of the Redi-Whip can at the pie pantry. Shit, I hope I'm not gonna get fired.*

I take a seat in front of Suzane's desk. Eighteen-years-old, on my own, and I feel like I'm in the elementary school principal's office again. What have I done now? *Last week Natalie let me feel her titties in the food pantry. But she seemed to like it. She wouldn't tell. Would she?*

Naw, Natalie's cool. It can't be that.

Whatever it is, I'll humbly apologize, and then go join my co-workers who are upstairs starting dinner.

Suzane spoke. "Rich, do you know about the Sunday buffet?"

"Yes ma'am." I didn't work on Sundays, but knew there was a spread for the after-church crowd.

"Well...when our customers check out, we ask them to write their account numbers on blank guest checks."

Thank God, this isn't about the floormats.

"And one sweet old lady found this." She slid my own artwork across the desk toward me.

Shit. Somehow the pad in Kenneth's storage slot made its way to the buffet line.

"You can't do this kind of shit, Rich. For Christsakes, what the hell were you thinking? I tried to tell my boss you're a good worker, but the customer demanded you be fired and my boss agreed."

"But…it was an accident, Suzane. Just a joke. I didn't mean—" My voice trembled. I paused for a moment to regroup. "Can I…talk to her? I need this job, Suzane."

"No, sorry."

Tears welled. I begged like a six year old trying to get ungrounded. "I won't do it again. Please. This job is the only thing I have. I have to pay rent. Can I apologize to the lady?"

"No, it's time for you to go. We'll mail you your last check. I've told Robbie he can drive you home. I hope you've learned something from this."

Learned something? Yeah, I learned something.

This was the heart of the Bible Belt—the capital of self righteousness and the county seat of hypocrisy—where the most foul-mouthed woman I'd ever known could tell me a lewd joke that planted the seed for the doodled image in my head in the first place, then fire her hardest working hand for obscenity because an old lady (probably racist to the core like so many of those Hide-A-Way snobs) demanded it as retribution for her being exposed to something so trivial. That's what I learned.

Work was hard to come by in the little town of Lindale. With five months until graduation, I had no money and no job. I checked with every business in town, but stores and restaurants were family run, and those places hired family members and friends. When rent was due, I confessed to Bob Staton that I'd been fired and had no money. I knew he had compassion; he and Gary weren't gonna kick me out, but Bob was also a businessman, and having a tenant who doesn't pay rent isn't very good business. He put me to work painting houses and mowing yards. Bob was both a shrewd businessman and a teacher of life, so I worked in exchange for rent and nothing else. Food was not part of this deal, and now, I had no money coming in—Zero.

My grandmother was the only contact I maintained with either side of my family. She was waitressing at my mother's restaurant in North Carolina. When I finally confessed to her I lost my job, she started sending money. Every Monday, ten dollars, like clockwork. *Thank you, Grandma. Thank you.* I wasn't too skilled at grocery shopping though; instead of buying enough beans, rice, and spam to last all week, I'd eat at Dairy Queen or the fried chicken place.

Grandma's money was good for about three meals a week. Even though Gary was upset with me for getting fired, once a week or so, he had me to his house for dinner. His wife, Susan seemed genuinely pleased to feed me. Sometimes she had me bring my laundry, and she'd wash a load while we ate. Come to think of it, Gary always called Susan before he left the office, so I'm pretty sure the dinners were as much Susan's doing as Gary's.

On the nights I wasn't working for Bob, I made certain to hang around when Gary left his office around five. Sitting in my room with my door open to the hall, I'd hear Gary hang up the phone and gather his things in the office. The floors creaked as he walked down the hall toward both my room and the exit. I tried to look weak, pathetic, like I was starving. *Please stop. Please stop and ask me over to eat.* Sometimes he would. *Thank you, Gary. Thank God for you.* Other times he didn't break stride, pretending not to notice how pitiful I looked. "See ya," his voice trailed off as he passed.

Gary kept the fridge in the kitchen, which served as a breakroom for all tenants, stocked with Cokes. When I didn't have dinner, I drank one or two Cokes. Then I'd go on a long training run fueled by thirty nine grams of sugar. Then I opened the fridge one night and saw a ceramic coffee mug sitting on the bottom rack in front of the drink cans. Taped to the outside of the cup was a note that read, "Cokes 30 cents". There was already 60 cents in the cup, either staged by Gary or the result of two legitimate sales to real estate agents. I grabbed a scrap of paper from Gary's office and wrote an IOU for 30 cents, then helped myself to a Coke. An hour later, after much consternation, I took the change out of the cup, replaced it with another IOU, walked across the street to T-Macs and bought myself a hot dog for dinner. The next time Gary restocked the fridge, he removed the mug and five dollars of IOUs. Mercifully, he never went more than a few days without sodas in the fridge.

One night, there was half a sandwich in clear wrap next to the drinks. Taped to the sandwich was a small piece a paper with my name, *Rich,* scribed in female penmanship. *This is for me! Somebody left me some food.* To anyone else, the sandwich was single slices of bologna and cheese between two pieces of mustard-glazed bread. But to me, it was equal parts food, faith, and hope. In *normal* circumstances, I wouldn't have eaten a sandwich with mustard on it, but I was living in a redefined *normal*. *Maybe, every day an anonymous Good Samaritan will leave me dinner. Maybe tomorrow, it'll be slice of pizza.* Like a castaway on a deserted island stuffing a message into a bottle, I left a note in place of the sandwich.

Thank you very much for the sandwich.
Rich

Over the next several days, I waited to be rescued from hunger. But the mystery sandwich was an aberration. On the nights that followed, each unceremonious opening of the refrigerator door brought a sting of disappointment—a sting somewhere below my eyes and behind my checks that threatened tears. *Grow up you big baby, what about those starving children in Africa who go weeks without eating?*

I was living on Coke, ten bucks a week, free school lunches, and an occasional dinner at the Camps. More than the loss of income, I missed those meals at the lodge. This was my senior year. People always said it would be the most memorable year of my life. And, it certainly would be. Nothing I envisioned about being a senior was happening for me. I had no food, family, income, or girlfriend. The need to work stole football and basketball from my senior year. All I had going for me was a few good friends, the compassion of two men letting me barter for a room, and the upcoming track season.

I trained hard, and was focused on winning district. I got up before school every morning to run. I did my track workouts in the afternoon at the school with the team, and sometimes did another run in the evening. On weekends I'd go to the track to do my own speed workouts. But after losing my job I came to dread the weekends. For two and a half days there were no free school lunches. Since Gary rarely came to his office, there were no dinner invitations either. Weekends meant hunger. One Saturday night, I hadn't eaten a crumb all day. After a long training run, I felt weak and faint. This wasn't my normal kind of tired, this was debilitating. I felt like a ninety-year-old man in need of a wheelchair. On a typical Saturday night, I'd walk two blocks to the pool hall, and watch my friends play video games. Doug Westberry could play Defender for an hour on one quarter. On a good Saturday night he might build up ten lives, get tired of the game and let me finish. But on this night, I was having severe hunger cramps and wasn't interested in anything except eating. I went to bed early, hoping to sleep it off, but my growling stomach wouldn't let me sleep.

For the first time during this whole ordeal I broke down. As I lay there, I began to cry. *Why am I being punished? Why me?* I wasn't always the best-behaved kid, but in many ways I was doing better than some of my classmates. Dope dealers, bullies, abusers, burnouts, and thugs. They were well-fed and some drove around town in sports cars. Their parents didn't abandon them. *What had I done to deserve this?*

I diverted my self-pity into anger—a savage resentment of my mother and father. When I had my job and was eating fancy meals at the lodge, I hadn't needed either one of them, and I had been cocky-proud of that. *To hell with you, Mom and "Hey", I don't need shit from you.* But this night, it was different.

In the absence of food, anger fed me, and it was more palatable than self-pity. If neither of my parents wanted me living with them, that was fine; but they could at least send me a few dollars to ensure I didn't go hungry. In fact, my father had been court-ordered sixteen years before to pay fifteen bucks a week. *I want my fucking money, you deadbeat. I'm hungry!*

I should call him. I should demand to eat, like his other kids.

No, don't bother. He doesn't have any money.

I thought about the day when I would be a grown man with my own family. *When they want to come over and see their grandkids and put on some kinda show like they were regular parents, I'll tell them to kiss my ass. I will never see either of them again.*

Saturday night, with no plan or prospect of food until Monday morning breakfast at school:

"Maybe I'll just go into T-Macs and steal something to eat."

"No, don't do that, you're eighteen now. The police..."

I lay in bed, trying to fall asleep but all I could think of was all the food in the houses around me. Pantries full of pork and beans, cream corn, coconut pies, and peanut butter. I considered knocking on my neighbor's doors to ask for food. But I knew that would frighten people and embarrass myself. I thought about going to the pool hall to try bumming a couple of bucks, but I knew I couldn't pay it back.

There has to be a better way than begging or stealing. Even in my intense hunger, I'd never resorted to those methods. Okay. One could argue that I was stealing Gary's Cokes. I looked across the street at Dairy Queen and tried to dismiss the idea of going to the dumpster in the parking lot. But the thought wouldn't go away. *I could walk over there, just to see if there might be something that's not disgusting...*

I was close to falling asleep when the buzz of a fly filled my room. The noise was more than distracting, it was deafening—like a chain saw. It must've have been flying in a circular pattern right next to my ear. Normally, I'd have jumped out of bed to hunt that fly. Maybe convert it from a fly to an oozing blob of yellow guts with a rolled up Sports Illustrated. Or, I might try to snatch it out of midair with my bare hand and then fastball it into the sink basin. But tonight, tonight I am like a lethargic cow lying in bed, exerting the least possible energy required to successfully shoo the fly when it stops to walk on my ear. I have no energy to compete. I have no energy to get out of bed and I'm, in fact, a bit afraid of even trying to do so because I'm not even sure I can. Above its maddening buzz, the fly delivers a more resounding message:

"Eating from a dumpster? You are no different than me. You are at bottom."

Thank you fly, for delivering this message.

As I walked across the street, I promised myself I'd never tell anyone what I was about to do. *If I don't tell anyone it will be like it never happened.* I smelled the rotten trash. I pinched my nose so the stink would stop. *That shit I smell—I'm not gonna eat that. The stuff on top is probably pretty fresh.*

I couldn't reach anything while standing outside, so I jumped in and ripped into a trash bag that was on top. Although the outside of the dumpster was illuminated by a street light, the inside was too dark to see. I saw trash bags, but after ripping one open while I was inside the dumpster, I couldn't see what I was sifting through. I grabbed two bags and heaved them out of the metal bin. I almost threw up as I climbed out. I dragged the bags away from the smell and toward a parking lot light. Although I was behind Dairy Queen, I could see cars passing on Highway 69. I saw people walking on the other end of the parking lot. *What if someone from school comes out and sees me going through the trash?* I ripped into the first bag and dumped most of the contents onto the asphalt. I scattered the packaging, cups, and plastic utensils, melted ice cream, and picked out the crust of a grilled cheese sandwich, a few French fries still in their original bag, a couple of half-eaten chicken fingers, and a third of a soggy chicken fried steak saturated with cold white gravy.

I wanted to sprint back home, but I couldn't risk being seen running across the main drag of Lindale with my hands cupped together holding scraps of food. I had to get further from the dumpster before I could eat this stuff. So I carried my dinner to a remote end of an adjacent parking lot, obscured from the highway by another building. I was hidden. I wolfed the stuff down in about a minute, gagging while wondering whose food this was. Thoughts of my classmates walking through the halls rolled into visions of them throwing away their food inside the DQ. Any one of them could unwittingly be my benefactor tonight. I could be eating some cheerleader's leftovers or Coach Robinson's (ok, probably Coach Robinson never had leftovers). I'd have no way of ever knowing, and it would change the way I viewed my classmates. How can one possibly ask a girl to the prom when he's surviving on her table scraps? I ate as fast as I could, not only because I was starving, but also because I wanted to get the hell out of there, without being seen. I ate so fast it felt like I had a chicken fried steak patty wedged sideways in my throat as I ran across the street back to my room.

How ironic, that not long ago my mother bragged to me that her insight and preparedness for the next depression would keep our family from joining the masses eating out of dumpsters. But there was no line to get into Dairy Queen's trash bin.

Repulsed, I washed my hands and rinsed my mouth out, glad that the food was already in my stomach, where I couldn't smell it. I chased the dumpster dinner with a can of Gary's Coca-Cola.

Back in bed, I remembered something I'd seen in my early teens, while on vacation in San Francisco with my grandparents. Homeless people everywhere. The first ones I'd ever seen. Several ate food from trashcans on Fisherman's Wharf. I recalled also, the pity my brain tagged to those to images. *How sad. Don't those people have anyone? How could someone not have anyone?* We ate fudge on a park bench at the piers and watched tourists toss their uneaten food down into the water to a group of seals. I couldn't resolve the juxtaposition of people throwing food into the bay while others ate scraps off the street right behind their backs.

My hunger remedied, I lay in my bed contemplating the parallelism between me and those vagrants on the wharf. *This may be who I am right now, but this is not who I will be.*

Tuna and Potato Chips

One night, Robbie knocked on my door at one in the morning. He held a bulging industrial trashbag. "I got something, man." He came in and dumped twenty cans of tuna and ten bags of *Lay's* potato chips on my floor. "Charity for the poor," he said, laughing.

What the hell?

"Hold on; there's more." He went back out to his car and came in with a bulkier hefty bag, slung over his shoulder, Santa style. More food: a box of saltine crackers, tuna, a six pack of Coke (yes, Coke), tuna, a box of chocolate cake mix (?), a gallon of milk, and more tuna—*Starkist*. "Charity more, charity more for the poor," he laughed.

I repeated his silly rhyme. "Charity for the poor, charity more…"

At the club, Robbie had taken two trash bags to the pantry and filled them with food. Then he carried them out to the dumpster as if he were taking out the trash. After the guard came and locked up the building, he drove away and circled back to retrieve the sack. Food—it was that easy. During his next shift, he borrowed a can opener so that I could open the tuna. How ironic, I'd graduated from eating scraps out of the dumpster to eating stolen food that had passed through a dumpster on its way to me.

Soon after the tuna and potato chip heist, Robbie was able to leverage his mother's friendship with a shift manager at Dairy Queen to get on as a cook there. It was a job for which I'd already been rejected. *It pays to know people in high places.* Right across the street, the DQ would have been perfect for me—a malnourished, high school student living alone, eager to work his ass off for three and a quarter an hour and half-price Hungerbusters and Dilly Bars—but in a town like Lindale, there was no hiding my reason for leaving my last job—fired for bestiality doodlings. On some nights, Robbie was able to sneak food out the back door. He'd call, then I'd run across the street for my dinner. Next to the dumpster I had been eating from was a bag, inside, a cheeseburger, hot, fresh, no bite marks, sometimes with fries. Beef was a nice reprieve from the nightly tuna ritual.

A place to stay, transportation, now food—these needs were met not by my parents but by my friends. In years to come, tuna would carry the stench of loneliness, a reminder of a time when neither of my parents cared if I starved. I wouldn't eat it. Years passed and my response evolved. Tuna became the aroma of perseverance, the taste of self-reliance and a testimony to the power of friendship. Nowadays, lunch at a *Subway* sandwich shop might turn into my personal Thanksgiving: a tuna sandwich, plain Lay's potato chips, and a Coke. Hypnotized by smell, taste, and imagination, I'm transported over space and time, to Lindale, Texas, February 1982. Sitting on the edge of my bed, alone in my room, my breathing heavy, having just completed my training run. Streams of sweat run down my neck and wick into the bib-shaped semicircle of perspiration that had formed under the rim of my T-shirt. I'm listening to *The Little River Band* on my *SoundDesign* stereo while wondering *who* I will become, *what* I will become. I imagine how proud Coach Davis, who's coaching at a nearby school, will be when he reads the Tyler paper and sees his favorite Lindale kid won a gold medal at Blackberry Relays.

I open a can of tuna and contemplate if I'll take a cold-water-only shower or just soak my shirt and wipe myself down. I scoop some meat with a chip like it's dip, reach up and grab a can of Coke off the old dresser, take a big swig to wash down the last of the dry tuna. For dessert, I spoon myself some bitter (Robbie didn't steal sugar) cake batter mixed with milk from a coffee mug. All I can think about is winning my race in front of my hometown, and I know within a few days, I'll get my one chance to make that dream come true. Butterflies form in my stomach. The Blackberry Relays—the single biggest day of my high school life.

The Blackberry Relays

In 1982, visitors coming into town northbound on Highway 69 passed fields of blackberries, peaches, pecans and an old weathered billboard declaring Lindale *Blackberry Capital of The World* and the *Home for Good Country Living*. I felt just a touch of pride each time I passed that old sign, since each spring I picked my share of the town's harvest. Just after the billboard was the obligatory generic green highway sign designating the entrance to town:

Lindale
Population 1631

A glimpse to the right, there was Lindale High School, perched on a hill a quarter of a mile off the main drag, its brown stone exterior panels separated with white rectangular columns. The town's sprawl, dense three blocks along the main drag each direction from THE four-way stop, consisted of the seven-unit Bonny Motel (the town's only lodging option), a café where good ole boys drank coffee, the office of the weekly town rag, Dairy Way convenient store, Dairy Queen, Piggly Wiggly, T-mac's gas station, and First Baptist Church. Just two blocks south of the four-way stop was a house serving multiple purposes as Gary Camp's CPA office, Howell Realty, and the bedroom of a seventeen-year-old high school student who believed he was on his way to the Olympics.

Soon franchise restaurants, supermarkets, home-improvement stores, and master planned communities would sprout up, reducing the old, orange brick buildings, home to the most vibrant and well-respected family-operated businesses in town, into marginal businesses like country knick-knack shops (where one could go to address all of their ceramic rooster needs), second-hand clothes stores (frequented only by parents who were hell-bent on embarrassing their kids by dressing them in their classmate's old clothes), and a Miranda Lambert souvenir shop. Wal-Mart and Lowe's would become the new places to see and be seen, leaving the Lindale of 1982 nothing more than a big wedge of memory in the minds of those of us who remain of that 1631—people now of a *certain age,* old enough to have once wondered why Marlin Perkins was always in the helicopter on Sunday nights, narrating, while his dutiful assistant, Jim, was down on the ground shooting tiny homemade tranquilizer darts at man-eating lions.

To promote its illustrious blackberry heritage, Lindale annually hosted the first east Texas track meet of the season, aptly named *The Blackberry Relays.* The meet represented my only chance to run in front of the hometown during my senior year. Ordinarily, track wasn't a big spectator sport in Lindale. But, with so many local athletes competing in so many divisions, and this being the only track meet hosted in Lindale, most of the student body and much of the town came out for this meet. At the time of my race, the stands would be nearly as full as at a varsity football game.

Early in the day, I pole vaulted twelve feet, good enough for a three-way tie for second place, creating a dilemma with medal provisioning. There were two medals, silver and bronze, but three athletes entitled to silver medals. They solved the issue with a coin flip. Predictably, I was the odd man out, and watched the other competitors walk away with medals. This was devastating; though I tied for second place, I didn't even get a medal to pin on my letter jacket.

It was the statement those medals made that first drove me toward track and field. There was nothing subjective about the sport. You were better than those you beat, and worse than those who beat you—period. In football, the opinion of people like Coach Robinson determined whether or not I even participated in the games, and I hated that about team sports. But in track, there were no coaches making me, with my agile legs and rifle arm, watch from the sideline as BJ repeatedly laid down in the pocket to avoid being hit. In track, if I was better than someone, I had every opportunity to prove it. Stopwatches didn't lie, and that's what I loved about it. At the end, you have an answer: You either win a medal, or you suck. But you don't stand on the sideline fretting about not being given a fair chance.

In junior high, one of my regular chores was to shine all the brass in the house. Mom had about ten pieces—mostly ashtrays spilling over with cigarette butts. After finishing my assignment, I'd gather my track medals and polish them. The smell of *Brasso* still reminds me of the first medal I won—a bronze I tried to make appear gold by shining the flat-black tint off it. The awards became validation—proof that I could beat a lot of people at something—and I studied every line and contour of the medal as I polished it. That runner in graceful stride and muscles rippling: that's me! I don't suck. The medals were like drugs and no matter how many I won, I wanted more, and I wanted gold.

You're mine. For the rest of my life I will have you. One day I will bring you out of a shoebox and you will shine proudly in the eyes of my children as I tell them exactly how you became mine. Then, twenty-five years later, I will do the same for my grandchildren. "Grandpa, show us your medals again," they will say. And seventy years from now, some old fogie who will soon be dying himself, will eulogize me. With tears welled in his eyes and a fond smile of remembrance, he will speak to the huge crowd that has gathered to celebrate my remarkable life: "When he was young, he could run like the wind, and pole vault like Bruce Jenner. At the end of his races, he'd kick past guys like they were standing still..."

The funeral coordinator would close the ceremonies. "...and to prove his life had meaning, his medals from the Blackberry Relays, his days at UCLA, and the Olympics are on display in the reception hall. Please pay your respects by viewing the medals while you're waiting in line for the ham sandwiches and potato salad which will be served following the services."

After the pole vault, I hung around the track all afternoon, watching my friends compete in the prelims while eagerly anticipating not only my race, but also the free dinner.

An intoxicating aroma of roast beef and peach cobbler filled the cafeteria air. I'd left school before lunch to pole vault, so I hadn't eaten all day, and I hadn't eaten well in several days. I was a junkie in need of a fix. I scarfed up all my food and uneaten portions of mashed potatoes, rolls, green beans and desserts from my friend's plates. By the time I left the cafeteria, I'd eaten in excess of two dinners. My gut was about to burst. As I walked back toward the track, I heard a PA announcement. "This is the first call for the Varsity Two-Mile Run."

I stretched on the infield. The high intensity bulbs beaming down from the towers were spotlights shining on me. *All these people are about to see me, Richard Ochoa-Schnabl-Hanson (whatever you wanna name me) take a giant leap toward something big. "I'll never forget watching him run at the Blackberry Relays back in '82," they will say someday. One day, this race will be one of my favorite memories. In a few minutes, I'll be on the victory stand, and all will hear. "The winner of the Two Mile Run, with a new Blackberry Relays record—Rich Ochoa. Then, this will be who I am, not some indigent eating chunks of corny dogs out of the DQ dumpster.*

About twenty runners from seven schools gathered at the starting line on the cold February night. Richard Cooper, my teammate, and one of a handful of guys in east Texas to whom I conceded defeat before the start of a race, was not among the group hopping around, shaking their legs, trying to keep warm as the official assigned lanes. Our relationship had evolved since that night three years earlier, when I nearly heaved him through a window onto a bed of coleslaw. Earlier in the day, I was sitting at my locker, putting a fresh wrap of tape on my pole when he came over.

"Rich, man, the Two (mile) is yours, Bro."

"I'm right behind you, Cuz. (When around black people, I thought it polite to talk like them). One-two, just like we talked about."

"Naw man, I done told coach I wanted to do the Half and the Mile."

"Why'd ya do that? The Two is your best race."

"You're a senior, man. This is your last chance to run in Lindale. I'll take the Mile and the Half; you win the Two. Ain't nan one of us gotta be second tahnight." He smiled and extended his hand for some kinda soul shake.

We did the handshake thing, probably less gracefully than how he was accustomed. "But you gotsta promise me one thing, Bro," he continued.

I was boiling over with excitement. "Anything, Man."

His big-toothed smile spread across his face. "You gahsta break my meet record from last year."

So gifted was the sophomore that the year before, he broke the Blackberry Relays meet record as a freshman.

"Sure thing," I said. "Ain't no problem to beat a freshman's mark."

He then reminded me that in the improbable event I actually did break his record that it would stand exactly one year. "You need tah give me sumpin to shoot fo next year, cuz I be takin' it back."

With Richard not running in the Two Mile, my victory was just a formality. "You got it, bro, ain't no thing. Maybe I'll come back and cheer for ya next year."

***

The grounds around Lindale's stadium is elevated above the playing surface, and the whole facility is circumscribed by a tall, stone wall built during the *Great Depression* as part of a government jobs program. In a distant corner of that wall, far from the field, there was a gap for vehicle access; spanning across that gap, a chain link gate. Sometimes, during football games, kids who didn't have money to get in clung to that gate, clasping the diamond grid as they peered through the gray, criss-crossing metal to see what was happening on the field. The view from atop that perch was horrible; it was too far away from the action. Our school didn't charge admission to track meets, so no one hung around outside that gate to watch people run. If they were interested, they simply walked into the stadium.

I'm eager for the race to begin. The nerves, the cotton mouth, the heart pounding, I know it'll all go away once I start running. I look up at that gap in the brick wall and remember the first time I ever won a race, my first gold medal—three years ago in the Mile

Run at a ninth-grade meet, here on my home track. After that victory, I noticed our station wagon parked up on that plateau behind the gate. I left the stadium and jogged up to the car. Outside the car was a pile of cigarette butts—Salems and Marlboros—Mom and Doug's brands. My parents were inside waiting for me when I approached the driver's side window.

"Did you see that? Did you see me blow them away?"

"Oh, you won?" My mother's tongue was in the way of her words. "I told Doug that was you, but he said 'no.'" She was drunk—ridiculously drunk.

They hadn't even gotten out of their car. I looked down at the track. Even with perfect eyesight, I had a hard time making out people's identities. No wonder they didn't know I'd won.

"Yeah, I won." *Five lousy minutes. That's how long it takes me to run a mile. You two can't leave your drinks for five minutes?*

"Really? That's nice." She was empty of excitement. She sounded like Robbie's Mother.

Doug started the car. "Let's go," he said.

"Mom, they're getting ready for the last event. If we beat Van in the Mile Relay, we win the meet!"

Doug shook his head, grunted, and snarled with impatience. "I thought you said you already won?"

"Well, I won my event, which puts our team in position to win the whole track meet. I wanna see my friends run the relay. It'll be over in ten minutes."

My mother sided with Doug. "We've been here over an hour already. It's time to go."

A few minutes later, twenty-nine of the thirty members of our track team shared a victorious group hug at the finish line of the Mile Relay. We'd just arrived home, when I answered the phone. A friend's voice modulated over music and giddy lockerroom hollering. "What are you doing at home, Schnabl? We won. We fuckin' won! Coach Anderson just brought the trophy in. He was looking for you. Everybody's looking for you."

That was three years ago—just a freshman meet. But *this* is the Blackberry Relays—varsity division. The starter shouts. "On your marks..." *The next ten minutes will be mine.*

My mile split is slower than it should be. Even though I'm sitting on the leader's heels, it's not good enough for Richard Cooper. He shouts from the infield as we pass on the back stretch. "5:20 Ochoa, quit bullshittin'!"

He's right; I'm holding back. I'm scared to pull away from everyone else. Could I really be that much better than the field to leave them now?

Five laps in, three to go and our lead pack is whittled down to five runners. *This is easy. I'm not even tired.* Richard Cooper's voice plays in my head. "Go for the record, man. Give me sumfin to shoot for next year."

It's time to show these people who I am. Coming out of the turn, we pass in review, glide past the stands, in front of the fans—in front of *my* fans. I lengthen my stride a bit and take the lead. *This is where it starts. I'm about to define who I am.* Yells and claps from my hometown fans spur me on. Voices and faces I recognize.

Robert Collins, editor of the *Lindale News*, sits in his wheelchair in the infield. He's focusing his camera on me, the lead runner. The flash goes off, travels through my eyes and sends a signal down to my adrenal glands. He wants a picture of the winner. Maybe that picture will be in the paper. Yes, it should be **my** picture in the paper. Richard will win the Mile and the Half but he's only a sophomore; he'll have plenty of chances for glory. I'll talk to Mr. Collins after the race; stroke him a bit. Maybe I'll even ask him for the front page.

I'm pulling away.

Everybody take your pictures, because you have never seen anything like this before. Watch me and shoot me, as I run around in circles slightly faster than twenty other boys. This is my moment. This is my reward for the dues I've paid. You other runners, so long suckers, eat my dust because you have not trained like I have. You did not outrun wolves at midnight because your legs were your only way home. This is mine dammit, and you are helpless as—

Then, a different feeling hits me—something far different than cockiness or confidence—intense stomach cramps. There's a knife inside my stomach, an alien in my bowels, or maybe an alien with a knife. Something's ripping at my guts. I slow down a bit. The pain does not abate, but intensifies. My twenty-yard lead narrows quickly. Four guys pass me single file. *I swear to God, giving birth could not be this painful.* My pace slows to a trot. *This can't be! I'm not even tired!* The high jump pit is just a few feet from the inside lane. As I round the turn, I belly-flop onto it, bury my head into the padding and cry in agony and shame. *I need to shit. I need to throw up. I need a doctor. I need to have this baby. I don't know what I need, but I need something.* My Blackberry Relays are over.

The pain comes in waves. My bloated stomach pushes up more mashed potatoes and roast beef than it was built to hold. Between the pain's peaks, I think back to my status two years before. I'd won district in the ninth grade Mile, made the varsity track team as a sophomore. I was positioned for junior and senior years full of glorious sports accomplishments, maybe all-district in three sports! I was on my way to UCLA. Then, the broken ankle, the move, Coach Robinson, his pistol, work. My prospects, once promising, are gone. A senior who's fallen off the sports radar, now I've fallen onto the high jump mats during my last hometown sports appearance.

Even as the lead pack comes back around on the next lap, I lie contemplating my failure at the one thing I thought I was good at. I'd been dreaming of this race for months, to the exclusion of everything else. I was obsessed with it. I hear some runners laugh at me as they pass.

The pain peaks, and I forget about the race for a moment and just beg God to heal me. *Just take it away for two minutes. Please God, give me a two-minute break from the pain.* And he does. I use the time to wonder how Lindale would remember me. I'd been having this premonition. It's the fall of 1988. Fresh off my Olympic gold medal, I'm back in Lindale, for a speaking engagement at the high school. I stop by Tindal's Drug Store with Gary Camp and Bob Staton to have a burger and a cherry Coke. As always, there's a cute high school girl working the grill. At the counter, a group of junior high boys whisper to each other about my identity. "That's him," one would say. The boldest among them would get up and come over to our table where we were sitting and ask me for an autograph. Gary would laugh. "Can I have your autograph?" he'd say, mocking the kid after he left.

Lying there on the mat, I come to grips with reality. *It's not gonna happen for me.* There will be no UCLA, no Olympics, that day at Tindal's Drug Store will never come. And tomorrow, if I'm not sick, I'll probably be scouring a dumpster for food. The Blackberry Relays was not a coming out party for me—rather a wakeup call.

Twenty-five years after that race, I'm in the attic and find a shoe box full of track medals and ribbons. I bring them down to the living room to show my two daughters—my girls, great athletes with closets full of trophies, medals, and ribbons. Leanna, the youngest, is a better pole vaulter in sixth grade than I was in eighth.

"Hey girls, wanna see something?"

Leanna, twelve, glances up from her *Gameboy*. "Okay."

Lindsay, eighteen, a bit more skeptical, pauses her *iPod* and looks at me. She does not speak. Her look does that for her. *What can possibly be more interesting than Kelly Clarkson?*

I place the open shoebox between them on the couch. "My track medals…"

They look into the box that holds the only evidence of the dreams I once had. The bronze I once tried to polish into gold is green with oxidation. The shoebox does not hold stepping stones to an Olympic medal realized, but only high school consolation prizes. Neither of my girls are interested enough to touch the medals. I thought Leanna might want to count them, or lay them out in a line on the kitchen table, like she had her Barbie dolls. But their eyes stare into an empty shoebox. Lindsay gazes at the mementos politely for about five seconds, "That's nice Daddy," then smiles and presses her earbuds back in. Leanna returns to saving the princess. They are not awed. They are not impressed. They don't even care.

Worms in My Turds

You probably don't want to read this chapter during dinner

Bob came by my (his) place after school one day to pick me up for chores, which on this day was to mow at one of his other rental properties. "I heard you done quit another race. You sick or somethin'?"

Suffering from another episode of those intense stomach cramps, I'd walked out of second place and into the shitter at the *Vandal Relays*. It wasn't just nerves because I was having labor pains during training runs as well. A week before district and I couldn't even run a hard mile without doubling over. I'd been too embarrassed to tell anybody, too poor to go to the doctor, so for months, I'd done nothing. Now was my chance to speak up. I looked at the ground when I told him. "I got worms."

"Do what?"

"I said, I got worms, Bob."

"What kinda worms you talking about, son?"

"I don't know."

"What do you mean, you don't know? They in your shit?"

"Yes. They're swarming on it."

"They alive?"

"Yeah, they're alive, so many it looks like vanilla frosting on my shit."

"Frostin' on your shit? Don't reckon I'll be eatin' any dessert tonight. How big are they?"

The little bastards were crawling out of me twenty-four hours a day. At school, my asshole itched so bad I counted the minutes for the bell to ring. The highlight of my school days occurred in the bathroom stalls where I'd wipe the sonsofbitches off and mash them. Wipe, crush, flush, attend class, repeat. Not wanting to be discovered, I stopped showering at school, which meant giving up hot showers, altogether.

Bob dropped me off to mow. An hour later, he returned. He handed me a green twelve ounce tin can of Gatorade and a pill. "Ya got pin worms. Pharmacist says to take this."

"Just one pill?"

"That's what he says. 'Course, I ain't never had frostin' on my shit, so I ain't speaking from experience."

In a few days, the worms were stillborn. They thinned out over the course of days until they disappeared altogether, about the same time as my disappointing track season ended.

The encyclopedia at school said pinworms were caused by unsanitary conditions, prevalent in third world countries. *In the U.S., seen mostly in small children.* If you're ever in Lindale, I'd recommend avoiding the dumpster behind Dairy Queen.

Sumpin to Eat

You'd think a high school kid with his own "downtown apartment" would be popular at school. But only one friend of mine ever asked to borrow my place. Willie Jones would do his best to make it seem like he was there just to chill with me. But it wouldn't take too long before his real motive surfaced. "Say, Rich man, why don't chu go get yo'self sumpin to eat." He'd extend three one-dollar bills toward me. "Hey, while you's out, can I borrow yo' pad for a lil' bit?"

Willie was a sophomore but already ranked as one of the top athletes in our school. He'd call girls from Gary's office phone. I was amazed how Willie got straight to the point with his girlfriends. Girls seemed to crawl over one another to be with him; kinda like a black *Fonzie*. He could transform the anxious voice I knew to something soothing, slow, contrived—something Barry White-like. He sounded so cool, so relaxed, like he was doing the girl a favor by calling.

"Hey lil thing, I got some work fo ya.

"What?"

"You don't wanna work taday? Baby this is the second time you done me like dis. If you don't wanna work no mo, let me know. Know what I mean, Cuz, I leave ya lone and move on."

"Whatchu talkin' 'bout, It's plenty girls up there wanna work with me but I called you...shit."

"Awright then, see you over here in bout ten minutes."

"Whatchu talking 'bout, I needs to come git you? Why come your sister don't give you a ride?"

"If she giv'ya ride here, I giv'ya ride back."

"Okay baby, hairy up. I'm waiting fo ya."

He's gotta be bullshitting me. You can't possibly get a girl acting so rude.

"Ya gahstah let the bitches know who's boss." He said it like he was coaching me. Sure enough, fifteen minutes later a girl from school would show at my door. I'd leave my room, go across the street to the chicken place and have dinner—compliments of Willie.

I'd sit at the table and wait for Willie's car to leave my house. With my hunger resolved, guilt set in, like I had turned the girl out for a two-piece dinner with mashed potatoes, a hard biscuit and a plastic spork. *What if she got pregnant? Would I be partly to blame?* On the other hand, a part of me admired Willie's self-confidence and how easily he could get girls. In that way, I wanted to be more like him. How did he do it? Why was I more concerned about his girlfriend's welfare than he was? Was there something wrong with me? Of course there was. I was a seventeen-year-old boy. And, at seventeen, there were times I wished I had some bitches who thought I was the boss. Hell, I would've settled for one.

When I returned to my room, I found a nice little gift from Willie himself. Something very personal, right there in the middle of my bedspread. *Well, I don't think she got pregnant.* With no money for detergent, no hot water, and no in-house laundry facilities, cleaning up Willie's mess was no small annoyance. I hung the bedspread on a tree limb outside my room. I was hosing it off when a car full of the hot girls in school passed by slowly. Tracy Wine, the hottest of the hotties, stuck her head out of the window and yelled as they drove by, "Hey Rich, did you wet your bed?" They were laughing as they drove off. They got it all wrong. I was strong, independent, emancipated from my parents while still in high school, living in my own place, and these girls laughed at me while I hosed Willie Jones's cum off my bedspread like I was some kind of chump. *I'm boss; why don't you bitches realize that?*

***

Willie was one of my few friends who knew I was undernourished. In addition to buying me several chicken dinners, he once had me over to his house for dinner and to spend the night with his family. There were several places where Willie pulled back a rug and a piece of plywood and showed me holes in the floor. It was hard to imagine five people living in the small decrepit wood shack, and I felt sad for the poverty the family lived in. His mother, Irene, cleaned homes; I'm not sure if his father worked much. If he did, he drank most of his wages.

As we ate, it occurred to me that these people were actually better off than me. They had food and hot water, and were together in some semblance of a family, even though Willie's father didn't join us for dinner. Funny, how I'd been conditioned: I instinctively had pity on their living conditions, then realized I was there, eating dinner with them, because they had pity for mine.

After eating, Willie had me play my comedy tape (the one I made at my father's place) for his mother. Irene spent over an hour listening to every bit, rewinding to hear her favorite parts twice. She loved the tape and told me I was the craziest and funniest person she'd ever met, which I considered a compliment.

We talked after dinner; mostly Irene and I. Willie got bored and went off to his room. Irene wanted to know my story. She would be the first adult since the lady on the bus to hear it. I told her about the kidney beans, my mother's rage, my father's apathy. I told her my one way ticket took me to Lindale for the simple reason I had friends here. She cried. She hugged me. She thanked me for being in her home and for being Willie's friend. I thanked her for feeding me and then went to bed.

Willie and I had been lying in his bed for a while (for clarification purposes, there was a row of pillows between us). A man yelling outside the closed bedroom door wakes me up. "How many times I done told you bitch!" Willie's Father was home.

Irene is trying to calm him. "Baby, keep your yo' voice down. Willie got a frien' up in there."

"So that's who et my goddamn dinner!"

"No, don't do this." Fear had replaced persuasion in her voice. "Not tonight, please don't—"

There's commotion: banging on the walls, stuff falling, the pounding of deliberate footsteps transmitting through the raised pier-and-beam support joists, the no-so-subtle vibration of the house.

Willie stirs in the bed next to me.

Irene is pleading. "No, Bobby. Pleeeease!"

I hear a thud.

Willie flies out of bed, opens his door, runs through it, and slams it behind him. *Family business is going down.* I lie and listen to the voices on the other side of the door.

"Didjah hit her?" Willie demanded. "You better get on outta here right now mothah fuckah or I'LL KILL YOU!"

Something inaudible from Willie's Father.

Willie, again, "I SWEAR TO FUCKIN GOD, I'LL KILL YOU! I AINT PLAYING WHIT CHU!"

Irene pleads with her son. "Willie put that bat down."

Two hard footsteps on the wood porch and the screen door slams against the jamb. Willie has run his own father out of his own house. Sixteen, and courageous enough to stand up to his father and defend his mother. In that way, I wanted to be more like Willie.

Willie and his mother talk—hushed voices; I'm unable to make out the words. *It must be over.*

Then, two more steps on the wood porch and the screen door slams against the jamb.

Irene yells. "Willie, come back here!"

He's gone, and Irene is sobbing outside my door. "Oh God, Oh please God."

More sobbing.

She's calls me through the closed bedroom door. "Richard? Richard, can you come here please?"

I come out. It's dark in the living room but I can see she doesn't look good. She's sitting upright in an old recliner, her head tilted back as she runs her fingers over a bloody gash on her cheek. I go to the kitchen and grab a towel from the handle of the refrigerator, douse it in water, return, and press it to her face. Her hand replaces mine on the dishrag. "Can you go fetch Willie and talk some sense into him, for he does sumpin foolish?"

I'm in the middle of this now.

Two footsteps on the front porch and the screen door slams against the jamb behind me. I'm running down the dark road toward a silhouette.

I yell. "WILLIE!" And, again. "WILLIE!"

I'm gaining on him. I see he's carrying a baseball bat. I get closer. He starts to run. I shout his name several more times. He just runs faster.

He's a champion hurdler. He's faster than me.

He's gone.

It's dark. I can't see him anymore. I'm tired. I walk back to the house. Two footsteps on the front porch. The screen-door slams against the jamb behind me. I'm in the living room. Irene is still crying. Her white night gown has soaked up some of her face blood. "Did you catch 'em?" she asks.

"I can't catch Willie Jones; he's too fast."

She's laughs, still crying some, but mostly laughing now. Her husband just beat her. Her son and husband may be beating each other's skulls in with baseball bats at this very moment, but I manage to make her laugh. I take the washcloth she's holding against her face into the kitchen and rinse the blood off, come back, press it against her face and hold her hand.

Finally Willie returns. "I don't know where bouts he went. It's okay Momma." He hugs her.

"Willie, don't chu ever be like him. Don't chu be like your father."

"I won't Momma, I won't."

***

Willie's been in my room for an hour. He's usually in there for twenty minutes. I'm getting impatient, so I knock on my own door.

"Come in," he says.

The girl is sitting on the edge of my bed crying. Willie's pacing back and forth. There's a problem. At first I think Willie is trying to help her with some problem. But then he scolds her as if I'm not there. "Look here, I'm tired of this bullshit. Why come you here if you don't wanna work? Whatchu think you here for? I ain't callin' you again. Ya hear me? I'm done whitchu."

"No, Willie. No." She buries her face in both hands. Her crying intensifies. He looks at me and shakes his head. Then speaks. "Can you believe dis bitch?"

I look at him. Then at her. Think about hugging her. Instead, I start to walk out.

"Where's you goin'? Git yo' ass here, Rich."

He's asking me to fix him. He's asking me to be the one to tell him he's a mother fucker, just like his father. He's asking me to teach him right from wrong.

Maybe I don't have the guts, maybe it's not my place, or maybe I figure it's too late. "Naw man, this ain't my business, bro."

"It's awright, bitch was just leavin'."

He needs me to have the same strength he showed in confronting his father. But I'm not sure if he respects me enough for it to do any good. I say nothing.

***

The next morning, Irene drove us to school. Her check has swollen her eye partially shut. Willie reminds her that he needs some meal money for the out-of-town track meet. She gives him five dollars. I guess she feels a bit awkward giving him money in front of me, so she tries to give me the same amount as her son. I know people with holes in their floor usually don't have money to spare, but when I refuse it, she almost starts crying. She insists I take it, but I don't have the heart to do so. She may be offering me her own lunch money. *If I take it, she may not be able to eat lunch today.* I tell her that I have enough money. Willie knew better, "You ain't got no money, you never got no money; go on Rich, take the money."

"I got money Willie."

"Show me your money then."

"It's in my locker."

"Bullshit, take the money."

When I finally accept the money and thank her, I sense how it makes her feel to help me. Thrown around her house last night, yet this morning, she's helping me. When I ate at the track meet, I couldn't stop thinking about Irene and whether or not she was eating today. Her plea to her son kept replaying in my head. "Willie, don't chu ever be like yo' father." I had seen a Willie she hadn't. Willie was already like his father. At that meet Willie won three events, but even in the euphoria of gold medal performances, I accurately envisioned Willie's future—and Irene's heartache.

One day, Willie and his father would serve time together in the same prison.

You Lose, Bitch

One evening after finishing a track workout, I was playing basketball on the junior high playground with a group of thugs who had been Lindale sports stars behind the protective shield of Coach Robinson. These punks epitomized everything Robinson was about—great athletes, violent on and off the field. Even though they had finished high school a year or two earlier, two of them by dropping out, Smite, Dogfood, and Tick still hung around the playground at school, living the lives of thieves, bullies, and dealers while awaiting fates they shared with a great number of athletes to come out of Lindale in the Robinson era—hard time.

There was a widespread rumor of how these three had sexually assaulted a younger, mentally challenged *brother*, Tim. A deep-voiced guy who was always laughing to fit in, Tim was playing on my team, shooting 4v4 hoops with the guys whom I had heard brutally violated him a year before. Tick blocked Tim's shot and followed up with typical trash talk. "Get down bitch! I'll fuck yo' ass like Smite did." Smite and Dogfood showed their approval with roaring laughter and hand slaps with Tick for such a clever insult. Later, the ball landed out of bounds and kicked off a coke bottle. It was Smite's turn. "Tim, go get dat bottle off da court or I'll have Dogfood shove it up yo' ass again."

"Nah man," Tick added. "Let's get the stick."

The insults were consistent with the stories I'd heard. Coke bottles, sticks, and dicks. This wasn't basketball; it was a dehumanizing salt rubbing of their alleged victim's wounds. I'm not sure Tim had the capacity to fully understand how humiliated he should have been. He offered meek resistance. "Fuck you, man, let's play ball, ho."

Dogfood got his insults in as well. Mocking Tim's response to the rumored gang rape, he cried out in a girly voice. "Stop it Smite! Stop! Get it out!"

Setting aside trying to comprehend the insidious attack, I couldn't believe the perpetrators were publicly boasting of such a depraved act. They didn't seem embarrassed by the homosexual aspects of the crime. In those days, suspicion of gay sex would normally result in the suspect being ostracized by even his close friends, especially in the world of high school sports. But, in their twisted minds, the incident, if it really happened, was worthy of reliving, retelling, commemorating with high fives. Perhaps they felt the need to remind the victim to stay in his place or it would happen again.

I got the ball on the left wing and pump faked the 6'5", once all-district, Tick. He left his feet and I drove past him toward the rim. I was high in the air, about to complete the trivial matter of laying the ball in when Dogfood came over from the back side and rammed his shoulder into my stomach as he slapped me in the face. In an organized league it would have been a flagrant foul resulting in ejection. But this was no organized league. This was the playground at Lindale Junior High. As I fell toward the ground, I waited a moment to see if the ball went in and when it didn't, about the time I landed, I called "foul." These guys played under a stupid playground rule that if you call "foul" and the shot goes in, you don't get credit for the bucket, which is why I didn't call the foul immediately on contact. "Bullshit," Dogfood said. "You punk; you can't call it that late." Out of the corner of my eye I saw a blur coming toward my head but I had no time to react. His punch landed squarely under my nose. Moments later, two guys were helping me to my feet. By then blood from inside my upper lip had filled my mouth and was running down my chin landing in splotches on the asphalt. I took my shirt off and pressed it against my lip. I wanted to fight back but I barely comprehended where I was and knew I'd taken a pretty serious punch already.

I walked alone a half mile to my room and rinsed my mouth with cold water. Pinching my upper lip between the thumbs and forefingers of both hands, I peeled the skin up toward the tip of my nose, and looked at my upper gums in the mirror. A blood-oozing fissure ran vertically from my upper left front tooth to a point where the inside of my upper lip attached to my gums just under my nostril. I gripped the front-left tooth below the gum damage and gently rocked it back and forth in its socket.

In 1982, Smite, Dogfood, and Tick were the closest thing Lindale had to a gang. Dogfood's sucker punch completed the trio's trifecta of physical assaults on me. Tick had once beaten me silly in one of Robinson's boxing matches. A couple of years earlier, I had a showdown with Smite in front of the whole basketball team. After practice, he was towel popping me and getting his buddies to join in. I responded with a less than original comeback. "Smite, you're stupid."

He slapped my face and dared me. "Say it again punk."

"You're stupid." I added a little more spice. "And you know what else? You're headed to prison."

His slap was harder this time. The sting brought tears to my eyes. "Say it again bitch."

"I ain't your bitch, but you sure will be a bitch when you're in prison, you stupid nigger!"

"What did chu call me? What did chu call me?" He repeated the question over and again as he slapped me all over the locker room. My racist insult excluded the possibility of any of my black friends jumping to my aid on this one…and…well…we were in a basketball locker room, so I had insulted pretty much the whole team, save a couple of benchwarmers. In classic Gandhi fashion, I took the ass whipping while asserting my prediction which incidentally would prove to be accurate. "Stupid, prison bitch." *If he's stupid, what does that make me?*

But this punch from Dogfood was more than a series of bitch slaps. Although my fat lip was painful and embarrassing at school, it was the less visible but more serious gum injury which caused me problems. Pus formed along the crack in my gum. The only school days I missed during my four years in high school were spent fighting a gum infection and fever. Gary's wife, Susan, brought me soup and medicine. Instead of training for my upcoming district race, I spent the next two weeks missing the tuneup meet, fighting a gum infection and ridding myself of pinworms. I'd be in no condition to challenge Edward Anderson or Richard Cooper.

A root canal, a series of subsequent infections and a slightly discolored purple patch on my gum in the area of the original trauma has always served as a reminder of Dogfood's punch. For many years I wished for the day I'd get revenge on him. Then I heard both Dogfood and Smite had been in and out of prison. Since then, I've wondered whether there were some punks in the joint who made Smite and Dogfood their bitches and, I wonder if, when Smite was doing time, if he remembered my prediction?

For the record, Dogfood, I was in Lindale a few years back and drove by the basketball courts—the scene of your crime against me. Realizing I had my daughter's basketball in my trunk, I pulled over, walked out onto the empty court, called a double technical foul on you and shot four free throws. And guess what? I made three of them, which incidentally is game. My team wins. Yeah I know…from your prison cells you and Smite might object I can't make a call twenty years after the foul but let me remind you of a lesson I'm sure you have already learned in prison: You don't make the rules no more.

Like I was saying in 1982, when I was rudely interrupted: "Foul."

You lose, Bitch.

What's an Editorial?

As if professing my love for Captain and Tennille at a school assembly wasn't enough to draw ridicule from my classmates, during freshman year, I competed in UIL poetry interpretation. I was pretty good—even won first place at one competition. I consciously repressed interests in anything that didn't involve running, jumping, or hand-to-hand combat after Coach Robinson began teasing me in front of the football team for my artsy endeavors. "Schnabl, what kind of tackle is that? Are you a football player or a poet? Why don't you go join Stan Denman and your sissy friends in that one act play? Maybe you can come over tonight and read my kids a bedtime story? Can you do that, Schnabl? Can you read a bedtime story to Bob and Tyson? Once upon a time, there was a stupid kraut who couldn't tackle his grandma…"

In spring of senior year, the speech/journalism teacher, Mr. Shell tracked me down. He was having a difficult time recruiting students willing to compete in the UIL district academic meet. He asked me to revive my freshman interpretation of a poem about a mountain climber who was mortally wounded as a result of his partner's mistake. Sports were over and Block was out of my life by now, so I had no reason to say "no."

I practiced *David* by Earle Birney, the night before the competition. The next morning, I tuned up in front of Mr. Shell's speech class before heading off on a short bus to the competition at Tyler Junior College. I had no expectations except to get out of class for a day and to be one of the few straight guys hanging around a bunch of cute girls. On the trip to Tyler, the morbidly obese Mr. Shell called me to the front of the bus. I sat across the aisle from him. At thirty-five, he looked fifty, and as it turned out, he only had a few years left. Wearing blue pants, a white shirt and a red tie, he looked like a gigantic ABA basketball with a flabby cartoon head sticking out.

His fly half-open, a swath of perspiration patches under each arm. I could smell him across the aisle. Each breath sounded like a heroic gasp to sustain life. His gray eyes peered at me through Roy Orbison's glasses. He took a breath deep enough to sustain himself through his upcoming question. "Rich, do you know what an editorial is?"

"Isn't that where you advertise something you're selling in the newspaper?"

He covered his blubbery checks with both hands, and slid the tips of his fat fingers under the lower rim of his glasses as if he were playing peek-a-boo. He studied me for a moment, trying to assess if I was serious. He saw that I was, then tilted his head down in disgust and slowly shook it, presenting to me his collection of dandruff crumbs the size of small cornflakes embedded within his thin, dark, graying, slicked-back hair.

"Come on Mr. Shell, tell me," I begged, curious where he was going with his question.

"An editorial is a persuasive argument that a writer makes [pause for air] usually on a controversial subject."

"Oh sure, I'm familiar with that," I said. The truth was the only kind of editorials I remembered reading were those that gave opinions on such issues like whether Larry Bird or Magic Johnson should be the first pick in the NBA draft.

"Well, I have an open spot in *Editorial Writing...*"

I didn't have anything to lose. "I'll do it. Thanks, Mr. Shell."

I took Mr. Shell's suggestion, and used the time before the contest to read a few columns in the university library.

The topic for the competition was:

A school board is having a meeting to consider this question: Should classic books be banned from high school libraries because of foul language?

The scenario gave several examples of literary works on the hypothetical chopping block, many of which I'd heard of only because I was supposed to have to read them in English class. I took a measured risk by using *gratuitous* profanity in my defense of *appropriate* profanity.

> *If we're going to take 'Death of a Salesmen' or 'To Kill a Mockingbird' out of our school libraries for using a 'damn', 'hell', or 'bastard' to develop a higher level of authenticity in their characters, while we are cleaning up our house, shall we, too, fire any teacher who has ever personally uttered the same offensive words? These books are not Penthouse Forum smut using foul language to degrade women, titillate, or otherwise shock the reader. They are artistic works that contain 'literary-appropriate' language that in another context might be used as profanity. The books transcend time, something that those who wish to censor them will not do. To those individuals I would say, "Censor at your church, censor in your homes, but not at our public schools. Let students get on with the business of learning to think for themselves. Let's not hide all the 'shit' from them.*

I turned in my paper, left the room and chuckled to myself. *I just blew my chance.* I probably just broke some fundamental law of journalism; like that thing English teachers always told us: "You cannot use the word that you are giving a definition of in the definition." Certainly there is some rule: "You cannot defend profanity by using profanity." I didn't beat myself up for too long; until a couple of hours ago, the only editorials I'd ever read were on the sports page. This would be a great story to tell my buddies: "Man, I crashed that dweeb party with *hells*, *damns*, and *shits*. Fuck them tightasses."

I went off to read in the poetry finals that I'd somehow advanced to from the morning prelims. The readers who preceded me were clearly more talented. I stammered several times near the beginning of my interpretation. I realized just how misplaced I was. *I don't belong here; I'm a football player.* One of my legs began to shake uncontrollably, which I knew would knock me out of contention even if inferior talent and stuttering had not already. I wasn't too upset. It wasn't like losing a track meet or something. I enjoyed the gay talent of the gay readers in the gay finals, and I'd gotten out of class. I went to the awards presentation with no expectations. When they announced the poetry winners, of the eight finalists, I failed to place in the top six.

Mike Morman, editor of our school newspaper, and preppiest of all the preps in our class, sat next to me during the award ceremony. Mike was in my collegebound English class. I should say Mike hijacked the class. The literature discussions often became Mike and the teacher debating author intent while the rest of the class listened. Since Mrs. Porsche was not one to allow me to lay my head down on my desk, I was forced to listen to all those pointless discussions. Mike was already espousing his views on the first chapter of *Macbeth* when I still thought it was the latest McDonald's sandwich for women. He talked so much about Macbeth that eventually I renamed it *The Book of Morman*.

When Mrs. Porsche assigned our class to choose a Shakespeare character and emulate their dress, Mike's mother sewed a special outfit, complete with a hat, and Pilgrim-looking shoes. Accessorized with props, he presented his character, Macbeth, while passing around a library book which had a color picture of the character whose outfit he had fully replicated. I think Mike made an A+ on that assignment.

I didn't even have enough money to buy toothpaste or deodorant. If I had five bucks to spare I would've bought some socks without holes or underwear without skid marks before buying a medieval vest for an English assignment. Robbie and I actually forgot about the assignment until the due date. When we saw Mike in the hall before first period, already dressed as a medieval dork, sporting a plastic sword, we knew we were screwed. The grade for this show-and-tell was weighted so heavily, that taking a zero on the assignment would make failing English for the year an absolute certainty for me. This would prevent me from graduating. I was in serious trouble. Robbie and I sat together during first period wearing jeans and T-shirts, wondering how we were going to morph into Shakespearean thespians. He threw out the first idea. "I'll be Romeo and you be Juliet. We can get Dia to put some makeup on you and I'll get up on my desk like I'm talking to you from the balcony."

"Juliet's on the balcony, dumbass. Romeo's down below. Even I know that. But that's a great idea. We can…like…drink poison and fall over desks. But you should be Juliet; I ain't wearing makeup."

Robbie didn't want to wear makeup either. "No way, man, it's my idea, and you could put your long hair in a ponytail."

He had me on that. "You have softer skin," I replied.

The Juliet thing wasn't gonna happen. We were each too stubborn. As soon as the bell rang ending first period, we ran down to the boy's locker room. We had five minutes. We were looking for something, anything remotely Shakespearean that we could wear or exhibit as props. Showing up in our normal clothes would give us a big fat zero on the assignment. We came across some scraggly cutoff PE shorts. In the adjoining janitor's closet, we found some white button-up cafeteria worker shirts.

"We're lunch ladies?" Robbie asked.

"No." I ripped the sleeves off one of the shirts, grabbed a rake and a shovel. "We're farm workers. Let's go outside and rub dirt on our faces."

Robbie objected. "Farm workers? There's no farm workers in Macbeth."

"There are today, dude."

With three minutes left, we had nothing else.

We rehearsed our presentation while running to class. It was decided I'd do the talking, and Robbie would play off me.

We watched and listened to our classmates present their characters wearing robes and gowns they were so proud of—outfits they and their normal parents had spent hours on, making them one stitch at a time. When it came time to explain our characters, we got up in front of the class together. I held the shovel with both hands, extended it out from my chest, offering it for the class to inspect. "We are Macbeth's farm hands, and we spend all day working in the fields." Like my second grade book report about UFOs, I just made stuff up. "We tend to the crops so that Macbeth and all his family can eat…"

I looked at Robbie. He's silently working his rake trying so hard not to break character…such a serious look. He's selling it so well—too well. I start losing it when I see how determined he is to salvage a D from this chaos. "And that is why we have dirt on our faces." I managed, between bursts of laughter. "Master Macbeth (Robbie nods his head and extends his upturned hand toward a seated Mike Morman) is cruel and won't provide us with shoes. That is why we are barefoot."

I can't speak anymore. I'm laughing so hard, it's all I can do to breathe, but somehow Robbie's still holding it together. He stops hoeing and assumes the speaking role. "And we live in little huts next to the fields we work... and there is no water to wash, that's why we are so dirty." I point to the dirt on his face. We are making a mockery of the most serious class in school, and it's so funny, a little snot blows out my nose, and tears began welling in my eyes. I bite my lip, try to self-inflict pain. I think of the repercussions. *I'm about to flunk out of high school.* I still can't stop laughing.

Our college bound classmates, wearing their literary garb, look at each other and shake their heads in disbelief. Most start laughing...at us, not with us. Mrs. Porsche strokes her forehead back and forth with her fingertips, raises her eyebrows. *She is not laughing.* She slightly cups her hand and presses her thumb to her temple while her fingertips rest in the middle of her forehead. She puts her elbows on her desk, holds her chin in her hands and looks straight down. *Maybe she's smiling; it's hard to tell because of her downturned head.* Undeterred, Robbie babbles something about sharecropping until John McCarty's outburst. "THAT'S STUPID!" I look at him for a moment and the irony hits me: a geek wearing knickers, black socks over his calves, a pilgrim hat with a buckle, and a three-inch wide fabric belt hiked up just below his chest, is calling us "stupid." Our presentation is over. *Entertaining people—this is my calling.*

Robbie and I got our D's without knowing anything about Macbeth, other than what we'd heard Mike babble about in class. I actually tried reading the first few pages, but in my humble opinion, Shakespeare's spellin' and gram'ar were so poer, apostrophes in r'ndom places, I gave up.

A photographer came in and took a group photo, each of us in our Shakespearean getups. In the Lindale 1982 yearbook, there's a picture of the thirteen students in the Honors English class. Situated strategically in the first row, in front of a collection of the most studious kids in our school dressed as Duncan-King of Scotland, Macduff, Lady Macbeth, and the three witches, are two guys wearing cutoff shorts and lunch-lady shirts with dirt rubbed on their faces. A 60 sure averages in better than a 0, so by putting on shorts and that shirt and rubbing dirt on my face, I kept my chance for graduation alive.

As I'm sitting next to Mike at the ceremony, I start to fidget like a little kid in church as the ceremony drags on–and-on: Slide Rule, shorthand, numbers sense...*Who knew there were so many contests for geeks to compete in?* Finally, they're ready to announce the winners for *Editorial Writing,* I half expected them to make a special announcement, "The most offensive entry goes to Lindale—Rich Ochoa."

There were twenty-four people entered in these events (three each from eight schools in the district), so when they announced sixth through second place, without mentioning Mike, I figured he had a good chance of winning. As was the practice, they always announced the school before the student's name. "First place—Lindale—"

I studied Mike, expecting to catch the reaction of the winner. Erect posture, fingers dovetailed on his lap, stylish business jacket accented with cufflinks, fashionable tie, and slacks. He may have looked like a winner, but I was seeing him as Macbeth.

"—Richard Ochoa."

Macbeth's jaw dropped and his eyes almost popped out of his head. I lost my breath and my heart pounded in shock. Mike looked sick. I walked to the front of the lecture hall to accept the award for my profanity-laced prose in my dirty jeans and the finest slightly-food-stained T-shirt I owned, pus oozing from my cracked gums and worms crawling out of my asshole, fully expecting the presenter to issue a sudden retraction. "Oh dear, I'm very sorry, silly me, I had the list upside down. Mr. Ochoa is actually the last place finisher, not first. He's the disruptive force in the back of the class who shoots spit wads into Mike Morman's hair when the teacher is not looking." But there was no mistake; the kid in jeopardy of not graduating because he'd spent more of his senior year playing paper football than studying, and didn't know the difference between a classified ad and an editorial column when he got out of bed this morning, had just won an award for being the best writer in the district. This was bigger than the '69 Mets. The world had last seen such a shocking upset when David slew Goliath.

After the bus returned from the UIL contest, Mr. Shell opened up the teacher's lounge so students could use the phone to call their folks for rides. Of course I didn't have anyone to call. But it was only a mile from the school to my room in town, so I didn't really need a ride. I'd have no problem lugging my huge gold medal home on foot. Nevertheless, I wanted to check out the normally forbidden confines of the teacher's lounge.

Prior to this occasion, I had been in Lindale High School's version of the *Forbidden City* only once, for that coffee and business meeting with Bob Staton. While other kids made calls, I perused the lounge to see what kind of minor mischief I could get into, giddy from my performance. I noticed the adjoining open door to guidance counselor's office. *Jackpot.* I sneaked into Mr. Scott's office intending to set a little booby trap. You know…something like he walks in the door and a *Dixie* cup of water falls on his head. I nosed around his desk and discovered the senior class rankings. I knew my grades weren't very good, but I wasn't prepared for what I was about to learn. I ranked fifty-eighth in a class of ninety-five. I looked at the names of those just ahead of me and couldn't believe what I was seeing. I had a low C average and ranked in the bottom half of my class, behind girls whom I'd helped with homework and slackers who had no intention of going to college—guys whose career hope was to get a job at *Star Canning* while waiting for their big chance to get on at *Tyler Pipe*. How can that be? There had to be some mistake. I needed to arrange a meeting with the counselor. *It's April of my senior year. I need to figure out how to get into college.* Assuming Mr. Scott would be in better mood if he wasn't soaked with water; I skipped setting up the booby trap and paid him a visit first thing Monday morning.

"I need to pick a college and get financial aid," I told the counselor.

"Well, for four-year colleges it's too late to apply, even if you had good grades. Why have you and your parents waited so late?"

Good question, let's call my mother and ask why she hasn't sent off my application for Stanford.

"You could go to Tyler Junior College, get the grades there and with your SAT, Rich, you could get into a pretty good four-year school."

Tyler? My plans are bigger than that, mister.

Junior college? I hated that adjective, *junior*. The word sounded so condescending. Like a rude man addressing a child as he pats him on the head and cuts in front of him in line. "Excuse me, junior," or a junior cheeseburger, which is certainly not big enough to fill me up, or a *Dr. Pepper Junior Ranger* whose membership includes a bumper sticker, a bat too small to strike a ball, a fake autographed picture of Al Oliver, and two free tickets for bleacher seats at a *Texas Rangers* home game, excluding Fridays, Saturdays, Sundays, and holidays.

He ended the discussion by giving me a brochure and application for TJC. I lamented the fact that I hadn't booby-trapped his office. I went home and tried to fill in the admissions paperwork. I came to the section about my parents: Father's social security number, gross household income of my parents for 1981, monthly mortgage, a list of bank accounts and investments of each of my parents...? This was much harder than the free lunch application. I hated those questions. *I'm not even on speaking terms with either of my parents, how can I produce all this info?* I considered making things up until I read the legal text on the instruction form: It is a federal offense to inaccurately report financial information on this form. *Mike. The Big House. CPS. No, better not make stuff up on this one.* Who am I kidding? Even if junior college tuition and books were paid one hundred percent, I couldn't live the way I had been any longer. Right now, at this very moment, I was hungry and had no money to eat and I was sitting in my room that I hadn't paid rent on in months, looking at this financial aid form, contemplating four years of college to be an I-don't-know-what when I grow up. It hit me. I'm not going to college. Forget UCLA, I can't even manage *Tyler Junior College.*

High school would soon be over and my good-hearted landlords weren't going to let me stay in my room rent-free after commencement. *I should've made better grades. If only I'd handed the ball off to Kunkel instead of keeping it myself, I could've gotten a scholarship. I wish I could do it again...If only I had another chance to go to high school...hey, maybe I could...*

Perhaps it was the ease with which my mother was able to change my name every time I went to a new school that made me believe I could pull it off. In 1982, there were no computerized tracking systems, schools didn't ask for student's social security numbers. I had moved enough to know that one could pretty much show up at a high school and start attending classes without a lot of redtape. If I had one more year, I could probably get my half-mile time down three or four seconds to something like 1:58. *Yeah, 1:58 would certainly get me a track scholarship.* In some states, I might even be able to compete for a state championship. I could forge a transcript that would present me as a senior-to-be with three years of high B's and low A's. I'll move to another state, stop acting like a class clown and redo my senior year. This time, I might even have a girlfriend. Where could I go and get away with this?

I was back in the same place I was a year ago—pick a place and go. This time, I'd do it right. I would start fresh; take a Greyhound and land in a new place. I thought about Carla, the girl from the Gatlinburg, Tennessee skating rink, with whom I spent three wonderful hours until my grandfather abruptly ended our evening. The wheels in my head turned. That area has a huge tourist industry. I could get work at a miniature golf course and arcade, or maybe at the *Ripley's Believe It or Not* museum. I bet there are plenty of jobs there. Jobs that weren't as back-breaking and filthy as washing dishes. Maybe Carla would even be my girlfriend, and invite me to her place for hamhocks, black-eyed peas, and cornbread. Maybe I could win state. If my mother could pull off changing my identity twice, surely I could manage a little handiwork on my school transcript.

Icees and Nukes

One night I was hanging out at the Dairy Way convenience store where Jim Ahmey had recently started working, discussing my senior year redo idea with him. He liked the idea. Jim was as delusional as me. "That's badass, dude. You should get there in June so you can do two-a-days football practice. You could be the starting quarterback, man."

"Jim, let me have some food."

"Rich, man, these people know when one candy bar is missing."

The owners kept a watchful eye on inventory and had already lectured Jim after suspecting he was linked to the disappearance of *Swisher Sweets* mini cigars, which he was. "You can have some *Icee*, but you can't use a new cup. I have to record the number of cups at the end of my shift."

I went out front and checked the trashcan for a semi-clean cup, but there was a layer of nacho cheese and assorted slop coating everything. I went back inside and wrapped my lips around the *Icee* nozzle and pulled the lever, nice and easy, but not easy enough. The cold sludge gushed into my mouth, slammed against the back of my throat, and splattered everywhere. Before I could push the handle shut, red *Icee* had covered my face and exploded all over my old tattered Roger Staubach jersey. About then, the front door opened, the little entrance bell rang, and Jim's Navy recruiter walked in smartly wearing his dress blues. Uncle Sam looked at my cherry red lips, Icee running down my jaw and dripping from my long scraggly hair with one thought on his mind—Quota. "I have found the young man this country has been looking for to maintain our submarine-launched nuclear missile systems." It was the recruiter's second visit with Jim, and he was happy to let me sit in on his pitch. He talked to us about the high-tech opportunities in the Navy. There'd be travel, a salary nearly double that of a dishwasher, endless food. One brochure showed I'd get eight thousand dollars for college when I got out.

"Advanced Electronics. That's where it's at," he said.

Interested in any ideas anybody had for my future, I talked military style to the Sailor as if he were my Boot camp Company Commander. "Sir, I don't know anything about electronics, sir."

"Relax son, you don't have to. Let me pull your ASVAB scores and see if you qualify. I'll call you tomorrow."

The recruiter didn't call the next day. Instead, he came by the school and had me called out of class. "Rich, I checked your ASVAB scores. You scored in the top ten percent. Pending a background check, you qualify for the ultimate training—nuclear weapons. On submarines."

"Nuclear Weapons? Like a scientist?"

"Well, not exactly, but pretty damn close. And the best part is you can see the world. Submariners are the Navy's elite. Son, with your brains, you could have a great future in the Navy."

Background check? What about the lawn chair? Brains? Maybe he has the wrong guy...

Until now, the most viable plan for the rest of my life began with me deceiving my way into another year of high school in Tennessee. I couldn't get a prom date and this guy was telling me about all these ports where exotic women would be waiting for my ship to dock to meet American boys like me. "The Filipino girls, Rich, they can suck the chrome off a trailer hitch."

"Really, wouldn't that make them sick?"

"You're a fucking riot, Rich. I'm telling you, your shipmates will love your wit. You are the kind of guy who everyone will want to hang with. Those girls will love you, too. You ever had an Asian girl, Rich? You can have two at once over there. I'm not shittin' you."

"Did you bring the papers? I'll signup right now…"

I spent the next Saturday at the recruiter's office watching videos about nuclear weapons and submarine service, and getting more details from the recruiter. "Oh, did I mention there was extra pay for submarine duty? And the food on subs is renowned for being the best in the Navy."

It just kept getting better. I knew computers were the wave of the future. I'd read an article that predicted one day everyone working in an office would have their own computer at their desk. Among the most complex computer systems on submarines were the ones used to launch ballistic missiles. I would program targeting data into the launch computer, run diagnostic programs, troubleshoot hardware failures on the launching systems, even crawl inside the missiles and set the arming devices. I weighed the pros: technical training, the promise of wine, women, and song, extra money, against the cons: I might be called on to blow up Russian children. *Oh well, if it ever comes down to doing that, maybe I'll just make myself throw-up and run off to the bathroom.* Eager to see what that two-at-once thing was all about, I was a bit disappointed when I learned I'd be spending the first eighteen months of my enlistment in a series of training programs: Basic training, submarine school, electronics school, and then weapons school. But, finally, I had some path to follow. For the first time, "the future" did not mean my upcoming game. The only things left for me to do to wrap this up were to pass the background check, physical, and to graduate high school.

I thought I should let my mother know that her son had joined the Navy. I hadn't talked to her in a long time, but wanted her to at least know what I was planning to do with my life after graduation. Maybe I even wanted her to be proud of me, so I told my Grandmother about my enlistment during one of our occasional phone calls. An hour later, I got a call from my mother. I knew if a call came in this late, she'd be under the influence. It was obvious from her speech pattern that this was the case tonight. Her negative attitude surprised me a bit. After all, less than a year earlier she had tried to convince me to quit school and join the Army before I was even old enough to enlist.

"Why didn't you sign-up for the Coastal Guard, Richard? Doug was in the Coastal Guard, you know. Doug says the Coastal Guard is the place to be in. Only the best and brightest get in. Did you try to get in with them, first?"

"No, I didn't." I knew the Coast Guard didn't have ports-of-call in the Philippines. "I don't wanna be in the Coast Guard."

"So you signed up with the Navy, without even trying the Coastal Guard?"

Doug had brainwashed her, led her to believe that only a reject from the Coast Guard would enlist in one of the other branches.

"Mom, I don't wanna go to the Coast Guard. I like the opportunities the Navy has offered me."

"Richard, talk to Doug."

Doug got on the phone. "The Coast Guard doesn't fight wars."

"Doug what was your rate in the Coast Guard?"

"I was a Boatsman's Mate."

"A Boatsman Mate?" I laughed at the irony. Here was a drunken ex-boatsman's mate, whose primary duty was to mop decks, tie ropes, and paint the ship, telling me I had screwed up by securing a year of advanced training in electronics and computers. Insulted that I had laughed at him, he quickly passed the phone back to my mother.

Mom rambled aimlessly. I heard her lighter click, her cadence interrupted by her pursed lips sucking on one cigarette after another. One statement contradicting the next:

"Richard, you don't even know what you've signed-up for; those people will own you."

"You don't have the discipline for the Navy." *But I do for the Coast Guard?*

"Mom, I've signed with the Navy. I'm joining the Navy."

Unable to convince me to change my mind, she threatened me. "I'm gonna call the Navy tomorrow and get you out of this."

Although I frequently disobeyed my mother, I'd only stood up to her once before. Never had I told her, "No, I'm not doing as you say." I had always feared retributions on the order of *The Plagues of Egypt*. But during this conversation, I was thankful for the control a thousand miles gave me. I was eighteen. She had nothing I needed, not a roof, a hot meal, nor a bed. She couldn't ground me to my room for the rest of my senior year. She had no leverage—a shark without teeth. I was now free to say whatever I wanted. So I did. "Mom, you can call anyone you want, but it's not your decision. You no longer have legal authority over me. You're so drunk you probably won't even remember this conversation, and I'm not talking to you anymore."

There was silence in my earpiece.

"Mom, did you hear me?"

Her tone changed. She responded with a hint of resignation. "I heard you, Richard." I think she was shocked. "Is that all you have to say?"

"No. There's one more thing. I'm not eating another fucking kidney bean for the rest of my life, and you can't make me."

I had abruptly seized control from her. It was that easy.

Money for Nothing

A few months before graduation, our senior class was herded into the cafeteria where we were inundated with sales people hocking an assortment of graduation products. We listened to their pitches and perused ceremonial merchandise displayed on rows of silk-covered lunch tables. So much rich-people crap: announcements with medieval coats-of-arms, name cards (with fancy but barely-legible cursive fonts) that one affixes inside the announcement, translucent rice-tissue inserts to supplement the announcement *in case the recipient happens to be out of toilet paper*, deluxe ivory envelopes with pattern foiled lining in your choice of gold or silver, RSVP envelopes, return address labels, envelope seals *in the event you get cotton mouth and have difficulty conjuring up spit*, thank you cards for those who send gifts, diploma frames, key chains, ball caps, jewelry, bumper stickers *for graduates with cars*, extra tassels *for those with more than one rear-view mirror*, and my personal favorite: appreciation gifts—"a thoughtful way to thank your parents and others who have supported you throughout your high school years."

The graduation sponsor gave a short speech. "As previously announced, we will need to collect that cap and gown fee by Friday for those of you who have not already paid. Friday is absolutely the last day."

A cap and gown fee? Shouldn't that be supplied by the school, the PTA, Booster Club, Alumni Association, Lion's Club, Fellowship of Christian Athletes, PTL, CPS…somebody? *I'm a taxpayer dammit, and my taxes should cover a cap and gown.*

I approached the sponsor as my classmates filed out of the cafeteria. "How much is that cap and gown fee?"

"Twenty dollars." She smiled.

Twenty dollars! I don't need to <u>buy</u> a gown. I just wanna <u>wear</u> one for two hours.

"Can I pay in two weeks?"

"I'm sorry; we've announced it several times. Friday is the last day."

"Well, my parents are out of town."

"Perhaps you could call them and have them overnight a check to you."

Perhaps you should save your idiotic suggestions for a kid whose Mother spends her days volunteering to make mimeograph copies at school, her weekends sewing Macbeth outfits for her honor student son, and her evenings baking cookies.

I wanted to make her feel like shit, for making me feel like shit. "Perhaps that would be impossible," I replied sarcastically. "I don't have parents."

I reveled in her pity. *Fuck her and her apple pies and picket fence.*

I was frustrated with this notion that I had to pay to graduate, and was taking it out on the messenger. I didn't care about a stupid cap and gown. I didn't care what I was supposed to wear. I just wanted to walk across that stage among my classmates and know that I had achieved the same thing they did. I just wanted to be included, like everyone else.

"Okay, can I just walk the stage without a cap and gown?"

"I don't think so, I'm sorry," she replied.

"So, if I don't pay twenty dollars in the next three days, I don't get to be in my graduation?"

"I'm sorry," she said.

I'm sorry, I'm sorry. This is bullshit. I'm going to write an editorial in the Lindale News about this.

I went to the Principal and got him to intervene on my behalf, getting an extension until blackberry season.

***

I was amazed how the preppies and Hide-A-Way kids wrote three hundred dollar checks for tricked-up stationary. "How can you afford all that?" I asked one guy.

"This shit is an investment, man. You shotgun these announcements out to everyone you know then sit back and wait for the checks to start rolling in. Easy money, man, easy money." *Hmmm. It really does take money to make money.* I started hearing stories from other seniors and seeing wads of their cash. "I haven't seen my uncle in ten years, and he sent me fifty bucks." *Damn, I'm missing out on an opportunity here.*

I had to get in on this. I sneaked into the teacher's work room and snagged a box of carbon paper and some business envelopes. I took them home and wrote the same heartfelt letter on five masters, each spawning five carbon copies beneath. With deliberate pen strokes, I explained how I'd been on my own for the last year. "Times have been tough, and there's not always enough money for food, but I'm almost done…"

I considered mentioning dumpsters and pinworms, but in the end, I left it out. I devoted a paragraph to summarize my modest accomplishments and another to my Navy plans. Then I scraped together three or four bucks for postage, and sent my homemade announcements to anyone whose address I could get from my grandmother. I sent them to all my relatives without regard for the fact that my mother would be both embarrassed and upset when her apathetically-estranged cousins, aunts, and uncles found out she had kicked me out of the house.

The cash I got in response to those homemade announcements and the chance to harvest blackberry fields that stretched from eye to horizon meant my struggles to avoid hunger were behind me. In a month, I'd be a slave to Uncle Sam. With the power of a few dollars, I set my sights on a social life. Our end-of-year sports banquet was coming up and I was determined to not let my senior year pass without a date. I'd already been priced out of the senior prom. This event was more affordable and less formal. I knew this girl, Lori, who I'd met at a skating rink two years before. Even though she lived only twenty-five miles away, since neither of us had a car, she might as well have been on the other end of the world. We talked on the phone for hours, but had seen each other in person only three brief times. Robbie said he'd loan me his car, and Jim would let me borrow his suit. When Lori accepted the invitation, I was all set for the first date of my senior year.

I picked berries after school and revived my rose-selling career for a two-day encore in Dallas on Mother's Day weekend to earn the money for the banquet tickets, the corsage, gas, and dress socks without holes. On my last rose-selling day, I was the oldest kid in the truck and not only did I sit in the front, but when the boss got sick, I drove most of the way home.

During our nightly talks, Lori seemed as excited about our date as I was. Then, two days before the event, she cancelled, citing a generic excuse stolen from Marsha Brady—"Something suddenly came up." Forty dollars—a whole weekend of selling roses in Dallas, and several lugs of berries—gone. I skipped the banquet. The "best year of my life" would pass without me going on a date.

To Study or Not To Study? That Is the Question

I took six classes my senior year. To graduate, I needed to pass only English, Civics and any two electives, one of which was Athletics. Because I rarely started my English homework until an hour before it was due—while sitting in Civics—and I didn't give a rat's ass about politics, zoning out when the teacher started talking about delegates, I found myself in real danger of failing both English and Civics. Those two teachers acted as gatekeepers for the graduation walk, and took their roles seriously. Two weeks before finals, during separate private counseling sessions, each informed me of the exact scores I needed to make on their respective exams to pass their class and graduate. I needed a 75 on my Civics test. I knew the teacher, Mr. Sitzer, disliked me based on his frequent I-wish-I–could strangle-you-you-smart-ass-punk looks. This was only his second year of teaching after two years of driving a school bus, and he struck me as uncompromising. This was a man who'd have no reservations in scoring one of my subjective essay questions 6 (instead of 7) out of 10 points, giving me a 74 on the test, a 69.4 for the course, preventing my graduation, taking away my Navy plans, and sending me on my way toward a career refilling Coke machines.

Mrs. Porsche, a tall, wide, orange-haired, freckled English teacher with oversized teeth, who once inspired me to read the first five pages of Macbeth, told me I needed a 78 on my English final to graduate. I locked eyes with her. That moment, her look, would leave an indelible stamp on my consciousness. She looked sad, maybe disappointed, perhaps guilty (like she'd failed to extricate the best writer in the whole district from the grip of the smart-ass who refused to release him). I don't know what emotion hid behind that look, but it was serious. Her mood was that of a doctor speaking to the family, "I'm so sorry, we did all we could."

I resorted to what I knew best—humor. "Mrs. Porsche, you coached me to a district championship in writing. Based on that alone, you should ask for a raise. Don't ya think I could get a few extra-credit points for that?" I smiled big, hoping to charm her.

She studied me with her sad, disappointed, guilty face. "I don't think so."

Come on lady, lighten up. We both know I'm smart enough for the real world. Just because I don't like reading all that "where-for-art-thou" shit written by those irrelevant, pompous snobs from the middle ages... I got big plans to be a scientist. Just give me a 78 and let me go into the Navy and learn about real-world stuff like nuclear bombs. I need to go to the Philippines, lady. You hear me?

She'd always been one of the hardest teachers for me to get a laugh from, but I wasn't about to give up. "Mrs. Porsche, how can I possibly make a B on this final when I haven't read any of the books?" I added a smile.

"You should have thought about that a long time ago," she said, as she raised her eyebrows and rotated her head slightly, her body language inviting my response.

I didn't know if she knew about my parentless situation. I didn't tell her what I wanted to. *Mrs. Porsche, I've spent all school year either working or starving. I have no parents. I have no structure. I have no one. When I'm sick, I take care of myself. I don't have a Mother to take me to Fabric World and sew costumes so I can make A's on your assignments. Please consider that when you're grading my test. Please understand you're not sending an illiterate out into the world. You know this...*

***

All year I'd put minimum effort into each of these important classes. I justified my laziness by blaming the teachers for not inspiring me. Instead of occasionally studying and doing homework and performing at a comfortable C-level in those key courses, I placed misguided emphasis on the classes I enjoyed. I had a 99 average in World Geography, an elective, not required for graduation, but I was failing the only social studies class that mattered. An F in either Civics or English would render my whole senior year a waste. I wouldn't walk the stage. I wouldn't get my diploma.

I called my recruiter.

"What exactly happens if I don't graduate?"

"What? What are you talking about? Did you quit school?"

"No, I'm just having a hard time in a couple of classes."

"How could you not graduate? You're in the 90th percentile on your ASVAB?"

"Well, I think everything's gonna be fine. Hypothetically, I'm just asking 'what if'? What exactly would happen to my enlistment agreement?"

"Well, your contract would be void. You could still go in on your enlistment date, if you still wanted to, but you wouldn't qualify for any technical training. After boot camp, instead of being an E-3, you'd be an E-1, and you'd get assigned based on the needs of the Navy. You'd be a cook or a deckhand. It would cost you a lot of money, over the course of your enlistment, thousands of dollars. After a year of good performance you could request technical training from your commanding officer, but there's no guarantee he'd approve it or that what you want would be open."

Failing English could cost me money? Instead of getting advanced electronics training and a spot on a submarine, I'd be cooking omelettes everyday at five a.m. on a naval air base in Memphis. Or worse yet, I'd be a Boatsman's Mate, just like Doug.

How could I be about to fail high school? I was too smart for that. I could name the fifty largest cities in the U.S., in order, according to the 1970 Census. I knew all the presidents in order from Washington through Reagan, all forty-eight prepositions, the difference between a participle and a gerund. I never used the word *ain't* or ended sentences with *at*. In fourth grade, I often won the class spelling bees. In fifth grade, I won the checkers championship. I was a district champion editorial writer. But these teachers were gonna fail me. How can this be? This must be some kind of cruel joke.

I hadn't put any effort into those classes because I assumed the faculty would pass me anyway knowing I was smart enough. I knew my grades were marginal going into finals, but I figured they'd give me a chance to write an essay or do a book report for extra credit. What advice would Coach Davis give me now? What lesson did this fall under? I knew the answer. "Don't expect anything to be handed to you. You are not entitled to anything."

I indeed had a sense of entitlement—entitled to graduate based on what I'd overcome just to be in school. The memory of cliché-laced lectures from the man who wore wide clown ties with plaid pants was powerful enough for me to understand I was wrong to feel entitled.

The meetings with the graduation gatekeepers shook me up. I couldn't let all I'd been through be for naught. I knew that failure on these finals and not graduating high school greatly increased the chances I would continue a life of poverty and hunger. Over the last few months, I'd many times been tempted to shoplift food. My friend had already stolen food so I could eat. I knew enough to know that's exactly where I was heading. Maybe it would be me, not Smite, who would go to jail first.

I thought about all the things I did not want my life to be. I didn't want to ever have that "kill-or-be-killed" attitude that the ex-con bus pervert had. I didn't want to get head from a man in prison, and I certainly didn't want to give it. The prospect of living hand-to-mouth, like I had been, scared the hell out of me.

I caught a glimpse of the path my life might take: At twenty-two, I'm washing dishes at a diner, sixty hours a week, scarfing up overtime, trying to string a few paychecks together so I could move off my buddy's couch. At thirty, I'm fired from a forklift operator's job at *Star Canning* for stashing a pallet of tuna behind a dumpster, so I could steal it later. With no savings, no job, and no Gary Camp or Bob Staton looking after me, I was worse off than I was when I was eighteen. I lose my room at the Bonny Motel, forcing me to sack out in the roach-infested trailer of a snaggle-tooth truck stop waitress who, in a fit of drunken desperation, I had slept with a month before. And she's anxious for me to hit it again, but I couldn't stand the sight of her face unless I was drunk, and now she's late for her period, which made me want to drink, and nobody would hire me because the man at Star Canning was telling all my potential employers that I was a thief.

While she sleeps next to me, her only redeeming quality is that she is kind enough (or desperate enough) to let me stay with her—which is the only thing keeping me from a cardboard box under a bridge—I stare at the ceiling, waiting for sleep to come. And I use this time, to practice my nightly ritual of pondering my past and the prospects for my future. *How did I end up here? What was the tipping point? Macbeth—I should have read Macbeth.* I felt my whole future being erased. Like in a time-travel movie, my pictures in photographs not yet taken were dissolving. My future, evaporating.

***

I thought the conversation with Mrs. Porsche was over. Her message—"You Are Not Graduating." But she had a surprise closing. "You can do this if you try." Puddles of tears formed in her eyes. "Don't let this year of your life go to waste." *She knows. She knows I am alone.* "I have four or five in my other classes in the same situation. They aren't going to make it. You could. You have enough time. It's in your hands, Rich."

This lady who, all school year, had been so distant, hard to crack, impervious to my charm, was pulling for me.

I'd worked harder outside the classroom than any other student in school. But no points were given for overcoming personal problems. It took those teachers sitting me down, looking me in the eye while explaining their obligation as educators to uphold academic standards for me to finally assert myself. *Mrs. Porsche is right. I can do it.*

In a sudden burst of intellectual energy, I studied. English was particularly difficult because there was so much test material from books I hadn't read. Winning the writing contest gave me a jolt of confidence that I could do it. While my friends were winding down, skipping classes and partying, I completed the test reviews, went to early morning study sessions in near-empty classrooms and buried myself in books for two weeks leading up to the finals. I skipped my trivial classes to study the important stuff in the library. I even picked Mike Morman's brain about Macbeth. When the test review sheets came out, I completed every section. For the first time in my life, I actually studied hard. These teachers were serious people, and my future was serious business. How disgraceful it would be if I didn't graduate. Imagine if after all this, my parents could say, "You see what a screw-up he is? He can't even pass high school!" I learned what motivated me more than anything—it wasn't as much the drive to enjoy the fruits of success, but the fear of failure. The consequences of such failure were clear. And that vision of my future self—what my life might become if I didn't focus on completing the steps needed to avoid it—was too vivid not to act upon.

I made the grade on both finals; weaving a tapestry of prose on the Macbeth essay question.

As I sat on the stage, preparing to walk, I thought about a lot of things: About how all those corny Coach Davis clichés were really true. *If it's worth having, it's worth working for.* How two teachers that I didn't particularly like, lit a fire under my ass to help me understand that lesson. About my friends, some of whom were on the stage with me, others sitting in the audience, in the same auditorium in which I jumped up and excitedly claimed my love for Captain and Tennille, who in small ways or large, helped me along the way. How would I ever repay them?

And on that night—the last in my hometown—I understood my journey was just beginning. The world I had lived in as a child was largely beyond my control. The life I will create for myself—my world—wouldn't be a function of my parents' decisions, but of my own. When Mary offered me a one way ticket to anywhere, I perceived it merely as freedom to go finish high school any place I chose. Something that was obscured then, but was clear to me now, was that the One Way Ticket to Anywhere was not only about the past year, but a metaphor for the rest of my life—all of our lives. You do something, anything, everything, whether it's a conscious decision rolling into a series of new choices based on previous actions, or an apparently trivial moment that, retrospectively becomes a fork-in-the-road, once-in-a-lifetime decision, YOU do it. YOU write your own slate. When it's done, it cannot be undone.

And on that night—the last in my hometown—I understood that the world is full of strangers, some unknowingly destined to become my friend and weave themselves alongside the lady on the bus and the redneck truck driver into the fabric of my self. People I hadn't met, some of whom weren't even born yet, in countries I'd only read about, would someday join me for a leg of my journey. We will change one another, perhaps in profound ways as the lady on the bus had changed me. Others, some in this auditorium tonight—people I have talked to thousands of times—I will never see again. Sal Ahmey, Marsha Ballard, Robbie, the pervert on the bus, Gina, Coach Robinson, Gary Camp, Mike Morman, Eddie, my mother, father, step-fathers, surrogate fathers and bikers who tried me to get me to fuck their girlfriends—I am the summation of each of them, and no one else on earth will ever be their confluence.

I'm leaving this place in the morning. It'll be a long time before I come back, and when I do, it'll never be like this again. It won't be the same, and neither will I. All the flux capacitors and DeLoreans in the world will never take me back to the convergence of this place, time, and feeling. This moment is a time capsule—my time capsule. And maybe one day, I will gather my journals and memories and write an intimate book that will open that capsule to anyone who cares to discover the joy, despair, acceptance, resentment, forgiveness—all those components of the human condition that crafted the man I was becoming. Maybe they will find a piece of themselves in my time capsule.

And on that night—the last in my hometown—I realized high school graduation in Lindale, Texas was not my destination, but just the first stop on my One Way Ticket to Anywhere.

Epilogue

    When I was sixteen, had a fortune teller told me all the things which were about to happen, I couldn't have imagined how I'd be able get through it. But, as I lived those years, I didn't really see the day-to-day struggles as insurmountable obstacles. Even as tribulations in this book and many more untold built upon one another to become my past and my reality, I always believed my life would soon turn a corner. I grieved over the death of my girlfriend, yet while doing so knew that, out there in my future I'd meet someone special. While enduring an abusive coach, I reminded myself that someday soon he'd be out of my life, forever. As the primary target of my mother's depression and alcoholic-induced anger, I kept telling myself that my independence would make her powerless, allowing me to set the terms of any future relationship. And the relationship became better when I had a managerial role in it.

    There will always be tiny pieces of my past traveling with me. I left something more than just my childhood back at those bus station sendoffs in North Carolina and Idaho. But I've also gained something from those experiences—the power of self determination and perseverance. Things don't get much worse than being seventeen and having nothing in life but twenty dollars, a garbage bag full of clothes, and a few good friends. If I can build a happy life from that, I can do anything (except become an Olympic athlete...although...I still dream of moving to some Caribbean nation and taking up curling and representing them). The world did not beat me down then and it never will. Whether I got that attitude from my parents as part of a master plan, from apathy, or accident, I can thank them for it.

    Through the Internet, ten years ago I learned that Coach Stan Davis was still in east Texas, coaching and teaching at Carthage High School. I had spent ten years going to college part time, while working full time to support my family. When I graduated with an engineering degree and got a great job offer, I thought about the lady on the bus who had advised me to accept help and years later thank those who provided it. Her request compelled me to let Coach Davis know how much he had contributed to my modest success and to my self esteem. I knew the most valuable gift a teacher could possibly receive is to have his life's work validated by a former student. So I sent my old coach, algebra teacher, and mentor a heartfelt letter and a Mahogany sign I hand carved and stained. It read, *There Ain't No Free Lunch.*

The messages of perseverance and to reject an attitude of entitlement he taught twenty years earlier meant so much to me that in my letter I asked him to hang his message, carved with my hands, in his classroom. I hoped that one day that lesson would touch at least one of his students in the same way it inspired me. In my letter I also asked him to have his children or grandchildren return the carving to one of my daughters upon his passing. I hope there is a day out there, many years from now, when one of my daughters will sign for a mysterious package. She'll open it and instantly remember that day when she was eleven years old and we talked about that carving and the phrase. And she will see to it that her grandkids understand what that lesson means.

Two weeks after sending the carving, I got a small package from Coach Davis. I opened it and found the most meaningful gift I will ever receive. A red covered, cliché-laced book of lessons and positive attitude quips written by Zig Ziglar. Inside the book, *See You At the Top*, were tons of expressions I had always previously attributed to Coach Davis's imagination. A lot of the lessons in the book were scoffed at by me and my classmates. They were still corny and idealistic, but those lessons and principals held greater value to me than they did when I first heard them.

More important, in the package was a handwritten letter—a letter that exemplified at the same time both the writer's emotional restraint and his passion—a letter from the man who in my mind will always epitomize the word *teacher* and whose face I will always conjure when I hear the word.

Rich,

Congratulations on your accomplishment. I have some idea how difficult it has been to be a provider, Father, and student all at the same time. Thanks for the kind words you wrote and the plaque. I'll be honored to hang it in my classroom and tell everybody I can about it and the man who made it. My boys know the story behind it and will get it back to your family. Stay in Touch.

I wanted to get you something that might mean something to you since you provided a gift to me that says so much. After the Bible, this book has influenced my life more than any other. A coach I greatly admired told me about it. It is a book I started class with when I was teaching you, and I still rely on it today. It has the story about "No Free Lunch." I hope you value the gift as much as I value yours.

In His Love,
Stan Davis

It is the perspective as a father of two teenage girls that motivated me to write this memoir. I'm determined to be the kind of parent I never had.

How ironic that even though they might not have always lived up to my expectations of what a father or mother should be, my parents have raised a man who asks himself every day, "Have I done the best job possible today to be a good father?" And for that, over anything else in my life, I am proud of myself.

About the Author

After several years of distinguished service maintaining the nuclear weapon systems aboard a US Navy Submarine, Rich settled in Keller, Texas, where he still lives with Carrie and his two girls. While serving in the Navy, Rich achieved great athletic success. Competing in the decathlon at the 1984 Boston College Relays, he finished ninth out of ten competitors after failing to clear the opening height in the high jump. Undeterred, he then entered the pole vault and nabbed eighteenth place in that event. With nothing else left to prove, he immediately retired from college sports to focus for the first time on using his brain.

Despite having once failed high school algebra, he eventually earned a B.S. in electrical engineering from the University of Texas. Rich works as an engineering manager at Nokia Mobile Phones, which for many years has helped him live his dream of seeing the world. In 2007 he scaled back his business travel and created a program within Nokia which has, thus far, provided technical jobs for over forty ambitious college students. He's helping his older daughter, Lindsay, finish college and teaching his younger daughter, Leanna, how to pole vault and solve math problems.

Rich is currently working on several projects, each with varying degrees of completion. *One Way Trail to Anywhere* will be a personal account guidebook of his backpacking trips. *When Mommy Hates Daddy* will examine how, for generations, state's family court's mother-biased policies have inherently diminished divorced father's roles in their children's lives. *The Lady On the Bus* will praise the virtues of kindness among strangers. Look for these books coming soon to *Amazon* and *Barnes and Noble*.

To ensure you're notified when his next book is published, Rich Ochoa invites you to either friend request him on *Facebook* or join the *Facebook* group, *One Way Ticket to Anywhere*. He'd also like it if you "liked" the book, *One Way Ticket to Anywhere* on *Facebook*. Hardcore fans may even follow him on *Twitter* and write a book review of *One Way Ticket to Anywhere* on www.amazon.com. For sample chapters of his ongoing projects, you may visit his website, www.onewaytickettoanywhere.com.

Made in the USA
Lexington, KY
24 June 2011